Learning to Lead for Transformation

AF079545

ALSO AVAILABLE FROM BLOOMSBURY

Sustainable School Leadership, Mike Bottery, Wont Ping-Man and George Ngai

Collaborative School Leadership, David Middlewood, Ian Abbott and Sue Robinson

Educational Leadership for a More Sustainable World, Mike Bottery

Leading Disadvantaged Learners, David Middlewood and Ian Abbott with Roberto A. Pamas

Strengthening Anti-Racist Educational Leaders, edited by Anjalé D. Welton and Sarah Diem

School Leadership and Education System Reform, edited by Toby Greany and Peter Earley

Understanding Educational Leadership, Steven J. Courtney, edited by Helen M. Gunter, Richard Niesche and Tina Trujillo

Preparation and Development of School Leaders in Africa, edited by Pontso Moorosi and Tony Bush

Race, Education and Educational Leadership in England, edited by Paul Miller and Christine Callender

Learning to Lead for Transformation

An African Perspective on Educational Leadership

Emmanuel Ngara

BLOOMSBURY ACADEMIC
LONDON · NEW YORK · OXFORD · NEW DELHI · SYDNEY

BLOOMSBURY ACADEMIC
Bloomsbury Publishing Plc
50 Bedford Square, London, WC1B 3DP, UK
1385 Broadway, New York, NY 10018, USA
29 Earlsfort Terrace, Dublin 2, Ireland

BLOOMSBURY, BLOOMSBURY ACADEMIC and the Diana logo are trademarks of
Bloomsbury Publishing Plc

First published in Great Britain 2022

Copyright © Emmanuel Ngara, 2022

Emmanuel Ngara has asserted his right under the Copyright, Designs and Patents Act, 1988, to be
identified as Author of this work.

For legal purposes the Acknowledgements and Dedication on p. v constitute an extension
of this copyright page.

Cover design: Charlotte James
Cover image © Yellow Dog Productions / Getty Images

All rights reserved. No part of this publication may be reproduced or transmitted in any form
or by any means, electronic or mechanical, including photocopying, recording, or any information
storage or retrieval system, without prior permission in writing from the publishers.

Bloomsbury Publishing Plc does not have any control over, or responsibility for, any
third-party websites referred to or in this book. All internet addresses given in this book
were correct at the time of going to press. The author and publisher regret any
inconvenience caused if addresses have changed or sites have ceased to exist, but can
accept no responsibility for any such changes.

A catalogue record for this book is available from the British Library.

A catalog record for this book is available from the Library of Congress.

ISBN: HB: 978-1-3502-6407-6
PB: 978-1-3502-6406-9
ePDF: 978-1-3502-6408-3
eBook: 978-1-3502-6409-0

Typeset by Newgen KnowledgeWorks Pvt. Ltd., Chennai, India
Printed and bound in Great Britain

To find out more about our authors and books visit www.bloomsbury.com and
sign up for our newsletters.

Acknowledgements and Dedication

This book is dedicated in a very special way to Mrs Bernice Teboho Ngara, my late wife. Teboho, who passed on in 2020, was not only my marriage and life partner but also an invaluable and indispensable partner in the teaching of Leadership. Together we gave up our careers in order to devote ourselves to the teaching of Leadership and the training of leaders. Together we taught Leadership in South Africa and Zimbabwe and together endeavoured to inspire those with whom we have had the opportunity to share our passion for leadership development.

There is a real sense in which this book would have been poorer were it not for Mme Teboho's contribution. Born and brought up in Lesotho, Mai Ngara was a great admirer of Moshoeshoe I of Lesotho and was the source of much that is said about him in this book. There is therefore a sense in which the late Teboho Ngara can be regarded as something of a co-author of Learning to Lead for Transformation.

Contents

List of Figures ix
Preface x

Introduction 1

Part I Understanding education and leadership

1 **Education for development and leadership** 11

2 **What is leadership?** 25

3 **General and educational theories of leadership** 35

Part II Approaches to leadership

4 **Educating people for domination** 51

5 **The *Ubuntu* approach to relationships and leadership** 59

6 **Educating people to serve: Servant leadership** 77

Part III Education for personal development and leadership

7 **Discovering one's purpose in life** 87

8 **Personal mastery, self-awareness and leadership qualities and habits** 95

9 **Educational leadership and the development of intelligences** 113

Part IV Education for transformational organizational leadership

10 **Vision and organizational leadership** 125

11 **Strategy as the road map to the desired state** 131

12 **Execution as the key to the actual destination** 137

Part V Beyond the organizational context of educational leadership

13 **Issues and principles of educational leadership** 151

14 **Leadership development at meso level** 179

15 **A new globalization and a new epistemology** 197

Appendix: Reflection exercises for students and interested practitioners 213
References 221
Index 229

Figures

1. The undialectical concept of teaching and learning 16
2. The dialectical and developmental concept of teaching and learning 17
3. The interaction of areas of need (John Adair) 40
4. A modified Johari Window model – for illustration purposes only 101
5. The broad functions of strategic leadership 132

Preface

The book is divided into five parts with each part consisting of three chapters which stand as a unit. The contents and place of each part are briefly explained below.

Part I: Understanding education and leadership

This first part of the book introduces both education and leadership as concepts. With regard to education, the focus is on teaching and learning, and on the principles of designing curriculum content. The position taken in this book is that educational leadership is not only about the officials who run educational institutions or those who sit in high government offices. These institutions exist for the purpose of learning and teaching. Principals of schools and colleges and vice chancellors of universities are there to ensure the processes of teaching and learning take place effectively. They are therefore also educational leaders who do an excellent job of teaching to ensure effective learning by students. They also need to understand what is meant by leadership. The development needs of those who facilitate the processes of teaching and learning as vice chancellors, administrators and so forth are discussed in detail in Part V. In this introductory part of the subject of educational leadership, the focus is on the following topics:

- Education for Development and Leadership
- What Leadership Is and Is Not
- General and Educational Theories of Leadership

Part II: Approaches to leadership

In this part of the book we deal with three modes or forms of leadership which could be referred to as 'philosophies of leadership' as they are concerned with issues of how people should or should not lead. A philosophy of leadership implies that somebody has developed or propagated ideas about how people should lead. The term used in this book is 'approaches to leadership'. The thinking here is that an approach to something is a way of dealing with it or thinking about it. It can reasonably be argued that there is a distinction between 'a philosophy of something' and 'an approach to something'. The former suggests a complicated theoretical explication, whereas the latter may or may not include theoretical explanations. It is simply a way of dealing with something, or doing something, or perhaps even thinking about something with or without elaborate definitions or explanations.

The 'forms' or 'modes' of leadership explained and discussed in this part of the book are the following:

- The Leadership of Domination
- *Ubuntu*-Based Leadership
- Servant Leadership

Those who practised the *Ubuntu/Botho/Unhu* or *Utu* approach to leadership were influenced by a certain philosophy of human relationships but did not necessarily consciously develop an elaborate philosophy of leadership. Similarly, many who practise or practised the Leadership of Domination may or may not have been influenced by certain thinkers but did not necessarily conceive an elaborate philosophy or theory of leadership. Both approaches were or are based on certain traditionally held beliefs about the relationship between the leader and the people he/she leads. On the other hand, Servant Leadership, as has been used in secular society since the second half of the twentieth century, is a well-thought-out approach to leadership. We have used the term 'approaches to leadership' because it is a more inclusive concept which denotes theoretical underpinnings as well as simply held beliefs and practices that may or may not be based on elaborately developed and consciously held theories.

There are what may be called 'types of leadership' that relate in one way or another to these three major approaches, including dictatorial, democratic, collegial and populist leadership. These are referred to as and when necessary but are not discussed in detail in this book.

Part III: Education for personal development and leadership

Leadership is a discipline which involves *being*, *knowing* and *becoming*. Assume that as a reader of this book you are registered on an educational leadership course. When embarking on this course or starting to read this book, you became aware of your being, your state and potential as a leader. Having gone through Parts I and II, you are now quite well informed about educational leadership; you know quite a lot about the discipline. What you need to focus on now is the process of *becoming*. This is about you personally working your way to become the leader you would like to be. Educational leadership is no longer an idea, a concept or practice out there that others have applied but something you have to personally grapple with. There are no fruits without roots. To lead others, you must be able to lead yourself. To do this you need to embark on the process of Personal Leadership Development which this part of the book is designed to guide you through. The process involves going through the following topics:

- Discovering One's Purpose in Life
- Personal Mastery, Self-awareness, Leadership Qualities and Habits
- Developing Leadership Intelligences

Part IV: Education for transformational organizational leadership

Part III highlights the importance of the leader being able to lead herself/himself in order to lead others. However, one's leadership ability is in the final analysis judged on ability to lead others. This takes us to the fourth element or *process* of leadership development, namely *applying*. The developing leader *applies* leadership principles to a group of people. One can lead teams or amorphous groups of followers, but in the final analysis, as Howard Gardner (1995: 292) correctly points out, 'enduring leadership ultimately demands some kind of institutional or organisational basis'. This part of the book is intended to help practicing and developing leaders develop the skills, attitudes and behaviours that enhance their leadership for their institutions, companies and whatever organizations they are called upon to lead. These skills, attitudes and behaviours are built on the approaches discussed in Part II and the disciplines, habits and intelligences that are the focus of Part III.

In this part of the book we focus on the nuts and bolts of leading institutions and organizations. We are talking about direct leadership here where you have a specific group of people looking up to you to lead them. What skills, what methods and what strategies are you going to use to ensure success? The focus is on three elements:

- Vision
- Strategy
- Execution

The rest are components of these three elements. Because of the unity of these three in the leadership of an organization, the appendix presents one *Practical Organisational Exercise* that is developed in stages starting at the end of Chapter 10 and getting completed at the end of Chapter 12.

Part V: Beyond the organizational context of educational leadership

Focussing on the education domain and higher education, this part of the book examines some of the complexities of educational leadership and the demands on educational leaders within and beyond organizations. Chapter 13 deals with knowledge of the education field with special reference to higher education, specifying some of the complexities of the field caused by such factors as globalization and the coronavirus (Covid-19). Chapter 14 focuses on an approach to the training needs of educational leaders, while Chapter 15 presents a new approach to the development of such leaders, an approach that suggests a diversified epistemology in place of what the author sees as the Western bias of the present epistemology.

The reader will see that there is a chronological and thematic development in the way the various parts of the book are organized. The uniqueness and contribution of the book to the field of educational leadership are explained in the introduction.

Introduction

There are numerous books on the subject of leadership. It is true to say that leadership has become one of the most popular topics in the book writing industry, with probably hundreds of titles being added to the existing list every few years. A cursory glance at *Writers on Leadership* (Penguin Books, 2001) by John van Maurik will give an indication of just how many authors had shown interest in the subject of leadership by the beginning of the twenty-first century. There are popular and renowned authors such as John Maxwell, Howard Gardner, Stephen Covey, Peter Senge, John Adair and the list goes on. Some of these have produced what should appropriately be called *classics* in the field of leadership. Among these may be included *The 21 Irrefutable Laws of Leadership* (John Maxwell), *The 7 Habits of Highly Effective People* (Stephen Covey), *The Fifth Discipline* (Peter Senge), *Effective Strategic Leadership* (John Adair), *Leading Minds* (Howard Gardner) and many others. These and numerous other books have clarified different aspects of leadership and have given guidance to leaders and to those who intend to lead. Some of the books, such as Stephen Covey's *The 7 Habits of Highly Effective People*, are principal sources of information on some of the issues this book deals with.

All the books mentioned above belong to the earlier period of conceptions of leadership and are all written from a Western perspective. There have been new developments, and we are beginning to see perspectives that are not presented from a purely Western viewpoint. African perspectives on leadership are explained in the following, among other publications: *Let Africa Lead* (Reuel Khoza, 2005), *The African Way* (Mike Boon, 2007) and *The Spirit of African Leadership* (Lovemore Mbigi, 2005). These books attempt to portray the African philosophy of *Ubuntu* as an approach to leadership that works for the people of Africa. Part of what Khoza attempts to do is to explain how culture, in particular what is referred to in the book as African Humanism (meaning *Ubuntu*), can become an organic part of business ethics. The concept of *Ubuntu* (*Utu* in Swahili) is important to the approach adopted in *Learning to Lead for Transformation* and is dealt with in some detail in Chapter 5.

Among the most powerful new additions to the literature on leadership is Katie Anderson's book, *Learning to Lead, Leading to Learn: Lessons from Toyota Leader ISAO YOSHINO on a Lifetime of Continuous Learning* (2020). This book presents a fascinating account of Japanese perspectives on leadership, viewed through the life, reflections and development of Isao Yoshino. Reading Anderson's book truly broadens one's understanding of leadership. One of the key concepts in the book is 'the fabric concept'. According to Yoshino (Anderson 2020: 7–8), the fabric concept, as in the clothing industry, entails identifying both the vertical warps and the horizontal weft that runs through one's life, similar to the pattern of a clothing material: 'The vertical threads are those themes and dreams that run mostly unchanged throughout your life – the "known" elements that are deep inside. The horizontal threads are ones we discover along the way and choose to incorporate into our life, making our unique pattern in life.' The vertical threads are the themes and dreams that run through one's life such as ambitions, goals and desires, while the horizontal threads are the episodes and experiences that come our way as we chart our way through life, helping us to see our purpose in life more clearly.

If in addition to the fabric concept you add the Japanese concept of *hansei* (self-reflection) and the principles of *continuous improvement* and *respect for people* (Anderson 2020: 24–5), you have a new way of understanding leadership development and a deeper understanding of how to chart your way through life. This enriches one's concept of leadership whether one is an Asian, a Westerner or an African. Similarly, one's understanding of the phenomenon of leadership is further enhanced and deepened if one learns and understands the African concept of *Ubuntu* which is one of the key elements discussed in this book.

An interesting development is that the study of indigenous knowledge systems seems to indicate that there is complementariness and consistency between different ways of knowing. This author's daughter, Rutendo Ngara (2017), writing as a scientist and a specialist in indigenous knowledge systems, has shown there is consistency between Chinese traditional medicine and African indigenous knowledge systems and goes on to argue that Einstein's theory of relativity 'is consistent with the indigenous African and Chinese ontologies that see all things as interdependent and inseparable parts of the cosmic whole' (see Ngulube 2017: 348). She posits that quantum theory reveals a basic 'oneness' of the universe and argues, 'This is consistent with the African indigenous notion of the all-pervasive *NTU* or interconnectedness of *Ma'at*, as well as the Chinese concept of *Qi*, which exists in all phenomena' (ibid: 349). Relating this logic to the subject of leadership, it is logical to argue that understanding the African concept of *Ubuntu*, which is discussed in Chapter 5, will enhance the understanding of the phenomenon of leadership for African, Asian and Western theorists and practitioners.

The reference to Japanese and African concepts of leadership naturally leads to the importance of understanding leadership in relation to the context in which it is practiced. As Philip Hallinger (Bush et al. 2019: 291–309) correctly points out, leadership models in the twentieth century were based on the experiences of Western scholars without due consideration for context. Factors such as increased international interaction and the growth of higher education in developing countries have raised awareness about the need for understanding leadership concepts and practices in non-Western contexts. With particular reference to school leadership, Hallinger (ibid: 297) has pointed out, 'Scholars have concluded that, in order to achieve results, leaders must adapt their leadership styles in ways that are consonant with the prevailing values and norms *in the socio-cultural context*.' There are at least two dimensions to considerations of leadership in the sociocultural context: first, for students of leadership in a particular sociocultural context, the study of leadership becomes more meaningful and more relevant. Second, scholars and practitioners from outside the particular sociocultural context will have their understanding of the phenomenon of leadership further enhanced as has been exemplified by the Japanese example above.

This book is on the subject of leadership with a specific focus on educational leadership. As we shall see, before the concept of educational leadership was in vogue, the work of principals or head teachers was conceived of in terms of management or administration. A very influential book in this regard was the Frenchman Henri Fayol's book on management published in 1916 with the title *Industrial and General Administration*. Educationists were influenced by Fayol's ideas on management as can be seen by the publication of the book in English in 1930 (Sir I. Pitman & Sons). A good number of articles are found on the internet on Fayol's influence on education. A good example is Daniel A. Wren's article titled 'The Influence of Henri Fayol on Management Theory and Education in North America' (Wren 2003). With the coming of the idea of educational leadership development, the number of publications on school leadership development began to grow steadily as can be evidenced by the appearance of the following among others: Philip Hallinger (ed.) (2003), *Reshaping the Landscape of School Leadership Development: A Global Perspective*; Harry Tomlinson (2004), *Educational Leadership: Personal Growth for Professional Development*; Rick and Shera Melick (2010), *Teaching That Transforms*; and others. A key publication in the field is Bush et al. (2019), *Principles of Educational Leadership and Management*. While its focus is on school leadership, the publication is an important reference book in that it examines theories of educational leadership and examines the subject in a variety of contexts such as globalization, the sociocultural and economic contexts and post-conflict situations as in Rwanda and Cambodia. It also gives valuable information on such issues as ethics, professionalism and the influence of stakeholders in school leadership and management. The question that may arise is where does *Learning to Lead for Transformation* come in, and how does it fit into the field of educational leadership discussed and analysed in the books just cited and others referred to in the references section?

It is appropriate to begin by stating that the book is a result of the author's long and enduring interest in leadership practice and his concern about leadership problems in our time. The concern is primarily about how failure in leadership has led to the suffering of many people in Africa and elsewhere. It is this interest and concern that caused the author (i.e. this writer) and his fellow teacher and life partner, the late Teboho Ngara, to resign from their secure jobs in Durban in 2005 with the intention of going to Pretoria to set up an academy called the Lead and Inspire School of Leadership and focus on leadership development. This book is about a very important area of leadership that has just been referred to above – educational leadership. The book deals with both instructional leadership, which is concerned with excellence in teaching and learning, and the leadership and management of education institutions, with a focus on higher education institutions. These are two important and complementary dimensions of educational leadership. The quality of teaching and learning is what makes an education institution an asset to a nation. But for the teaching and learning to be enhanced, the people who run the institution must be people of vision who understand what good education is and have the ability to ensure good education takes place in the institution.

At this juncture it is appropriate to mention four key characteristics of this book: first, it is worth noting that the book begins by outlining the approach to teaching and learning that facilitates development for both the learner and the country in question. It is the education system that has the best approach to teaching and learning that will foster the development of the best leaders. More importantly, as a further development to the publications referred to above, this book attempts to set out what it is that someone who wants to be a leader should know and do in order to be a fully rounded practitioner of leadership. It is not just about how to lead but also how to become a leader, what leadership is, what its purpose is, what society expects from a leader and how to then exercise one's power and abilities in leading others.

The brief comment above leads to something critical: We can define the disciplines of Mathematics, Engineering, Philosophy, Physics, Linguistics and so on. Specialists know the content and boundaries of each discipline and the body of knowledge that the learner must master for him/her to be awarded the qualification in question. It seems to the author of this book that many higher education institutions are still unclear about Leadership as a discipline – what to teach and how to distinguish it from the more established related disciplines. Consequently, what this book does, in part, is to attempt to define the body of knowledge that a specialist in Leadership should master – starting with what leadership is, theories of leadership, approaches to leadership and so on, and going on to show how one can develop as a leader and what it means and entails to lead organizations, and so on. It then goes beyond organizations to show how educational leadership is impacted by forces both within and outside organizations, taking into account the role of macro issues such as governments and what the text defines as 'supra-macro' issues such as globalization, Covid-19 and internationalization of higher education. In that context, the book further asks what are the epistemological issues that higher education institutions in our time should consider for students from both the South and the North? And what are the implications for educational leadership development? The book is therefore a unique fusion of two disciplines: Leadership as an academic discipline and Education from the perspective of both teaching and learning and the development of people who run education institutions. The fusion produces an individual who is truly qualified as both a leader and an educationist, namely an educational leader.

The explanation immediately above leads to a very important consideration: It is this author's view that disciplines such as History, Theology, Chemistry, Political Science, Geography, Philosophy, Linguistics and so on entail going through three processes: *being, knowing* and *applying*. *Being* is the state you start from. You have little or no knowledge of History, Theology, Chemistry, Geography and so on. You then begin the process of knowing and when you know enough you are able to apply your knowledge as an historian, a theologian, a geographer and so on. However, in your attitudes, values, natural inclinations and way of life, you have not necessarily become a different person – you have not been transformed to see life differently. You are merely applying the knowledge and skill that goes with the mastery of the particular discipline. To put it simply, the mastery of the English Language by an African second-language speaker of English does not necessarily turn them into an English man or woman. This is different from when you go through leadership training that includes elements such as personal leadership development, self-awareness and personal mastery. This kind of process entails a new understanding of self and the development of a new set of values and attitudes that transforms one into a better person. It is something similar to being converted to a religion such as Islam, Hinduism or Christianity. In this regard, the process of leadership development and practising leadership entails going through four processes: *being, knowing, becoming* and *applying*.

The last point made above explains the difference between this book and purely academic books on educational leadership such as *The Principles of Educational Leadership and Management* by Bush et al. The information provided in these books is extremely valuable and essential but tends to be purely theoretical and intellectual. They present the learner with information about *what* educational leadership is and *not* with the process of *how to become* a leader. In this book, educational leadership becomes a field in which the principles, attitudes and behaviours that go with leadership are applied by the leader. In other words, there is *formation* involved in the process advocated by this book. The learner is not just acquiring knowledge and habits but is also motivated to *become* the leader that the book talks about. This is the second distinguishing characteristic of this book. What this means is that leadership is analysed and discussed as both a practice (as leadership with lower case l) and a discipline (as Leadership with upper case L) that is applied to the field of education.

The third important contribution that this book makes is to discuss a traditional African approach to leadership, that is, the *Ubuntu*-based approach, in relation to what have been identified by Western writers such as Ron Boehme (1989) as the two dominant types or approaches to leadership, namely the Leadership of Domination and Servant Leadership. Africa is mentioned here with special reference to sub-Saharan Africa which excludes Arab-dominated North Africa. While traditional African approaches have been written about by writers such as Lovemore Mbigi (2005) and Mike Boon (2007), what this book has done are two things: first, to bring the *Ubuntu* approach into the mainstream debate about leadership approaches or philosophies that help future generations of leaders to better understand what leadership is about and what needs to be done to improve the current practice; and second, to give practical and historical examples of how the philosophy was put into practice by real traditional leaders. In other words, the philosophy is not presented as a purely abstract theory but as an approach that was practised by historical figures. The issue being what can those who want to improve leadership practice learn from authentic traditional African experience? And indeed, what can African political leaders of today and tomorrow learn from their own ancestors about leadership for nation building and development?

Thus the book enriches our understanding of leadership across cultures in a manner similar to, though not in as detailed a manner as, Katie Anderson's book, *Learning to Lead, Leading to Learn* which has been referred to above. The argument here is not that the African way is the only way of knowing and practising leadership. It is one valid way of knowing and practising leadership which should be known not just by Africans but also by leadership students and practitioners from other cultures. In this regard the book attempts to do two things: On the one hand, it enhances African learners' understanding of leadership by explaining African leadership traditions; on the other, it challenges learners from other cultures to think about approaches to leadership that have been developed in their own cultures and traditions. The argument here is that indigenous knowledge systems from around the world have much to offer to us, the modern people of our age.

In traditional African society, particularly in the southern part of the continent, storytelling was an important way of teaching values and motivating the young to develop desirable characteristics such as courage and service of others. In some societies storytelling after dinner was also a way of both teaching values and providing entertainment during the dry season between harvesting and planting when there was no urgency for young people to get up early in the morning to go and work in the fields. Now the tradition of storytelling to teach values and other lessons is fully exploited in this book in which illustrative stories are used to exemplify the type of leadership under discussion. Some of the stories are anecdotes based on real-life situations, while some are taken from the lives of real people such as Julius Nyerere of Tanzania or Alexander Fleming, the Scottish boy who later discovered penicillin. Typically, there is a 'Tuning in Exercise' related to the story. This is explained below.

The fourth characteristic has to do with bringing together different cultural traditions and leadership practices. From an instructional point of view, the book's approach is international and inclusive in that it explores learning and instructional leadership from different cultural and theoretical perspectives. Starting with Jurgen Habermas's (German/Western) theory of cognitive interests (technical, practical and emancipatory), it goes on to draw on Paulo Freire's approach to pedagogy (Latin American), leading to the decolonized epistemology and *Ubuntu*-based developmental approach that this writer developed in an earlier book (Ngara 1995). Furthermore, there is another significant way in which the book presents an African perspective combined with an international and inclusive approach. In addition to the *Ubuntu* approach, two other perspectives are highlighted in the book: the Japanese approach to leadership and the Nordic system of government which, combined with Servant Leadership as developed by Robert Greenleaf (1977), represent good and exemplary Western approaches to leadership. The position taken in the book is there is one human race with a multiplicity of cultures and traditions. It is to the advantage of all peoples to make use of that which is good in the cultures, traditions and practices of the people of Africa and other formerly colonized countries, and from the West and the East. For the people of the West and formerly colonized people, there is currently only one epistemology, based on modern Western concepts of ways of knowing. For the people of Africa and other peoples of the South, it is essential that they know who they are, understand their own good cultural traditions and use these to enrich their own and the world's understanding of what leadership and educational leadership are about.

What remains is to comment on the target groups and on the structure and presentation. In terms of the target groups, the book is first designed as a textbook for postgraduate students and their teachers, especially master's degree and postgraduate diploma students of Educational Leadership. (Some lecturers/professors might also consider it as a recommended text for Bachelor of Education students specializing in Educational Leadership.) In addition, the book is also designed as a handbook for practitioners and policymakers. Policymakers in ministries or departments of education and practitioners who want to improve their leadership abilities would find this to be an easy to follow handbook. The structure of the book is partly designed with these target groups in mind. For students there are first 'Tuning in Exercises' at the beginning of each chapter. In addition there are more challenging activities and exercises in the appendix before the references section. The activities-cum-exercises are arranged according to the fifteen chapters of the book with typically two activities/exercises for each chapter. There are exceptional cases where there is one or three exercises per chapter. Practitioners and policymakers need not work on the activities and exercises in the appendix, but they would do well to read the story or stories at the beginning of each chapter and to familiarize themselves with the Tuning in Exercise of the chapter.

There are four further features that deserve highlighting in this introduction: first, the book is divided into five parts as explained in the preface. These parts are arranged in what the author sees as a logical sequence in the teaching and learning of Leadership. This kind of progression is what seems appropriate for a programme for students specializing in Educational Leadership. The structure is similar to the structure of the diploma programme which the author and his colleagues ran at the Lead and Inspire School of Leadership in Pretoria, South Africa, from 2010 to 2012 – although that was at a lower level than the level envisaged for the users of this book.

Second, as already indicated, many chapters feature illustrative stories and Tuning in Exercises. The 'Tuning in Exercise' is the method used at the Lead and Inspire School of Leadership to draw the attention of students to the topic of the day and to invite active participation from them. It is the equivalent of what is conventionally called a 'teaser' but is intended to go deeper than the ordinary teaser by inviting learners to reflect more seriously on the questions and to then give the rest of the lesson the attention it deserves. In the context of a class many of the exercises are meant to encourage discussion and sharing among the learners. The Tuning in Exercise is followed by substantive presentations and further discussions.

Third, from the point of view of the approach to teaching where students are involved, the following are the key pedagogical features:

1. Tuning in Exercises as a way of introducing each topic.
2. Illustrative stories to demonstrate the type of leadership or issue under discussion.
3. Lecture presentations: These are not marked as such, but the reader should understand that the key content features are intended to be presented in the form of lecture presentations. As virtual teaching has become an essential approach to teaching resulting from the Covid-19 experience, some lectures could ideally be presented as additional online resources.
4. Group discussions and group reports.
5. The activities-cum-exercises in the appendix.

Finally, it is worth mentioning the use of the first-person plural 'we' and the first-person singular 'I' in the narrative. The text is written by a single author who uses the 'we' to include the reader in the narrative in the spirit of *Ubuntu*, suggesting the writer is telling the story of the book together with the reader. Where it is inappropriate to include the reader, the first-person singular 'I' is used.

Part I

Understanding education and leadership

1

Education for development and leadership

Tuning in Exercise

Reflect on the following questions and answer them as individuals first, and then as a group. Bring your group reports to the plenary session:

1. What do you consider to be the purpose of education in society?
2. Who is more important in the classroom, the teacher or the student?
3. What is the main purpose of the student in a lesson: is it to be taught or to learn?

The purpose of education

Education that is meaningful and that adequately fulfils its purpose in society must have three main functions:

- First, it must be able to preserve the values, beliefs, customs, traditions and knowledge that ensure the long-term survival of the society in question.
- Second, it must be able to facilitate development. Society should not remain static if it is to face the challenges that are brought upon it by the changes that are taking place globally and cosmically. There are threats to our environment that are caused by advances in technology; the advances in technology also mean that if any particular nation is not able to keep abreast of those advances, it cannot compete on an equal footing with other nations; a nation that was once a colony has to change its way of thinking and doing things so that it can operate fully as an independent state that has its own identity which gives respect and recognition to its citizens. There is a dialectical relationship between education and economic development. It is what the education system can do

to its people that can enable the people of a country to transform the economy and propel industrialization. With appropriate education, people can become powerful agents of change and transformation. All this entails changing the consciousness and skill levels of the people.
- Third, education provides the individual with the skills and capabilities that will enable him or her to fit into the structure and value systems of the society by empowering him or her to perform such tasks as teaching, nursing, computer programming and leading a company or a government department, among many other tasks. In that way, the individual is not only helped to fit into the society and survive but is also empowered to play a role in the development of the nation.

This book is about the development of educational leaders. It looks at what is done to future educational leaders both from the point of view of the education given to them and what is done to them to become effective leaders. In this chapter our focus is on the kind of education that facilitates the development of educational leaders. An appropriate starting point in this regard is the curriculum.

The curriculum and ways of knowing

Very often when people talk about the curriculum, they are referring to what is taught or curriculum content. In *The African University and Its Mission* (Ngara 1995) I make this statement: 'By curriculum we mean what is taught as well as the methods of teaching it.' I quote Grundy (1987: 5) as saying, curriculum is 'a way of organising a set of human educational experiences'. An important point of reference in discussing ways of knowing is the German sociologist, Jurgen Habermas's theory of cognitive interests. In terms of this theory, Habermas identified three basic cognitive interests which constitute three ways of knowing: technical, practical and emancipatory. Habermas posits that these are three ways in which knowledge is organized and generated: the technical use which is only concerned with the technical aspects of knowledge; the practical interest which in part means making meaning of our lives through reading, dialogue and intersubjective reflection on reality; and the emancipatory which is learning to create social change. The question here is whether the approach to teaching should be based on the technical, the practical or the emancipatory interest. In *The African University and Its Mission* (Ngara 1995: 43–4), I explained the implications of the three interests as follows:

- A curriculum that is based on or dominated by the technical interest can be oriented towards controlling the pupil or learner. This can be explained by reference to Fundamental Pedagogics, a theoretical discourse which is said to have dominated the approach to teacher education in Afrikaans language and historically Black institutions in apartheid South Africa. In terms of this approach, politics and economics were excluded from educational discourse as they were said to be extraneous to the educational process. The acquisition of knowledge was therefore conceived of in purely technical terms. In reality this approach was meant to perpetuate the apartheid system by denying the learner the opportunity to question the system. According to Penny Enslin, by means of Fundamental Pedagogics, teachers were 'required to perceive and treat children as helpless, incompetent and … in need of authority to save them from their own evil inclinations' (see Nkomo 1990: 86). While this is so, it is important to note that the development of skill is a primary preoccupation of the technical interest.

- A curriculum based on the practical interest promotes interaction between pupil and teacher in the process of making meaning of the world. It entails recognition of the other and dialogue, with the teacher recognizing the pupil and the pupil recognizing the teacher. There is an emphasis on understanding the world, interpreting it and promoting the appropriate action. Consequently judgement is the central disposition of this interest.
- The emancipatory cognitive interest was defined by Grundy (1987: 14) as 'a fundamental interest in emancipation and empowerment to engage in autonomous action arising out of authentic critical insights into the social construction of society'. A curriculum informed by this interest promotes freedom, self-reflection and action that is intended to question and change the status quo. With reference to their own research, Donella Caspersz and Doina Olaru (2014) have put it this way: 'We argue that developing an emancipatory interest is critical in learning to create social change, that is, wanting to create a better world and society for self and others.' Now, to change the world for the better, one must see what is wrong with what presently is. From this it is logical to conclude that the central disposition of the emancipatory interest is critique as argued by Grundy (ibid: 124).

The question that arises is whether these three interests are necessarily mutually exclusive. As argued in *The African University and Its Mission*, a properly educated learner will need skill, the ability to judge and take appropriate action, and the ability to critique. The question, therefore, is not whether any should be excluded but which should be the dominant interest that informs the curriculum. The conclusion we are bound to arrive at in this regard is that provided skill and judgement are part of the education of the learner, a curriculum that is predominantly informed by the emancipatory interest provides a sound basis for the education of university students. This leads us to a discussion of the approach to teaching and learning advocated in this book. An observation that should be made at this point is that in our scheme of things in this book, 'ways of knowing' should include consideration of the role of indigenous knowledge systems in the education of learners in previously colonized countries. This is a subject that comes up for discussion at various points in this book.

A teaching/learning model for development

Reproductive and constructive learning – lessons from Paulo Freire

There are two opposing concepts of learning that we should be aware of – reproductive and constructive learning. Constructive learning is learning with understanding in which the student applies his/her critical faculties to a text or body of knowledge, questions the assumptions of the author, connects one part of the text with the other and passes judgement on the arguments and conclusions of the author. Reproductive learning is passive learning in which the student directs his/her attention towards learning the text itself and is therefore involved in rote learning which is characterized by the memorization of facts. For them to become productive or critical thinkers, students should go beyond the mere recognition and production of facts and must, as Behr (1980: 44) has argued, acquire methods and techniques for using data by '(i) changing information into different symbolic forms; (ii) discovering relationships among facts; (iii) applying facts to solve problems and (iv) making judgments on the merit or value of data'. By achieving this students master the content and become subjects of the learning process so that they are no longer just reproducing undigested facts but are themselves participating in the organization of knowledge and consequently becoming independent of the author of the text.

In order to appreciate fully the implications of constructive and reproductive learning we should realize they have an ideological dimension in so far as each is designed to produce a certain kind of social being. The one questions values, assumptions and conclusions, and the other accepts them on their face value. The implications of these two types of human beings have been eloquently articulated by Paulo Freire in his theory of 'banking education' and 'problem-posing education'. In the banking approach to education students are dumb depositories of information, passively receiving the gift of knowledge from the teachers who consider themselves to be the ultimate authorities with whose choice and views the students must comply. According to Freire (1972: 46–7), banking education maintains a contradiction between students and teachers through a series of attitudes and practices (ten in all) which can be roughly summarized as follows:

- The teacher being the only one who teaches while students maintain the position of those who are taught.
- The teacher thinking that he/she knows everything while students are presumed to know nothing.
- The teacher thinking that he/she is the only one who can think while students are essentially reduced to objects of his/her thoughts.
- In other words, everything in the learning process, including talking, disciplining, the choice of the programme and so on, is done from the perspective of the teacher while students are passive, ignorant and meekly obedient participants.

The relations between teacher and pupil portrayed here are very much akin to those based on Fundamental Pedagogics that we have already discussed. Now, in place of banking education Freire (1972: 52–3) proposes the problem-posing concept of education which sees 'men as conscious beings and consciousness directed towards the world'. Problem-posing or liberating education 'consists in acts of cognition, not transferrals of information. It is a learning situation in which the cognizable object ... intermediates the cognitive actors – teacher on the one hand and students on the other.' Accordingly, problem-posing education demands a resolution of the teacher–student contradiction by insisting on 'dialogical relations' through which a new relationship emerges: 'teacher-student with student-teachers'. Banking education domesticates while problem-posing education liberates. Freire's approach is akin to the Habermasian concept of the critical interest which is emancipatory. It also incorporates the practical interest in promoting dialogue.

At this juncture it is appropriate to point to the two sets of relationships that are implicit in the dichotomy between the two opposing sets of concepts we have outlined above: first, reproductive learning versus constructive learning; second, banking education versus problem-posing education. The two sets can be characterized as representing an undialectical approach to teaching and learning (reproductive learning, banking education) and a dialectical approach to teaching and learning (constructive learning, problem-posing education). The former may under certain circumstances be compared to the Habermasian concept of the technical interest and the latter to the critical interest.

The stage we have reached in our analysis takes us to a crucial point in our effort to develop an approach to education that facilitates the development of educational leaders and the transformation of nations. As indicated at the beginning of this chapter, the curriculum consists of two main elements: what is taught (or curriculum content) and the approach to teaching that content. We will address curriculum content later; for now we need to draw the discussion on teaching and learning to a conclusion by positing an approach to teaching and learning. For the curriculum to produce the desired results, our approach to teaching and learning should be designed to establish a new set of relationships: first, between the learner and knowledge; second, between the learner and the teacher; and third, between the learner and the world out there, that is, the world of work and society at large. To understand this we should first reflect on what I have referred to as an undialectical approach to teaching and learning.

The undialectical concept of teaching and learning

The undialectical concept regards the learner as a dumb depository of knowledge, a passive recipient of information and facts, an object of history and of the influences of the world in which he/she lives. In the process of teaching and learning, the teacher feeds the learner with information and facts and the learner gives nothing back to the teacher; the knowledge is deposited into the learner's mind and the learner receives it passively and memorizes it without transforming it, reconstructing it or adding to it. As a product of history, the learner is impacted upon by the world out there, outside the educational institution, and is subjected to its various pressures – economic, political, social – without reacting in a positive and active way to these pressures or attempting to pre-empt them; what is more there is no deliberate attempt to link the knowledge the learner acquires (passively) and the needs of society out there. The learning process is characterized by passive cognition and a passive attitude to the world and the teacher. This kind of relationship between the learner on the one hand and the teacher and the world on the other can be represented schematically as shown in Figure 1 (see Ngara 1995: 50).

The learner we have in this approach to teaching and learning may have the capacity to receive, and perhaps retain, large amounts of facts, but without the ability to use that information to transform his/her environment. Such a person may become a perfect functionary, a robot who carries out whatever instructions he/she is given, but has no capacity to think and therefore cannot change the face of the world. Such people

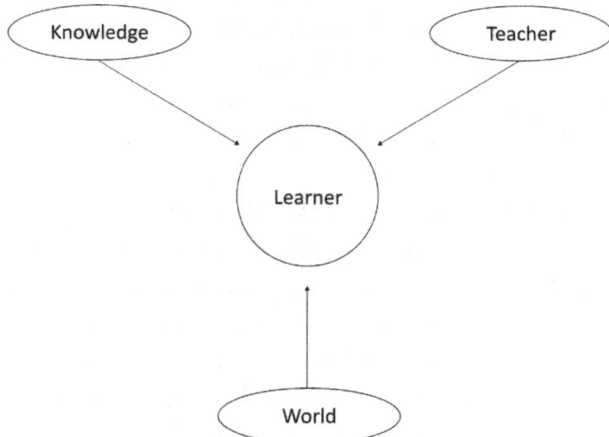

Figure 1 The undialectical concept of teaching and learning
Source: Created by Emmanuel Ngara for the 1995 publication.

will fill high-level positions in society and perform their functions as 'efficiently' as possible to keep the system going or to maintain the system that was left by the colonial masters or whatever authorities were previously in charge. Graduates of this calibre can, at best, maintain the status quo without bringing about any meaningful change. What we need is a theory of teaching/learning which helps the learner to be the subject of history and producer of knowledge who understands his/her society, can critique the society and participate in that society's development to a higher level. The model proposed here can be represented as shown in Figure 2 (Ibid: 52).

What we have here is a dialectical and developmental concept of teaching and learning. It is not unidirectional; rather, it produces a dynamic and dialectical relationship between the learner and knowledge, the learner and the teacher and the learner and the learning process. What is more, as the arrow between the circle for 'Knowledge' and the circle for 'World/Society' in Figure 2 shows, the knowledge the learner acquires comes back to society in the form of the learner's influence on society. (The same applies to the dotted lines between 'Teacher' and 'World' and between 'Teacher' and 'Knowledge'). There are two observations to be made about this approach to teaching and learning: First, it observes the principles of connectedness in the teaching and learning process. The learner is connected to the teacher, to her/his society and to knowledge, just as the teacher is connected to the learner, to society and to knowledge. This is in line with the interdependence principles of the philosophy of *Ubuntu* that will be discussed in detail in a later chapter. Briefly, the philosophy says, 'A person is a person on account of other people' (*Motho ke motho ka batho* in the Sesotho language of Lesotho). This means a student is the kind of student he/she is in relation to other students, and in relation to the teacher and the world he/she comes from. The import of this is that ideally learning is a social

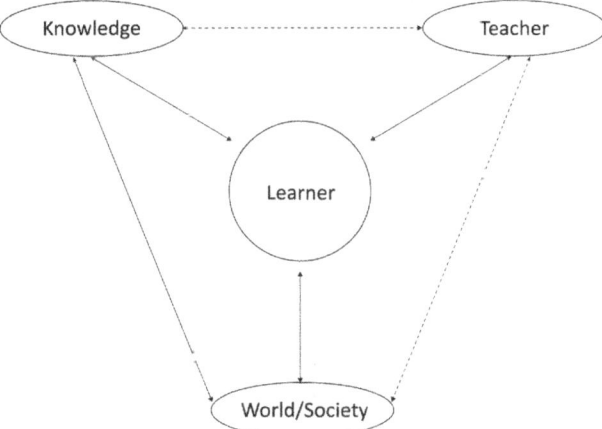

Figure 2 The dialectical and developmental concept of teaching and learning
Source: Created by Emmanuel Ngara for the 1995 publication.

process. Similarly, the teacher is a teacher in relation to students and the society he/she comes from. Consequently, there is no teacher without students, just as there is no army general without an army. Extended further, it is not only the students who learn from the teacher; the teacher also learns from students. In this regard, it is interesting to note how true leaders like Isao Yoshino of Toyota acknowledge that as teachers they can learn from learners. Thus Katie Anderson (2020: 14) comments, 'While I considered myself the learner and Mr. Yoshino the teacher during our earliest encounters, Yoshino told me that he too learned from me.'

As we shall see later (Part V), this book is being written at a time when Covid-19 has made digitalization an important aspect of teaching and learning. We have to acknowledge the need and importance of digitalization and realize that this is the way for the future, even post-Covid-19. However, the *Ubuntu* philosophy warns us that learning is a social process. The contact between the teacher and the student and between student and student is an important part of learning and teaching. What this seems to indicate is that while it is possible for students to learn from their homes and the teacher to teach from her/his home, there is something missing in the kind of learning that is characterized by the solitariness of both student and teacher. This is an issue that we shall come back to in Part V, but the implications seem to be that digitalization needs to be enriched by some kind of social contact between student and teacher, and student and student.

The second observation is that this is a developmental approach to teaching/learning in that it sharpens the learner's intellectual faculties and social consciousness and consequently helps him/her to make a positive impact on the state of knowledge and on the world, and thus propel the wheels of history forward. The developmental concept is therefore a model which is not only concerned with the process of learning; it is not only concerned with constructive learning in relation to a text or body of knowledge but also seeks to explain the relationship between the process of acquiring knowledge and the phenomenon of development. The dialectical and developmental model thus subsumes the constructive learning theory as propounded by Behr but is more inclusive as it takes into account issues of social consciousness as articulated by Paulo Freire, and also seeks to foster a sense of social responsibility during the learning process. However, to have a fuller understanding of the developmental concept, we need to bring in an element that has not been fully discussed here – curriculum content.

Curriculum content and the developmental model of education

The model of education advocated in this chapter works on the premise that the educational experience is dependent on two primary complementary variables or elements – teaching/learning and curriculum content. The one refers to the process the student should go through, or the *how* of the educational experience, while the other is the body of knowledge to which the teaching/learning process is applied, and this constitutes the *what* of the educational experience. The understanding here is that a learning model which neglects or minimizes the importance of either of these elements presents an incomplete view of the educational experience and is consequently flawed.

The question that immediately arises as far as curriculum content is concerned is what to include and what not to include in the syllabus for a particular group of students. There are a number of considerations to take into account here: First, the corpus of knowledge in all disciplines keeps on increasing as more discoveries are made or more knowledge is created. In the field of literature, for example, new works of art continue to be produced and a university department of Literature must from time to time review its syllabus in the light of these new developments. Second, knowledge is generated and discovered in a social and historical context. This perhaps applies more to the humanities and social sciences than to the natural sciences but has a general application to all forms of knowledge. For example, works of art have a more or less direct relationship with historical and social developments. A related issue is that there is no education system which is ideologically neutral. The education system of any society to a large extent reflects the ideological value systems and cultural prejudices of the dominant social groups of that society. It could be argued, for instance, that the content of British education reflects not only values that have been handed down from generation to generation but also contemporary British middle-class values, the middle class being the social group that has dominated British values since the overthrow of feudalism in the country. Similarly, there is no gainsaying that during the colonial era, education in Africa reflected colonial values and generally negated African values. It is said that French colonization was more thorough than British colonization, and so we are told that students in Gabon deep down in Africa would be taught exactly the same content as French students in Paris, and consequently turning educated Africans into French men and women. Further south, Mokubung Nkomo (1990: 2) records how, in apartheid South Africa, Bantu education encouraged the domination of Blacks by Whites.

The arguments presented above point to the following: choosing the most valuable elements of the available quantum of material to form part of the curriculum for the particular group of students; selecting content that facilitates the preservation of the values, traditions, identity and aspirations of the society the students come from; and selecting content that facilitates the development of that society. This argument relates to the appropriateness and relevance of the curriculum to the society the students come from. It would not do, for instance, for a literature syllabus in a British university to have French literature as the largest component. Such a syllabus would be out of sync with the cultural values and aspirations of the people of Britain. Similarly, a literature syllabus for African students which projects British literature more than African literature would be out of sync with the cultural values and aspirations of the people of Africa. But there is more to curriculum content than societal and cultural considerations. The content must be such as to meet the needs of the student as well. As indicated earlier, a properly educated learner will need skill, the ability to judge and take appropriate action and the ability to critique. University students will need to have knowledge and skills that enable them to be employable and to generate employment in the relevant areas of specialization. This means university students, for instance, will need to know their accounting, law, medicine, psychology and so on and should be able to cope with related disciplines as well. They should have the skills that go with these professions. The Tuning Project (Onana et al. 2014: 63–5) which sought to harmonize the quality of the products of higher education institutions across the African continent by defining competences of graduates in various fields of study identified eighteen generic competences, of which six are listed here:

1. Ability for conceptual thinking, analysis and synthesis
2. Professionalism, ethical values and commitment to Ubuntu (respect for the well-being and dignity of fellow human beings)
3. Capacity for critical evaluation and self-awareness
4. Ability to translate knowledge into practice
5. Objective decision-making and practical cost-effective problem solving
6. Capacity to use innovative and appropriate technologies

These and the other twelve competences apply to all disciplines. It may be noted that while the emancipatory interest is not clearly articulated in the competences, all three Habermasian interests – technical, practical and emancipatory – are either explicitly or implicitly incorporated in some of these competences. The emancipatory interest which may not be discerned very clearly in these six comes out more effectively in competence number 16: 'Ability to evaluate, review and enhance quality'. An interesting point to note is that the philosophy of *Ubuntu* is included in competence number 2. This points to the importance of the *Ubuntu* philosophy to African students of both Education and Leadership. In designing the curricula for students, academics should therefore think of content that facilitates the development of graduates who have these qualities and competences.

The principles we have articulated so far have a general application to students from all cultures provided the necessary adjustments are made in respect of each specific culture. What we need to be conscious of is the fact that there is more to be done for students in formerly colonized countries than the general principle of making adjustments. In these countries, knowledge was seen through the lenses of the colonial mind. The colonizers' understanding of knowledge was based on their traditions which disregarded and/or undermined the knowledge systems of the indigenous people. In this regard, it is incumbent upon academic institutions in Africa and other former colonies to examine the whole epistemological system upon which the approach to education in the colonial institutions was based. The questions that need to be asked in the process of decolonizing education include the following:

1. Does the education system inherited from colonialism include or exclude indigenous knowledge systems?
2. Does the inherited system affirm the positive values, traditions, customs and other elements of the indigenous people that help to ensure the long-term survival and identity of the society in question?
3. What elements of the indigenous knowledge system of the people must be included in the decolonized epistemology?
4. What elements in the colonial system would enrich the decolonized curriculum?

In asking these and similar questions, it is necessary to take into account the debate on the concepts of coloniality and decoloniality with specific reference to the coloniality of power, the coloniality of knowledge and the coloniality of being as, for example, explained in Johannes Seroto (2018). These concepts are discussed in greater detail in Chapter 15. Of particular relevance to this chapter is the coloniality of knowledge. According to Seroto, the coloniality of knowledge poses epistemological questions that are linked to the following:

1) The politics of knowledge generation; 2) questions of who generates which knowledge and for what purpose; 3) the question of relevance and irrelevance of knowledge; and 4) how some knowledges disempowered/empowered communities and peoples. (Seroto 2018: 5)

With regard to the determination of appropriate curriculum content for African institutions all this entails the following:

- Understanding African history
- Having enough knowledge of indigenous African knowledge systems and cultural traditions
- Ability to identify the elements of knowledge that are common or relevant to all cultures
- Identifying the elements in the colonial system that are valuable and have the potential to facilitate the development of the people of Africa

In the next session we give some guiding principles to higher education institutions in Africa (see Ngara 1995: 78–89). The guiding principles may be used by higher education institutions in formerly colonized countries in other parts of the world to reflect on appropriate curriculum content for themselves.

Some guiding principles for designing curriculum content in African universities

1. There is a common core of knowledge which is the same for all cultures – African, European, Asian, American and so on; and learners from all cultures can benefit from this common core.
2. The accepted conventions governing the content and organization of knowledge in African institutions of higher education derive from the Western tradition which is based on Western epistemology and value systems.
3. If African institutions of higher education are to provide an education which is relevant to the needs of Africa and which speaks to the problems of the continent, their curricula should as far as possible be informed by the African environment and indigenous African knowledge systems.
4. By the content of the syllabus being informed by the African environment is not meant that African students should immerse themselves in the African environment to the exclusion of all other cultures and traditions, for that would not provide a basis for a sound education. What it does mean is that African curriculum developers should design syllabuses that are informed by an 'Africa-centred consciousness' but which incorporate knowledge of those parts of the world whose history, culture and languages have impacted Africa.
5. The following is a brief explanation of a syllabus that is based on an Africa-centred consciousness: A history syllabus based on this principle will present African history as the axis on which the history of every other continent revolves. Thus in addition to studying the history of the relevant part of Africa, the students will be taught about Africa's contact with Europe, the African diaspora, important points of contact with Asia and, if necessary and relevant, other countries in the world whose history and experiences are similar to those of Africa. Within these broad principles, a department will decide how much to include and what to leave out.

Conclusion: The universality of the basic principle

In this chapter we have dealt with the enormous task of developing educational leaders through instructional leadership. The basic argument here is that effective training of educational leaders for teaching and management purposes depends on two main variables: the teaching/learning process and curriculum content. In terms of the teaching/learning process we have analysed the Habermasian concept of the three learning interests and Paulo Freire's concepts of banking education and problem-posing education. The discussion of these concepts was meant to lead to the developmental concept of education. From the point of view of curriculum content, the developmental concept of education can be summarized as positing that curriculum content in an African university should meet at least two primary requirements: First, it should be based on sound educational principles that have a general universal application in the particular discipline. Second, it should be appropriate to the African context and reflect an Africa-centred consciousness. A curriculum based on these principles will play a major role in fulfilling the teaching and learning element of the training of educational leaders.

The case of Africa has been used as a concrete example to ensure the position taken in this book is not purely theoretical. In other words, the principles explained here have a general application depending on the countries concerned. The principles articulated by Habermas and Paulo Freire as well as the dialectical and developmental concept of teaching and learning are all relevant in some degree to all societies – whether Western, Asian, Caribbean, Latin American or African; whether in the North or the South. They have special relevance for Africa and other formerly colonized continents because of the need for the people of those continents and countries to make education more meaningful and relevant to their needs and the needs of their countries. For students in, say, Arab countries and India, what they probably need to do is to substitute concepts such as Africa-centred consciousness with Arab-centred consciousness, India-centred consciousness and so on. Students in some countries of the North need a liberating form of education just as Africans do, but because the present system is based on Western values and a Western epistemology, the system is a lot more meaningful for them than it is for formerly colonized peoples. What they need is an education system which puts more emphasis on the liberating elements in Habermas, Paulo Freire and the dialectical and developmental concept of teaching and learning.

What is also a primary requirement for all learners/leaders is to build into the curriculum the leadership component of the programme. It is with this in view that the next chapter seeks to clarify the meaning of the term *leadership*.

2

What is leadership?

Tuning in Exercise

Reflect on the following questions as individuals first, discuss them in groups and bring group reports to the plenary session. If you are studying Leadership as an Open and Distance Learning (ODL) student, or if you are a practitioner who wants to improve her/his leadership capacity, it would be useful to have an opportunity to discuss the questions with someone else who has similar interests.

- Whose interests are more important, those of the leader or those of the followers?
- Is leadership a position?
- Are all leaders born leaders?
- Are Leadership and Management synonymous?

What leadership is and is not

In the introduction, we noted that in this book we are going to examine leadership both as a practice and an academic discipline. To make a distinction between these two dimensions of the subject, we shall use leadership with lower case l to denote leadership as a practice and Leadership with upper case L to denote Leadership as a discipline in the same way as we would refer to Mathematics, Chemistry and English Language as disciplines. We also noted that leadership development entails going through three processes: *being, knowing* and *becoming*. The process of becoming an educational leader entails going through a fourth element, namely *applying* or *application*. This relates to the sphere of life in which one is operating as a leader, such as education, business, politics and so on. Consequently, the process of becoming an educational leader presented in this book involves *formation*.

What then is leadership? We may all think we know what leadership is, but there is a great deal of misunderstanding and confusion about the term. In this regard, leadership authorities have identified a number of myths that have developed about the concept which need to be clarified:

Myths about leadership

Myth number 1: Leadership is a position

The thinking here is that whoever is in charge is a leader; or whoever holds a position of authority is a leader. Consequently, to be a leader is coterminous with holding a position. The truth of the matter is that not all people in positions of authority have what it takes to be a leader. On the other hand there are people who do not hold official positions and yet possess leadership qualities and do the things that true leaders do. This point will become clearer as we interrogate the phenomenon in subsequent chapters. Suffice it at this point to quote one of the acknowledged gurus on leadership who in turn quotes one Stanley Huffty making this telling comment: 'It's not the position that makes the leader; it's the leader that makes the position' (Maxwell 2007: 15).

My late partner in teaching, Mrs Bernice Teboho Ngara, used to tell the story of a girl she taught at a school called Westville Girls High School in Durban, South Africa. The school had been a school for White girls only during the time of the apartheid system in South Africa when education was run on racial lines. Mrs Ngara became a teacher at the school just after the abolition of apartheid when Nelson Mandela had been elected the first Black president of the country. Mrs Ngara was one of very few African teachers in the school and was the only African on the staff who taught English. Most of the students were White.

One day a new Black girl called Iviwe joined the class. She was a few days in the class when she noticed how noisy, misbehaved and disrespectful of the teacher the students were. Suddenly Iviwe stood up, walked to the front of the class, banged the desk in front of her to call for attention and then said firmly: 'Girls, this is not on! We are here to learn, but you are depriving us of that opportunity by making it impossible for the teacher to teach. Is it because she is a Black teacher? Please stop this nonsense so that we can learn!' Suddenly there was silence, and the eyes of all the girls followed her as she confidently walked back to her seat. The girls looked at Iviwe with amazement, and order was immediately restored and the teacher could now teach. Iviwe had no position in the school. She was a Black girl; she was one of the youngest; and she was new. From that day onwards, the class recognized her as a leader.

The story of Iviwe shows that leadership is not necessarily coterminous with a position. There are many cases when position and leadership go hand in hand – when a person who occupies a position demonstrates the qualities and behaviour of a leader. There are, however, other cases when people in positions of authority are not able to demonstrate that they deserve the positions they hold.

Myth number 2: All leaders are born leaders

In Act Five Scene 1 of his play, *Twelfth Night*, William Shakespeare wrote:

> Why, 'Some are born great,
> some achieve greatness,
> and some have greatness thrown upon them'.

This was a very perceptive comment, one that is very pertinent to the issue of leadership. While some leaders are 'born leaders', there are many who achieve leadership by their own efforts, and by applying the principles of true leadership, while there are some who assume leadership responsibilities or inherit leadership positions without really deserving them. Shakespeare could have been aware that in many European countries at that time, the kingship or queenship of a country was hereditary. If you were the first born of a king or queen, you were likely to be the heir to the throne whether you had good leadership qualities or not. It is significant that Shakespeare used Feste, the Clown, to make this comment. It is reasonable to argue that this witty clown is in fact the wisest of the characters in the play; and that the playwright was using this clown to express some of his deepest thoughts. Coming to our time, there is a statement that has become popular in leadership parlance: 'Leadership is not an exclusive club for those who were born with it.' Yes, leadership is an art and a way of life that can be taught, developed and acquired.

Myth number 3: Leadership is synonymous with Management; or a leader is the same as a manager

Let us begin by comparing two companies that deal with motor vehicles. The one is a garage where vehicles are serviced. The other is a car manufacturing plant where new cars are built and assembled. The first company deals with existing vehicles. Its main function is to ensure that our cars continue to operate efficiently. Where a part is worn out, it is changed. When the oil is too old it is replaced by new oil. If the engine has done too many miles and is no longer doing an efficient job, it can be reconditioned. The function of this garage is to keep our cars running smoothly and efficiently.

On the other hand, the car manufacturing factory is to produce new cars, not to just keep our old cars running. What is more, if the people running the factory are really good at their job, they do not keep on producing the same models of vehicles. They keep on experimenting and striving to produce better models of vehicles than previous models. If they are to remain relevant and competitive, they have to be innovative and keep on researching to produce better-quality vehicles which they need to market and convince the customers that they are producing a new and superior product.

This comparison between the two types of companies can shed some light on the relationship between leadership and management. The two companies both deal with motor vehicles; their functions are related, but different. In a similar way, while leadership and management are related, they are quite distinct from each other. People often talk about 'leadership' while they are in fact talking about 'management'. They can talk about 'the leader' while they are in fact talking about someone who is a 'manager'.

We shall deal with the distinction between leader and manager in some detail below. For now, it should suffice to make the following points: A leader does a lot more than a manager. A manager focuses on the maintenance of systems, processes and practices, and on making sure that the machinery of the organization runs smoothly and efficiently. Leadership has to do with giving direction – with telling people where to go and why. Leadership is about influencing and inspiring people so as to move an organization from point A to point B and to point C and so on. The leader sees the organization recreating or reinventing itself; he/she is innovative. The manager generally follows laid down rules, procedures and practices. The manager does a maintenance job like the garage referred to above; the leader innovates and grows the organization.

Interrogating leadership, management and administration

We noted above that people often talk about leadership when in reality they are talking about management. There are in fact three concepts that can be confused with one another, and it is necessary to clarify the distinction between them. These are *leadership*, *management* and *administration*. With regard to the first two, it has been correctly said that you lead people and manage an organization. It is the people in the organization that the leader leads to change the organization which operates in terms of structures, systems and processes. But before we proceed we need to make mention of a fourth term that is associated with the running of organizations such as companies and higher education institutions, and that is *governance*. We shall return to this.

Leadership and management

In the meantime consider the following scenario: You are the chief executive officer of a higher education institution, and you and your executive team get a visit from two officials of the Ministry of Higher Education. They interview you and your team by asking a series of questions. We shall call them Mr Mafa and Ms Temba.

Mr Mafa

1. How many students are enrolled in your institution?
2. How do you capture the information supplied by the students onto your database?
3. How do you check the accuracy of the information?
4. Do you have an IT specialist on your staff?
5. Explain how you ensure that your student record system complies with government requirements.

Ms Temba

1. What do you want your student enrolment to be three years from now?
2. To what extent is your staff involved in planning the development of the institution?
3. Would you say you have a happy staff, and what incentives do you provide to get buy-in from them?
4. What contribution is your institution making to national development now, and what is your vision of the institution five years from now?
5. How do you motivate your students to reach for the stars and to develop in character and personality?

Question

Which of the two, *leadership* or *management*, is each official focussing on?

Explanation

Both sets of questions are necessary and useful, but they focus on different things. Mr Mafa's questions are about the efficient running of the institution. His questions focus on systems, processes and structures. Ms Temba's questions are more about people, the development of staff and students and the growth of the institution. Mr Mafa wants the chief executive and her/his team to run an efficient organization. Ms Temba wants the executive to have an impact on the growth of the institution, on its role in society and on the development of both staff and students. In other words, Ms Temba wants the executive to influence and inspire the people who work and learn in the institution. Mr Mafa's questions are largely management questions, while Ms Temba's questions are mainly on issues of leadership.

A leader does much more than a manager. While the manager ensures that the machinery of the organization runs smoothly and efficiently, the leader influences other people to follow so as to grow the organization and to move it both quantitatively and qualitatively to the next level. The leader has her/his eyes not only on the organization as it is today but also on the better and bigger institution it could be in the next three, five or ten years. The point must be made that quantitative development may not always be necessary but qualitative development is a must at all times. We shall see in later chapters that the leader is in part guided by a vision and influences other people to buy into that vision for the good of the organization.

Vision and influence must be complemented by the specifics of how you translate ideas and ideals into concrete reality. This requires management which has to do with putting structures, procedures and processes in place and making sure that conflicts are resolved and rules and regulations are followed. It should be clear from this that both leadership and management are necessary and complementary.

The influence of Henri Fayol

At this point, it is appropriate to refer to the influence of Henri Fayol who, as mentioned in the introduction, wrote a book entitled *Industrial and General Administration* in 1916 (see Fayol 1930; Wren 2003; Hatchuel and Segrestin 2018). Fayol significantly influenced the development of management thinking in both industry and education in Europe. Among other things, he defined what he called the five functions of management as well as fourteen (14) principles of management. We shall do no more than just list these here: The five functions were: Planning, Organising, Command, Coordination and Control. The fourteen management principles were:

1. Division of Work
2. Balancing Authority and Responsibility
3. Discipline
4. Unity of Command
5. Unity of Direction (this refers to teams working under one manager using one plan)
6. Subordination of Individual Interest to the General Interest
7. Remuneration
8. Centralization
9. Scalar Chain (the chain of supervision from the highest authority to the lowest)
10. Order
11. Equity
12. Stability of Tenure of Personnel
13. Initiative
14. Espirit De Corps (striving for the involvement and unity of the employees).

It is clear that except for principle number 13 (Initiative) these are all functions to be performed and principles to be followed, not qualities or characteristics that the individual is expected to have. Principle number 13 is somewhat different in that employees were encouraged to develop and carry out plans. It can be argued that while it was not directed at the manager as such, this was an ability (and therefore a quality) that employees were encouraged to develop. Leadership qualities are discussed in some detail in Chapter 8; and some African perspectives on leadership qualities are dealt with in Chapter 5 and other chapters. For now we briefly turn our attention to leadership and management issues in the school system.

Leadership and management in the school system

As this is a book on educational leadership, it is appropriate to briefly reflect on how the concepts *leadership* and *management* have been viewed in the school system. Traditionally, up to and until the 1980s, school principals were regarded as managers or administrators, representing the government or other authorities in the running of the school. It could also be argued that apart from the need for some evidence of general management abilities, there were no clear and specific competencies required for school heads or principals. Essentially, the school head was meant to maintain the status quo in line with the policy of the authorities and performing functions such as those defined by Fayol.

Starting in the United States in the 1980s, the idea of school leadership development began to emerge and grow. As Philip Hallinger outlines in chapter 1 of *Reshaping the Landscape of School Leadership Development* (Hallinger et al., 2003), the role of the principal began to be conceived of as that of instructional leader, transformational leader, leader of a learning community, among other functions, rather than that of just a manager of facility or a system administrator. The role of principal was thus assumed not to be just one of maintaining the status quo but of moving the school forward. School principals began to be seen as agents of change, leading others in the process we referred to above as of moving the organization from point A to point B and to point C and so on. By the 1990s globalization and other pressures were now leading nations throughout the world to begin to think in terms of principal competencies such as literacy, IT literacy, problem solving, critical thinking and others. The concept of school leadership development both in training and during service was now in vogue. The growth and acceptance of the idea can be seen in the publication of such books as *Understanding Educational Leadership* by Steven J. Courtney and others (Bloomsbury Publishing) and Harry Tomlinson's *Educational Leadership: Personal Growth for Personal Development* (Sage), among others.

Administration

Administration features little in the literature on leadership and management, but it is pertinent to refer to it, partly for the sake of clarity and avoiding ambiguity and partly because it is an important concept. There is a sense in which *administration* is an old-fashioned word. What is now commonly called the management of an institution was traditionally referred to as the administration. That usage still persists today in politics where you hear people talking about the Obama or Trump administration in America or the Zuma administration in South Africa. This is a reference to the government of the country concerned under the leadership of the president in question. Related to this is that universities teach programmes in what is called Administration Studies or Political and Administrative Studies. These programmes are about government systems and how governments are run. Our concern in this chapter is with the term administration as it relates to the day-to-day running of an organization, whether it is a company, government ministry, higher education institution or church organization.

Administration in the general non-political sense just explained above plays a role in the running of an organization, and it is necessary to explain how this concept differs from management, and consequently from leadership. A way of distinguishing between administration and management in today's world is to say that the administration element is that aspect of management which deals with routine work. This includes activities such as organizing and conducting meetings, pushing paper, putting appointments and functions in the diary, providing tea and coffee for people attending meetings, answering telephone calls and responding to emails and so on. Management deals with more complicated issues as explained above.

Is administration an essential part of running an organization? It is true to say that leadership and management without good administration can seriously affect the efficient running of an organization. Attention to detail is important. It is good administration that facilitates the implementation of goals and strategic plans; it is good administration that ensures that when rules and regulations are in place, they are properly implemented; it is administration that helps the executives and senior managers to work smoothly and efficiently with good order and in a systematic way. The chief executive needs an efficient personal assistant to make sure all the appointments are organized seamlessly, documents are filed and work flows continuously from the office. This brings us to the term *corporate governance*.

Corporate governance in brief

We refer to this term only for the sake of completeness. It is, however, necessary to point out that anybody who leads an organization, whether in the private sector, in government or in an academic institution, should be aware of corporate governance issues. Corporate governance is defined by some authorities as 'the system of rules, practices and processes by which a firm is governed and controlled'. In a company or an education institution, corporate governance is about ensuring the good running and effectiveness of the organization in relation to the interests of the stakeholders. The following examples should suffice to explain what corporate governance entails.

Example of corporate governance in companies

Some readers may know about or have heard about the King Report on Corporate Governance. This is a series of booklets (this author is aware of four such reports) on guidelines for corporate governance in South African companies, issued by the King Committee on Corporate Governance on behalf of the Institute of Directors in South Africa. It is named after the chairperson, Professor Mervyn King.

For example, King III requires companies to set up an internal audit function which guides them in ensuring good governance, risk management and good internal controls. King IV requires companies to be transparent in their corporate governance practices. There is also a King Code of Ethics which, together with the King Report, gives guidance on the exercise of ethical and effective leadership by the governing body of a company.

Corporate governance in an academic institution

In an academic institution, the normal practice is to have the management led by the vice chancellor or rector, who is the chief executive officer of the organization. He/she and the executive are responsible for running the day-to-day affairs of the institution. Over and above them is a council or board which oversees the efficient and proper running of the institution on behalf of the government and other stakeholders such as the community. If it is a church-related institution, the church in question becomes the primary stakeholder equivalent to the government.

In the example just given, there is a need to clarify leadership roles and issues of accountability. While the vice chancellor is the academic leader who should not only be concerned with management issues but should also ensure he/she leads the institution with vision, he/she is accountable to the council or board and ultimately to the government or church or other chief stakeholder in question. Good governance should also ensure that the roles of the chief executive and those of the chairperson of the board are clearly adumbrated. The chairperson of the board should not take over the roles of the vice chancellor, and neither should the vice chancellor seek to assume the responsibilities of the chairperson. Conflating the roles of the chief executive officer and those of the council or board chairperson by having the same person assuming both roles is a recipe for disaster as it flies in the face of accountability and can easily lead to problems like corruption, the abuse of office and misuse of funds.

Conclusion: Final clarification

In this chapter, we have endeavoured to explain the concept of leadership and to show how it relates to concepts such as management, administration and governance. The student of Leadership, the aspiring leader and the leadership practitioner should be clear about the relationship and distinctions between these terms. The leader has to work with these terms and be clear in her/his mind when each is applicable. In this regard, it is appropriate and useful to make the following observations: Leadership and management as practices do not necessarily contradict each other; rather they complement one another in an organization. Good leadership without good management can only lead to poor performance and poor productivity on the part of an organization. On the other hand, it is necessary to emphasize that for anyone at the head of an organization to focus only on management issues is to fail the organization and its stakeholders. As will become clearer in subsequent chapters, good, dynamic and efficient leadership is essential for the survival of any organization in the modern world. In addition, it cannot be overemphasized that a good leader should be clear about governance issues as adherence to the rules and norms of good governance protects the name and reputation of any organization.

We cannot bring this chapter to a close without reference to an aspect of the word 'leadership' which is not commonly addressed in the literature on the phenomenon of leadership, and that is the ambiguity between what we have defined as 'leadership' and 'leader' and another common usage of the two words. What we have called the management or executive of an organization is often referred to in common discourse as 'the leadership' of an organization. You also hear people talking about 'the leadership' of a country, church or political party. This is a reference to what we have referred to as 'people in positions of authority' as a collective. Similarly, the person at the head of an organization is often referred to as 'the leader' of, say, a company, church, country and so on, meaning the person who holds the highest office in the entity concerned.

The people who are given those titles in common discourse may or may not meet the requirements for a leader as we have explained in our comparison of 'leader' and 'manager', and in our definition of 'leadership' and 'management'. The usage of the terms 'leader' and 'leadership' in common discourse can, for lack of a better term, be referred to as 'the popular usage' of the two words, which is different from what we can call 'the technical usage' of the words. In this book, we use the terms 'leader' and 'leadership' in their technical sense.

3

General and educational theories of leadership

Tuning in Exercise

Reflect on the following questions as individuals and then share your findings:

1. Think of any subject you have majored in at university or any other tertiary education institution: Were you taught any theories relating to that subject?
2. Why is it necessary to understand the theoretical basis of a discipline?
3. What theory or theories of leadership are you familiar with?

Introduction

Now that we have interrogated the concept of leadership in its various aspects and contrasted it with related concepts, we need to understand its theoretical basis. A theory is an idea that is intended to explain something – an idea which is based on evidence or careful consideration of the subject in question. There may be different theories on the subject representing different views on it. Theories also develop with time as specialists in the field get to know more about the subject or phenomenon. The diversity of theories can also be an indication of the importance of the subject. Leadership is a dynamic and developing phenomenon and so we can expect to find different contestations about what it is and how best leaders can perform their roles as leaders.

What is interesting about leadership from the perspective of its theoretical foundations is that while it is one of the oldest practices, what are today recognized in mainstream literature as theories of leadership began to be developed in the Western tradition only during the last two hundred years or so. It is not clear why this is so. Empires were built thousands of years ago, great nations developed in the distant past and some great leaders arose and left their footprints on Planet Earth, but there were no theories of leadership comparable to theories of such fields as Theology, Philosophy and Medicine until the mid-nineteenth century in Europe. It is, however, necessary to add that ideas about leadership must have been developed in various cultures, although these ideas may not have been elaborate enough to be recognized by modern scholars as theories.

A case in point is that among the African people of Southern and East Africa there was a philosophy now generally known by the Zulu term *Ubuntu* (meaning 'personhood' or 'humanness'). In Sesotho the concept is called *Botho* and in Shona *Unhu*. In East Africa, the concept is called *Utu* in Swahili. The philosophy cannot in itself be regarded as a theory of leadership, but it gave rise to an approach to leadership that was discussed in a paper at a conference on Transformational Leadership a few years ago (Ngara 2013). We will discuss this in some detail in the relevant chapter on 'Approaches to Leadership Practice'. What remains to be noted here is that it is rather surprising that in discussing theories of leadership, mainstream literature seems to make no reference to Jesus' teaching on leadership. One is tempted to conclude that this is because the Christian Church in its various denominations does not (at least in the mind of this writer) put sufficient emphasis on the importance of leadership in Jesus' teaching. This is despite the fact that in the last two decades or so a good number of books have been published based on the Bible or specifically on Jesus' approach to leadership. The important thing to note here is that the theories of leadership discussed below are based on mainstream literature on leadership which excludes developments outside the Western tradition.

Six theories of leadership

In this chapter we are going to give a brief account of six theories of leadership in some kind of chronological order from the oldest to the most recent. The dating of one of the theories (i.e. the Functional Theory which this author associates with John Adair) is rather unclear. We will examine each theory as one theory, but what we call a theory may in fact be made up of a cluster of theories that follow the same basic approach. The six generic leadership theories we shall discuss are the following:

- The Great Man Theory (1840s)
- The Trait Theory (1930s–1940s)
- The Behavioural Theory (1940s–1950s)
- The Situational or Contingency Theory (1960s)
- The Functional Theory (1960s?)
- The Transformational Leadership Theory (1970s)

We shall then comment on how some of these apply to the educational leadership domain.

1. The Great Man Theory

As can be deduced from the name of the theory, the assumption here was that only men could be great leaders, and it was only the privileged few who were entitled to greatness and to great leadership. The theory assumed that the characteristics that made these men great leaders were intrinsic, and consequently leaders are born, not made. In that regard people like Julius Caesar, Napoleon, Confucius or Moshoeshoe I of Lesotho were born leaders. If you are not a man, tough luck. If you are a man and not born a leader, tough luck – you cannot be a great leader.

The Great Man theory is supposed to have been popularized by Thomas Carlyle (1795–1881), who was a Scottish philosopher, essayist, historian, mathematician and teacher. The theory was first challenged in 1860 by Herbert Spencer, one of the British thinkers of the time.

2. The Trait Theory

The Trait Theory, which is also called the Qualities Theory, was a natural development from the Great Man Theory. Like its predecessor, it held that leaders are born, not made. Its proponents thought that it was necessary to define the characteristics that made people effective leaders in order to identify those people who were likely to take the reigns of power. The traits or qualities identified include physical (e.g. appearance and height), intelligence ability, personality (e.g. enthusiasm, aggressiveness and self-confidence) and social characteristics (e.g. interpersonal skills and cooperativeness).

The Trait Theory did not pass the test of time. There were inconsistencies in the findings. Different studies did not agree on which were the common leadership traits. Not all leaders possessed what were supposed to be the necessary characteristics, some of which were shown to be possessed by people who were not leaders.

3. Behavioural Theories

The Great Man Theory and the Trait Theory focussed on the person, on the inner person, on who the person was. One of their weaknesses was that they did not give any clue about leadership behaviour. It was as if the proponents were saying that because one was born a leader, one did not have to make any effort to change one's behaviour in order to be more effective as a leader. In this regard, behavioural theorists changed the focus from *who* effective leaders were to *what* they did and *how* they did what they did – from the inner person to the person's actions. The focus now was on such issues as the following:

- How effective leaders carry out their duties
- How they delegate duties and tasks
- How they communicate with subordinates or followers and so on.

In an article in *Business Management Ideas*, Surbhi Rawat reports that Kurt Lewin of the University of Iowa and his colleagues made attempts to scientifically determine effective leadership behaviour by comparing the effects of three leadership styles: autocratic, democratic and laissez-faire. The behaviours exhibited by the different types of leader were as follows:

- The autocratic leader tends to make decisions without involving subordinates, spells out work methods, provides workers with very limited knowledge of goals and can even give negative feedback.
- The democratic or participative leader includes the group in decision-making, consults the subordinates in proposed actions and encourages participation from the subordinates.
- The laissez-faire leader gives the group complete freedom; subordinates set their own goals and decide on the means of achieving them. The role of the leader is to support the subordinates by providing information and acting as a contact point with the group's external environment. He/she avoids giving feedback.

The findings in terms of effectiveness and output were that democratic leadership appeared to result in both good quantity and quality of work, as well as worker satisfaction, followed by autocratic leadership. The results of the laissez-faire approach were the poorest.

4. Situational Theory (Contingency Theories)

Unlike the proponents of the Trait Theory, Situational theorists came up with something external to the leader which the leader had to respond to appropriately in order to be effective – or which determined the performance of the leader. The thinking here is that leadership depends on the situation. As this writer understands this theory, there are at least two scenarios here: On the one hand leaders are seen to be products of situations. Leaders become leaders because of various situations. Someone who is an effective leader in one situation may not be a good performer at all in a different situation.

The other scenario is that effective group performance can be achieved by matching the style of the manager (i.e. leader) to the situation or by changing the situation to fit the manager's style. The effectiveness of the leader depends on how he/she matches his/her leadership style to the demands of the situation. In this regard, the leader can choose to lead from the front, the middle or the rear, depending on the demands of the situation, as John van Maurik (2001: 19) observes.

Paul Hersey and Kenneth Blanchard

In line with Situational Leadership thinking, Hersey and Blanchard (1977) identified four key styles that were open to the leader. The four styles have been characterized as telling, selling, participating or delegating. Leadership ability was therefore determined by whether the leader was able to employ the right style in relation to the level of maturity of the subordinates. Singing from the same hymn sheet Charles Keating (1982: 23) echoed the two authors by saying, 'Good leadership depends upon good judgement, the ability to judge the level of the group and to supply the most effective kind of leadership for that level.'

Blanchard and other co-writers subsequently refined the four styles referred to above in a manner that makes them more intelligible, as has been summarized by John van Maurik (2001: 23–4). In this regard, it is useful to match each of the four styles mentioned above with its equivalent below:

Style 1: A Directive Approach: The leader gives a great deal of direction and very little support to subordinates who should not question her/his orders (Telling).
Style 2: A Coaching Approach: The leader acts like a coach who gives both direction and support (Selling).
Style 3: A Supporting Style: The leader adopts a collegial approach, giving high support and low direction (Participating).
Style 4: A Delegating Approach: The leader has confidence in the competence of the subordinate and trusts her/him, and so both support and direction are low (Delegating).

5. The Functional Theory

The Functional Theory of Leadership is based on the idea of leadership functions. The theory has been clearly explained by John Adair (2003: 76–86) who explains it in terms of needs. Adair sees three interlocking elements of need in a situation. The three elements are Task, Group (or Team) and Individual. When a leader embarks on a project or undertakes to do anything major he/she should be aware of the following factors: There is the Task that needs to be achieved; there is the Group (Team) that needs to be motivated and maintained; and there are the needs that the Individual member of the Team brings to the situation. Each of these areas affects the other two, as Adair shows in his three interlocking circles (Adair 2018) (see Figure 3).

Now for the Task to be achieved, the Team needs to be built and maintained; and the needs of the Individual need to be taken care of. That means that there are

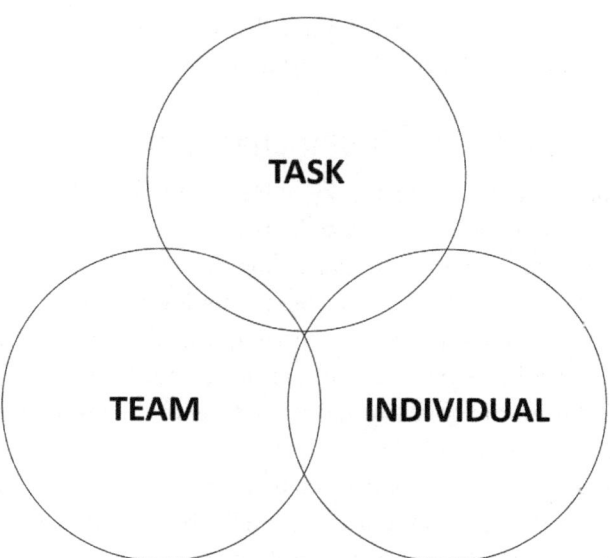

Figure 3 The interaction of areas of need. © John Adair, 2018, Lessons in Leadership, Bloomsbury Business, an imprint of Bloomsbury Publishing Plc

functions to be performed, and these are performed by the leader. Adair refers to these functions as *areas of leadership responsibility*. The following are the functions of the leader – in summary form:

- Defining the Task (purpose, aims, objectives)
- Planning (mapping out how the goal is going to be achieved)
- Briefing (communicating with the Team)
- Controlling (harnessing human, financial and material resources)
- Supporting (giving support and ensuring the maintenance of standards and values)
- Informing (giving information to the group, stakeholders and other interested parties)
- Reviewing (ensuring that targets, standards and criteria are kept)

In view of the above, Adair gives the following definition of a leader:

'A leader is the sort of person with the appropriate *qualities* and *knowledge* … who is able to provide the necessary *functions* to enable a team to achieve its task and to hold it together as a working unity' (79).

6. Transformational Leadership

In the five theories we have discussed so far there is what might be called 'a hidden progression' in terms of relationships between leader and follower and between the follower and the organization. In the Great Man and Trait theories, the follower is not in the picture at all, and there is no obvious reference to the organization. In the Behavioural, Situational and Functional theories, there is a relationship between leader and follower. That relationship is of two kinds: In the laissez-faire model that was only briefly referred to, the leader does not care about the follower at all. As Roger Gill and his fellow co-authors (1998: 49) have noted, 'The laissez-faire leader's followers or subordinates are left to fend for themselves even when they need help or support.' As the word laissez-faire implies, the leader adopts some kind of 'I don't care' attitude to the fate of the followers, a 'let them be' attitude. As we noted in the case of Kurt Lewin's studies, the laissez-faire approach led to the poorest results in terms of productivity.

The relationship between the leader and followers in the other models is some kind of transactional relationship for the sake of productivity. A typical transactional relationship takes place in the process of buying and selling in a shop. The buyer gives the required amount of money for the commodity he/she needs, and the seller hands the appropriate commodity to the buyer. In most cases there is no emotional relationship between the two, no deep relationship involved. Similarly, in traditional employer/employee relationships in a typical workplace, the worker 'sells his/her labour' as it were, and the employer 'rewards the employee' with a monthly salary. There may be no consideration of the relationship between worker and employer. The one is looking for her pay cheque, and the other is concerned about whether the specific task for which the employee was employed has been performed or not. There may not be any consideration of the relationship between the employee and the organization. What prevails here is a simple give and take relationship.

There is a sense in which relationships that prevail where Behavioural, Situational and Functional Theories of Leadership are applied resemble the simple give and take relationship that has just been explained above. In these cases, there is a predominantly transactional relationship between the leader and followers. The main concern of the leader is improved productivity or completion of the task. Except in the Functional approach where the needs of the Individual are part of the leader's responsibility, what happens to the worker is not a primary consideration. As Roger Gill and others have put it, where 'carrots' and 'sticks' are used, people may be made to 'feel like donkeys' because 'not enough consideration is given to people's ideas, feelings and needs' (1998: 49). This is where Transformational Leadership comes in as a leadership paradigm that differs significantly from the rest, and one which is giving a new understanding of what leadership is.

What is transformational leadership?

It is appropriate to begin with a quote that connects two founding fathers of transformational leadership, Jim Burns and Bernard Bass. Bass was being interviewed by Adele Bergstrom (2002). Bass had just published a book on Transformational Leadership, and Bergstrom asked him what the book was about and how it began.

In his response Bass said the book was the result of research he began in 1980. He first thought transformational leadership was a dynamic approach to leadership that did not concern itself with moral issues. He further explained, 'Jim Burns originally saw that a transformational leader was somebody who was uplifting – raised the moral values – as well as got people to do more than they expected to do.'

This incomplete quote gives some pointers: There are issues of morality and moral values involved in this approach to leadership. In addition, the transformational leader is one who uplifts and who has the capacity to influence and motivate followers to stretch themselves beyond the normal expectations. He/she is a leader who adds value to the life of workers and has the capacity to change and transform.

Before explaining what scholars seem to agree about the key characteristics of transformational leadership, it is apposite to mention the following which relate to the quotation above and the comment on it:

1. The transformational leader is a role model who inspires followers.
2. The transformational leader challenges and motivates followers to strive to achieve beyond their normal capabilities.
3. The transformational leader endeavours to connect the followers' sense of identity and self-worth with the identity and goals of the organization.
4. The transformational leader articulates a powerful and energizing vision which inspires the followers.

The four points here show that there is a three-way form of connectedness: connectedness between the followers and the leader who is viewed as a role model; connectedness between the followers and the organization as the followers now identify with the goals and vision of the organization; and, needless to say, connectedness between the leader and the organization as the leader is the one who is expected to champion the new organizational vision. This system of relationships makes positive change possible: The workers are prepared to change by buying into the leader's vision; and they, in turn, become agents of change facilitating the positive transformation of the organization.

Now, how does the leader manage to be the force that makes the change possible? Most specialists in the field now agree that transformational leadership is characterized by four features (or what has been called the Four Is):

- Idealized influence: The leader has a character and a vision that attracts others to follow her or him.
- Inspirational motivation: The leader has the capacity and disposition to motivate others to follow the vision.

- Intellectual stimulation: The leader challenges the normal beliefs and attitudes of the group or team and encourages innovation and creativity.
- Individualized consideration: The leader pays attention to individual members of the team or organization and helps them to achieve both their personal goals and the goals of the organization.

Some thinkers believe the whole purpose of being a leader is to bring about change – not change for the sake of change, but positive change. The leader is therefore a change agent. In this regard, Transformational Leadership Theory is an approach that powerfully facilitates change; it empowers the leader to facilitate change in both the followers and the organization. The reader may recall how we noted in Chapter 2 that with the coming of the idea of school leadership development, the principal was now expected to be a change agent, not just a manager.

Which of the six is the best theory?

Before we come to theories that have been applied to educational leadership, let us consider two issues: First, is any of these six theories outmoded and not useful to the twenty-first-century leader? There is possibly a sense in which the Great Man Theory and the Trait Theory can be regarded as outlandish, especially as they were both based on the notion that leaders are only born and not made, making leadership an exclusive club for those who were born with it. They are certainly not in line with the *Ubuntu* philosophy that is discussed in Chapter 5. Other than that, it is probably correct to suggest that the four other theories discussed here, and may be a few others, complement one another. Without doubt, Transformational Leadership Theory is, in the mind of this writer, the best of the six discussed here, but a leader applying that theory will benefit from the insights that can be gained from the experience of those who have applied the Behavioural, Situational and Functional theories. It is also pertinent to point out that combined with other theories, the Situational or Contingency Theory is very useful.

Viewing leadership theories from the perspective of education

Transformational leadership and education

So far in this chapter we have looked at leadership from the point of view of generic or general leadership which is applicable to various spheres of life. As this book is on educational leadership, it is necessary to examine some of these theories through the lenses of a specialist in educational leadership. In the first chapter of *Principles of Educational Leadership and Management*, Tony Bush discusses competing models of school leadership. The ones this author finds particularly relevant for this book are transformational leadership, distributed leadership, contingent leadership and managerialism and instructional leadership. Bush further enhances our understanding of transformational leadership. He observes, 'Transformational leadership is based on the assumption that higher levels of personal commitment to organisational goals, and greater capacities for accomplishing those goals, are assumed to result in extra effort and greater productivity.' We have already noted how transformational approaches can be contrasted with transactional approaches. Bush confirms this and demonstrates how transactional leadership can take place in the education sphere by giving the example of teachers providing educational services (teaching, pupil welfare and extracurricular activities) in exchange for salaries and other rewards. He then notes, 'This is a basic approach and does not lead to the level of commitment associated with the transformational model.' He adds, 'Transformational leadership remains popular as it accords closely with the emphasis on vision as the central dimension of leadership' (see Bush et al. 2019: 7–8). The downside to transformational leadership, according to some scholars (e.g. ibid: 8) is that, among other things, 'transformational language is used by governments to encourage, or require, practitioners to adopt and implement centrally determined policies'. South Africa is quoted as an example of this, but the majority of South Africans would agree that the government is right in focusing on transformation in order for the education system to reflect the needs of the new democratic dispensation and the majority of the people after the apartheid system. It is possible that the theory has been abused by some governments in the West. That is regrettable, but used as originally conceived of, it is a positive approach to education.

Distributed leadership

An important dimension of leadership in educational leadership is distributed leadership. All the models we have discussed so far are examples of solo leadership. Traditionally in academia, there has been a degree of collegiality and participative leadership. In the twenty-first century, as Bush points out, distributed leadership has become the normatively preferred leadership model. Among other things, 'distributed leadership concentrates on engaging expertise wherever it exists within the organisation rather than seeking this only through formal position or role' (Bush et al. 2019:10) . Bush quotes Harris (2004: 16) as arguing that 'successful heads recognize the limitations of a singular leadership approach' and adopt a form of leadership 'distributed through collaborative and joint working' (ibid: 10). Thus distributed is differentiated from other models by its focus on collective rather than singular leadership. This approach is not alien to African traditional leadership as can be seen in the example of Moshoeshoe I of Lesotho who is one of the exemplars of *Ubuntu*-based leadership discussed in Chapter 5.

Contingent leadership

There is a danger in leadership theorists and practitioners adopting a 'one size fits all' approach to leadership. There was wisdom in Blanchard and Hersey adopting the situational approach to leadership. Leadership often requires effective analysis and diagnosis of the problem at hand for the most appropriate response to be arrived at. This is where in educational leadership 'contingent leadership acknowledges the diverse nature of school contexts, and the advantages of adapting leadership styles to the particular situation, rather than adopting a "one size fits all" stance' (Bush et al. 2019: 13).

Managerialism

An approach to leadership which educationists should be aware of is managerialism. If we think of educational leadership taking place at macro (national), meso (organizational) and micro (individual) levels, it is easy to see that managerialism typically starts at the macro level, with government wanting to see greater efficiency, and consequently introducing strong bureaucratic structures, processes and procedures. As Bush points out (Bush et al. 2019: 7), 'Managerial leadership is the model which provides the greatest risk of a bureaucratic approach to school organisation.' Higher education institutions can also be subjected to managerialism with a strong focus on planning and the production of targeted numbers of graduates in key areas that are considered to be relevant for economic and industrial development. In Africa, state managerialism can be quite evident as in the case of South Africa (CHE 2016: 105–36). But as explained above, the South African government felt it had the obligation to help steer the transformation process in the interests of the majority following the discriminatory apartheid system. Managerialism can be initiated at the individual level in a case where a very strong vice chancellor with set views on how to transform an institution is appointed and comes to the organization determined to see it completely transformed to become a new institution with new structures and a new culture. While a managerialist approach may sometimes be necessary, the authorities must be careful enough to ensure that institutional values are not lost and people are not alienated. In a higher education institution, managerialism can result in a situation where the interests of academics and students are sacrificed on the altar of efficiency (see, e.g., CHE 2016: 133–4). As the CHE points out (ibid.: 131–6) a progressive alternative to state managerialism is a knowledge-based model of system governance in which 'government has a steering role in relation to the achievement of national goals through higher education' and universities understand that, among other things, 'they have a responsibility to be transparent about what they do with public and private funds' and the responsibility to educate.

Instructional leadership

Instructional leadership is important to the extent that it draws attention to teaching and learning as the core business of educational institutions. As Bush points out, other terms such as pedagogical leadership and leadership for learning can be used to refer to the same concept. As defined by the authorities on the subject, the concept is used with reference to school principals and this is why research has shown that leaders (meaning positional leaders) who are close to the core business of teaching and learning are more likely to make a difference to learners. The literature on school leadership development (e.g. Hallinger 2003) shows that in some advanced countries, school principals are, among other things, regarded as leaders of 'learning communities'. This means that the principal sees himself as a learner like everybody else in the school, but as a learner who leads the transformation process of the school in teaching and curriculum change – who has the role of helping the school to move forward. According to this author, there is another dimension to the concept of instructional leadership. While principals should play the role of instructional leaders, it is possible to look at the concept of instructional leadership differently by giving credit to the actual teachers whose excellence in the process of teaching and learning makes a positive impact on students. The thinking here is those who make the greatest positive impact on the learners are leaders in their profession and should be recognized as such and rewarded accordingly. Consequently, there should be two categories of instructional leaders in a school: the principal and those teachers in the school who make a positive impact on students through effective teaching.

Some concluding observations

Looking at educational leadership development as discussed in this chapter and the previous chapter, it becomes apparent that much of the focus is on school leadership development and less on university leadership development. Readers of this book will be aware that while there are many publications on university education, and while some universities have established teaching and learning centres, the majority of university leaders such as vice chancellors, deans and chairpersons or heads of department have not been trained for the posts they hold. There are in service programmes that are run by various bodies but leadership development for university academics is not taken as seriously as leadership development for school principals has been taken by various nations of the world. Related to this is the fact that for lecturers and professors there is normally no teaching qualification required. It is their qualifications in their fields of specialization that count. This book is intended to focus on educational leadership development with a particular focus on university-level training.

Part II

Approaches to leadership

4

Educating people for domination

Introduction

In *Leadership for the 21st Century* (1989) Ron Boehme has argued that there are two main types of leadership in the world: the Leadership of Domination and the Leadership of Servanthood, commonly known as Servant Leadership. From an African perspective, there is a third important approach to leadership that is not known to Boehme, and that is what can variously be referred to as the *Ubuntu*, *Botho*, *Unhu* or *Utu* approach which is based on what in the Zulu and Xhosa languages is called *Ubuntu* philosophy, *Botho* and *Unhu* philosophy, respectively, in Sesotho and Shona; and *Utu* in Swahili. In this part of the book we are therefore dealing with three modes or forms of leadership which could be referred to as 'philosophies of leadership' as they are concerned with how people should or should not lead.

Tuning in Exercise

Read the two stories below and answer the questions at the end of the narratives. (For students, the exercise is best done by two groups (or two sets of groups) with one group answering the questions on Anecdote 1 and the other answering the questions on Anecdote 2.) The names used are mostly from the languages of Southern Africa, namely Zulu, Sotho, Shona and so on, where English-language names are also commonly used.

The principal and the prefect

Anecdote 1: Mr Nkosi the principal

The school principal walked into the staff room. All the staff stood to attention, except for three teachers who were busy talking, unaware that the principal had just walked in.

'James, Janet and John, come to my office immediately!' the principal announced in an angry voice. 'I am the principal of this school', he said when he and the three teachers got to the office. 'When I come into the staff room, everyone – I mean everyone – should stand to attention and say, "Good morning Mr Nkosi", and then sit down quietly for me to make an announcement. Understand?'

At this point James tried to give an explanation, but the principal roared at him:

> Mr Mofokeng, you dare not interrupt me when I'm talking to you! Because you interrupted me, I have no choice but to impose a penalty upon you. Your penalty is this: Go and write a letter of apology which includes a vow of obedience to me as your principal. Bring the letter to me in thirty minutes. I must have order in this school, and all must respect the office of the Principal. Now, get out of my office all of you!

As the three were leaving the office, the principal said, 'Janet, go and tell the rest of the staff to go back to their stations. I'll make my announcement later.'

Within thirty minutes James Mofokeng came holding a letter. It was a letter of resignation. James was a brilliant Maths teacher who could find a job any time anywhere. The school was lucky to have had him on the staff.

Anecdote 2: Gibson the prefect

A young boy called Anesu has graduated from primary school and has been admitted at a highly reputed and wealthy boarding school. He is told he has a mentor who is one of the prefects. The mentor's name is Gibson. On the day they meet for the first time, Gibson hears a knock on his dormitory door. It is early in the morning. He opens the door and a timid-looking young boy enters. 'So, you're Anesu', Gibson says in a deep and powerful voice.

'Yes', the young boy says timidly.

'Sir!' thunders Gibson. 'Say "Yes, Sir!" Every morning you come, knock on the door, salute and say "Good morning Sir". You then make my bed, polish my shoes, salute again and say "Good bye Sir". Understand?'

'Yes, Sir', Anesu says with a salute.

Questions on Anecdote 1

1. If you were the principal of the school and found the three teachers talking, how would you react?
2. What does the story tell us about the principal's emotions?
3. Do you think James Mofokeng was justified in his response to the principal?
4. What does the story tell us about the relationship between the principal and his staff?

Questions on Anecdote 2

1. Is it a good practice to have school prefects who are given small boys to serve them? Explain your answer.
2. What attitude to leadership is a boy like Gibson likely to develop: that of a boss or that of a servant of the people?
3. This story is based on real events in some Southern African countries. Do you think the system should be improved, and if so, how?

Some manifestations of the leadership of domination

The anecdotes presented above in some way exemplify the leadership of domination. The principal's understanding of his relationship with the staff is that of domination, with the staff serving him in fear and trepidation. One can see someone who has been taught, and perhaps misunderstood, some of Fayol's functions and principles, such as command, control and order. Similarly, the young prefect sees himself as a big boss who is served by a younger boy, the latter being to all intents and purposes a servant of the older boy. This kind of practice used to be quite common in schools that were formerly for White students in Southern Africa. In some mission schools for African students in the 1950s and 1960s you had the practice of torturing 'new comers' who were ordered to do things like jumping, marching or performing chores at the behest of older boys and to the amusement of the older boys. What the missionaries or school managers in both types of schools did not seem to realize is that schools were becoming training grounds for future dictators.

But the leadership of domination is by no means limited to educational institutions. We find the leadership of domination in every sphere of life: a man who terrorizes his wife and children; a pastor or priest who dominates all the meetings he chairs or attends; a permanent secretary (or director general) in a government ministry who lords it over all the officials under him or her. In fact, the leadership of domination is glaringly apparent in government ministries in some countries. It becomes clear to any new arrival in a ministry or state-owned enterprise that survival and success often depend on how much you pander to the whims of 'the head of ministry'. You are putting your job at risk if you try to follow your conscience and do what you think is right in certain situations where issues of justice and fairness to workers are involved. If the head of ministry wants to use you as chief executive officer to un-procedurally change the conditions of service of the staff in the state-owned enterprise you lead, you must do so without questioning, or else you are putting your own job at risk.

The leadership of domination tends to support the persistence of certain unethical practices. People in positions of authority often abuse these positions. For example, promotions may not necessarily be based on merit, as the boss will want to promote his favourites – those who pander to the whims of 'the strong man'. This may extend to the appointment of relatives who become part of the leader's power base as they can be used to spy on fellow employees. Another very bad practice is the abuse of women employees. A woman subordinate who wants a promotion will sometimes be required to grant sexual favours to the boss, and this may result in her being unfaithful to her husband while the boss is unfaithful to his wife.

Yet another form of abuse where the leadership of domination prevails is the unlawful use of funds by people in positions of authority. A government minister who is in charge of a fund (such as a scholarship fund, for example) may instruct the accountant to divert the funds to the minister's personal use. The accountant may not necessarily want to commit such a crime but will do it for fear of losing his job. In a state-owned enterprise the senior management may grant themselves super salaries undeservedly or give themselves allowances that are not justified. There is a joke that used to be commonly told in one Southern African country. In the story the Minister of Health visited his counterpart in Malaysia. The Malaysian minister took his African friend to a new hospital. 'Do you see this hospital?', the Malaysian minister asked his African friend. 'The hospital was supposed to be twice as big as this; but half of the money went into my pocket.' The African minister subsequently invited his Malaysian friend to his country and took him on a tour of the city and the surrounding area. At one point they stopped facing a wild bush. 'Do you see this bush?', the African minister asked his friend, 'There was supposed to be a hospital there; but all the money went into my pocket.'

The examples given above show that the leadership of domination does not only manifest itself in undemocratic and dictatorial tendencies but can also lead to the loss of morality, the blunting of consciences and outright corruption. For political leaders the desire for power and prosperity becomes a major driving force which detracts the individuals concerned from the main purpose of serving the people. For individuals reporting to superiors who are driven by such a desire for material gain, there can be a real dilemma – whether to obey one's conscience and displease 'the boss' who has the power to deprive you of your job or position or to do as the powerful person wants to be done, and then live with a guilty conscience.

Machiavelli's philosophy in the background

The leadership of domination is currently the prevailing mode of leadership which has been practised by many leaders in the West and elsewhere for centuries and has also been propagated by some leadership theorists. It is reasonable to argue that whether consciously or unconsciously, many leaders adhere to the leadership philosophy of the Italian philosopher, historian and political theorist, Niccolo Machiavelli (1469–1527). Machiavelli is said to have propagated the view that opportunistic or amoral means justify politically desirable ends. Crudely put, this says 'the end justifies the means'. The *Internet Encyclopedia of Philosophy* says of Machiavelli that his influence has been enormous. It adds, 'Arguably no philosopher since antiquity, with the possible exception of Kant, has affected his successors so deeply.'

Referring to Machiavelli's work, *The Prince*, the Encyclopaedia has this to say: 'Almost from its composition, *The Prince* has been notorious for its seeming recommendations of cruelty; its seeming prioritization of autocracy ... over more republican or democratic forms ... Indeed it remains perhaps the most notorious work in the history of political philosophy.' Machiavelli was concerned with how to gain and maintain power. How one gets the power – whether justifiably or morally or not – was not the issue for him – as long as power is gained and retained. One can even resort to evil ways of achieving power, and that would be OK. In chapter 18 of *The Prince* he is quoted as saying that a prince must know 'how to do evil, if that is necessary, but must also strive to maintain the appearance of virtue in front of observers'. Consequently, in terms of this approach to power, 'So it follows that a prudent ruler cannot, and must not, honour his word when it places him at a disadvantage and when the reasons for which he made his promise no longer exist.' What all this means is that the end justifies the means. What matters is the acquisition of power and the stability of government by whatever means. In this approach to power, the difference between virtue and vice is blurred: Vice becomes a virtue if it can lead to the desired goal (see Skinner 1981: 44).

The leadership of domination is implicit in this approach as the implications here are that if you have to forcibly suppress the opposition or contender in order to gain and retain power, it is good for you to do so. Consequently, the spreading of wealth among the military in order to remain secure in power was a strategy for Machiavelli which is commonly practiced by oppressive regimes today. This leads to the question whether it is better to be loved or feared. On that Machiavelli was clear: 'It would be best to be both feared and loved, although it is necessary to be feared. That way your rule of law will not be changed. It is riskier to offend a man that is feared.'

Consequently, therefore, if you have to make a choice, to be feared is much safer than to be loved (ibid.: 51).

It is not inappropriate to argue that many leaders in today's world live by the dictum that to be feared is much safer than to be loved – whether they know about the Italian philosopher or not. For many leaders, leadership means the exercise of power and control of those over whom you have authority. They know that fear involves 'dread of punishment', as Machiavelli would have said, and so they lord it over their followers. It is said by far the strongest influence on one of Africa's worst dictators, Joseph Mobutu, who renamed himself Mobutu Seseseko and ruled as dictator of the country now known as the Democratic Republic of the Congo for thirty-one years, was Niccolo Machiavelli. One of his officers is reported as saying Mobutu knew *The Prince* by heart.

Douglas McGregor's Theory X and Theory Y

The kind of leadership we discussed above relates to what is popularly referred to as Douglas MacGregor's Theory X, which in part holds the following:

1. 'People have a natural dislike for work and will consequently avoid it if possible. Consequently it is necessary for management to adopt a stick-and-carrot approach to motivation which may be seen in company incentive schemes combined with rules and the measurement of productivity.'
2. 'Because people dislike work, it is naturally necessary to coerce, control, direct and threaten in order to ensure sufficient effort from them to ensure that organisational objectives are met' (see van Maurik 2001: 14–15).

A leader or manager who holds this view of humanity shows no trust for the people who work with him/her and will bully his/her subordinates, instil fear in them and perhaps use a stick-and-carrot method to get work done.

McGregor also proposed what he called Theory Y. A Theory Y manager believes, among other things, that:

1. 'To the average human being work is as natural as play.'
2. 'Control by threats or bribes is not the only way to get people to work for organisational objectives.'
3. 'The average person learns under proper conditions not only to accept but also to seek out responsibility' (van Maurik 2001: 15).

Clearly, Theory Y represents a very different view of humanity, and it suggests a very different way of dealing with subordinates from what Theory X proposes.

Theory X projects the ideology of domination, while Theory Y sees the potential in human beings to perform and be productive without the use of force. This brings us to some of the defining characteristics of the leadership of domination.

Some characteristics of the leadership of domination

The natural environment of the leadership of domination is a dictatorship where the leader has absolute control and can be despotic or tyrannical. Nevertheless it also flourishes in what may be called pseudo-democracies where the Constitution is based on democratic principles, but the culture of leadership is one that allows dictatorial attitudes and practices to persist. The following are some of the characteristics that the leadership of domination shows in such environments:

1. The system operates by force and control.
2. The leader exercises control of subordinates by using subtle or overt threats. Among other things, subtle threats can take the form of making certain categories of people feel that they are being watched, and consequently they do not feel free to express their views in public about the prevailing economic and political conditions.
3. To keep power, the leader instils fear in other people.
4. People often do not trust one another as they may spy on one another.
5. People may not feel free to express their views freely in meetings for fear of offending 'the boss'.
6. The leader finds it difficult to step down from power as leadership is not for the sake of serving the people but for the sake of power and prosperity.
7. He surrounds himself with bootlickers and flatterers.
8. Benefits tend to be enjoyed by supporters only and not by members of the opposition and the rest of the population.

Conclusion: Growing evidence against the leadership of domination

While practice informed by Machiavelli's theory still holds sway, research has shown that people generally work better when they do what they want to do, not when they are doing what they are forced to do. It is not by leading with an iron fist and maintaining a tight control on things that you get people to be more productive. On the contrary, people perform better when they are given greater responsibility, when the leader shows more faith and trust in the subordinates and when he/she empowers them and treats them with respect, courtesy and trust.

5

The *Ubuntu* approach to relationships and leadership

Tuning in Exercise

We begin with a story about King Moshoeshoe I of Lesotho. The story goes that at one point in the nineteenth century there was such a devastating famine in parts of what is now Lesotho that some people became cannibals or *malimo* in Sesotho. The leader of the group that resorted to cannibalism was called Rakotswane. This group killed and ate Peete, Moshoeshoe's grandfather. Meanwhile Moshoeshoe was providing for his people in and around his stronghold of Thaba Bosiu. The *malimo* heard about this and went to Thaba Bosiu in search of food. Moshoeshoe's councillors (ministers) or *matona* recognized Rakotswane and his gang when the group reached Thaba Bosiu. When they recognized the cannibals, the *matona* urged the king to kill his grandfather's killers.

Questions

1. What would you have done if you were in Moshoeshoe's position?
2. What did Moshoeshoe actually do?

The *Ubuntu* philosophy and leadership

We shall revisit the questions on King Moshoeshoe. In the meantime we need to put the discussion in its proper context by explaining the philosophy of *Ubuntu*. The *Ubuntu* philosophy has become the most famous philosophy of the people of Africa. For a summary of the etymology of the suffix *NTU*, one can read the analysis by Rutendo Ngara (2017) in which she summarizes what some scholars have seen as its four forms. Ngara explains *NTU* as referring to 'the causative, dynamic life-force or power responsible for all creation on Earth and the Universe'. The *Ubuntu* philosophy is said to have been popularized at the time of attaining majority rule in South Africa and Zimbabwe, but the concept exists among the various Bantu people of Eastern, Central and Southern Africa. Bantu is a word which refers to 'people' in the plural form, the singular form being *Umuntu* (a human being) in IsiZulu and Xhosa which are Nguni languages. The Nguni word *Ubuntu* has been popularized, but both the word and philosophy exist in other languages. In Sesotho the words are *motho* 'a person' and *batho* 'people'. In Shona the words are *munhu* 'a person' and *vanhu* 'people'. The word exists in such languages as Herero of Namibia, Chewa of Malawi, Swahili of Tanzania, Kenya and Uganda, and in many other languages.

As already explained, the word *Ubuntu* means 'personhood' or 'being human'. It also connotes such qualities as compassion, caring and humanness. *Ubuntu* as a philosophy is captured in the Zulu/Xhosa saying *Umuntu ngumuntu ngabantu* 'A person is a person through other people'. Nelson Mandela is supposed to have defined *Ubuntu* as an African concept that means 'the profound sense that we are human only through the humanity of others' (Stengel 2010). One of the most well-known proponents of *Ubuntu*, Archbishop Emeritus Desmond Tutu (2011: 22) has said, '*Ubuntu* is the essence of being human. It speaks of how my humanity is caught up and bound up inextricably with yours.' In other words, I am what I am through your humanity, through the humanity of others. This is given expression in the Shona expression *Ndiri nokuti tiri* 'I am because we are'. Another Shona expression says *Munhu munhu pane vanhu* 'A person is a person where there are other people'. Consequently, I cannot be a human being without other people. In Shona *Ubuntu* is *Unhu or Hunhu*, in Sesotho the word is *Botho*, in Swahili it is *Utu* – all meaning 'personhood' or 'being human'. Some scholars such as Professor Micere Githae Mugo will refer to the philosophy as the *Utu/Ubuntu* philosophy, to show that the concept is indigenous to both Southern Africa and East Africa. In this chapter we shall use the Sesotho expression to explain the concept.

The philosophy of *Botho* is captured in the traditional maxim *Motho ke motho ka batho* 'A person is a person through other people' or 'A person is a person on account of other people'. The expression is central to the traditional African idea of existence and relationships. It is an expression of the importance of community and family relationships among ethnic groups on the African continent. A person exists as part of community; he/she exists in a system of relationships. Thus, *I* am because *You*, the community, are. You as an individual are what you are because we are what we are. You exist in a system of relationships – with your parents, relatives, community, ancestors and the Creator. A human being is a social being. This is a far cry from the Western individualistic paradigm summarized by the French philosopher Descartes (1596–1650) who arrived at the Latin formulation: *Cogito ergo sum* 'I think therefore I am'. Descartes's formulation is an expression of individualism that is unthinkable in the traditional African context.

The philosophy of *Botho* is given expression in the traditional African attitude to relationships. Thus a family is not just a man, his wife and children. The true definition of family can only be seen in its extended form, in the tapestry of the system of relatives. Consequently every individual has a place in the extended family as an uncle, grandchild, grandmother, aunt and so on. Similarly, marriage is not just a union between two people, because marriage brings two families together. Because of this emphasis on family, the idea of an old age home for old people still sounds strange to African people even in this day and age. I, the writer of this book, hired a taxi one day to go and see a retired White Bishop who lives in an old people's home in Pretoria. When I explained to the taxi driver where I was going and who I was visiting, the driver commented very gently, 'This is very strange to us Africans – to keep someone in a place reserved for old people!' The conversation went on to discuss how in a normal environment an old man should be in a family playing with his grandchildren. Perhaps the reaction of this taxi driver explains what Archbishop Tutu (Tutu 2011: 22) means when he says, '*Ubuntu* speaks of spiritual attributes such as generosity, hospitality, compassion, caring and sharing.' To be truly human is to feel for others, to have empathy and to care for them.

The philosophy of *Botho* does not only have implications for the individual and his/her community. It is at the centre of what it means to be a king, a chief, a leader. When applied to the province of leadership the maxim becomes *Morena ke morena ka batho* 'A king is a king through the people'. This maxim answers a very important question: Who is more important: the king or the people? Who is more important, the leader or the people? Just as the individual cannot exist independently of the community, the king or leader cannot exist independently of the community. Perhaps the Pedi (Northern Sotho) version is even more telling in expressing the relationship between the king or leader and the people. It says *Kgosi ke kgosi ka sechaba* 'A king is a king through the nation' or 'A king is a king on account of the nation'. The nation comes before the king, before the leader. Without the nation there is no king, no leader!

If the people are more important than the leader, it goes without saying that the *Botho/Ubuntu/Unhu/Utu* approach promotes the stewardship view of leadership. This view says the leader does not own the country or company or organization or any other entity for which he/she has responsibility. The leader was elected or appointed to see to it that the people and the organization or country prosper. The leader is therefore appointed to serve the people, not to be served by them. The king or leader must rule in the interest of community, not in his/her own interest.

For a leader who understands this philosophy, interdependence becomes an important principle to abide by. The king depends on the people just as much as the people depend on the king. By accepting the principle of interdependence, the king or leader realizes that leadership entails interaction with the people. It entails consultation with and listening to the people or the people's representatives.

The actual interaction may be direct (in terms of, say, face-to-face interaction) or indirect (through the people's representatives and other means). By interacting with the people, the leader is given a platform on which to engage, challenge and inspire people.

At this point it is appropriate to explain Mike Boon's summary of the characteristics of what he calls 'tribal leadership' which succinctly expresses the principles explained here. Of the seven characteristics Boon (2007: 44) lists, only the first three are quoted here. They encapsulate what the chief ideally stands for in traditional society:

- 'The chief personifies the unity of the tribe …
- The chief is not an autocrat, and must rely on councillors representing the people to assist him.
- The chief must be guided by consensus. If he is not, the people will ignore his decision or his "law".'

Wangari Maathai (2009: 154) has correctly pointed out that African people should understand that the prevailing culture of corruption, theft and graft among African political leaders was not always the case, 'that the majority of their forebears were honest, fair and just, and that their societies were functional and people's basic needs were met'. What Maathai's comment points to is that many African leaders of today have lost their *Botho/Utu* or do not even know about it. They were educated in a Western paradigm which places emphasis on individual success, the acquisition of wealth and competition.

The purpose of giving the above analysis of the *Ubuntu* philosophy and its implications for leadership is to prepare the ground for a study of two kingdoms: the Mutapa Empire of Zimbabwe and the Kingdom of Lesotho. These are kingdoms that give concrete evidence of what Maathai is referring to. The chapter is based on two conference papers (Ngara 2013 and Ngara 2012) in which it is argued that by applying the principles of the *Ubuntu* philosophy in combination with strategic leadership and diplomacy, the leaders of these kingdoms were able to exert a positive impact on their subjects and to transform their territories into important and internationally recognized nation states. In the latter paper (Ngara 2013) an important theme was to find elements of transformational leadership in traditional African leadership. While that is important, the main focus here is to identify good leadership practices in the interest of the people.

The Mutapa Empire

According to the New World Encyclopaedia (2012: 1), the Mutapa Empire may not have been the equal of contemporary European empires in technology but its craftsmen produced high-quality artefacts while trade was carefully regulated with set measures and standards to ensure fairness. Knowledge of this empire, which was built up more through commerce than conquest, can help construct a balanced story of where, when and how human societies have flourished.

The founders of the Mutapa Empire were of the Shona group and were both culturally and politically connected to the builders of the Great Zimbabwe. Historians have reconstructed a history of the Mutapa dynasty from the founder, Nyatsimba Mutota (1430–1480), to the last king, Chioko Dambamupute (1887–1902). Thus the empire lasted in different forms for more than five hundred years. Most of the information on the empire is from written Portuguese records on which Mudenge (1988), Beach and others relied. Looking at the Mutapa state from the point of view of good and transformational leadership which could serve as an example to present-day leaders, it is possible to identify four themes:

- Relations between the king and provincial leaders
- The role of the economy in developing a stable state
- The king's involvement in the affairs of the people
- Relations with foreign countries

Relations between the Mutapa and provincial leaders

The Mutapas seem to have realized the benefits of giving relative freedom to the citizens and to regional governors, which strategy seems to have earned them the loyalty of both vassals and ordinary citizens. The New World Encyclopaedia notes: 'The Mutapa did not intervene needlessly in the lives of his subjects. He appears to have realized that if the people enjoyed a reasonable and a stable society, their loyalty could be expected' (3). And whereas the regional governors were expected to pay taxes to the king by way of cattle and other forms of wealth, this was not a one-way process. What often happened was that gifts were given by the king to officials and regional governors to ensure their loyalty. There was give and take with the king recognizing the importance of the *Ubuntu* principle of interdependence. This is what Chanaiwa refers to as the 'charisma, well-being and political wisdom of the Mutapa' (New World Encyclopaedia, 3). This can be characterized as a soft way to engage and influence followers, gaining their loyalty, not through brute force but by inspiring them. By showing trust and mutual respect, the king was able to endear himself to the provincial leaders and the general populace.

Creating a stable state by managing the economy

The wisdom of the Mutapas appears to have extended to the management of the economy. The Mutapa Empire enjoyed a thriving economy for centuries (Mudenge

1988: 161–94). The economy was diversified with agricultural farming and cattle as its backbone. Millet, rice and vegetables were grown. Large numbers of cattle were kept, and there was also poultry farming. Because of the system of paying tribute to the king, the Mutapa could store large quantities of grain and feed his people with this surplus in times of famine. Another important industry was gold mining. There were evidently reasonable reserves of gold, and this led Europeans to associate the Mutapa Empire with King Solomon's gold from Ophir which is mentioned in the Book of Kings (1 Kgs 10.11). In addition, elephant hunting was also a thriving business. As a result of such a rich and relatively diversified economy, a strong trade industry developed between the Mutapa emperors, the Portuguese and Far Eastern countries like India and China.

Obviously a thriving economy facilitated the development of a stable society while peace and stability facilitated the growth of a stable economy that would have led the subjects to be reasonably contented and loyal. That peace and stability prevailed during certain periods of the empire is evidenced by the fact that the houses of ordinary people needed no doors because the people expected to be protected from thieves and malefactors by the king (Mudenge 1988: 154). What is important to note here is that by paying attention to the economy and not just to their power and control of the state, the Mutapas were able to transform their kingdom into a relatively stable and thriving empire. This would seem to lend weight to the suggestion implied in the New World Encyclopaedia above that the economy more so than conquest has the potential to facilitate the development of a stable and flourishing society.

Involvement in the affairs of the people

A matter to which historians do not seem to attach the importance it deserves is the fact that the Mutapa was personally involved in solving people's problems brought to him. According to some sources, the people of the Mutapa Empire had seven holidays per month. On these days the king did not himself take a holiday but was very busy holding audiences to solve the problems brought before him. Mudenge (1988: 88) quotes Bocarro and Barros as saying, 'These audiences often last from morning till evening, without the King ever sitting down.' The audiences had to be held by the king himself, and if something prevented him from doing so, the responsibility would fall upon his most senior minister called the Nengomasha. What this seems to show is that the Mutapa did not live in an ivory tower. He was actively interested in the affairs of his people and was personally involved in interacting with them and listening to their problems.

In view of the above, it seems safe to suggest that the maxim 'The King is a king on account of the people' was put into practice by the Mutapa emperors. There was also evidence of servant leadership as the king saw himself as having the responsibility of serving his people. Undoubtedly, not every member of the dynasty would have performed the duties with the same degree of competence as the best of them, but the principle was there, and it appears that some Mutapas were able to elicit admiration and loyalty from the people.

Relations with foreign powers

This author has not done sufficient research on this topic, but it is clear that the Mutapa dealt with foreign powers. Perhaps the most important of these powers during the five hundred years of the existence of the dynasty was Portugal which was a powerful nation at the time. Portugal managed to colonize Mozambique and would have wanted to extend its rule into the Mutapa Empire. However, for the duration of five hundred years Portugal did not conquer Mutapa and was content with signing a treaty in terms of which the European nation kept a small army at the headquarters of the Mutapa. This arrangement seems to have suited both sides: For the Portuguese the intention was ostensibly to protect the Mutapa, but in reality the Portuguese would have wanted to be kept informed about what was going on at the Mutapa headquarters. On the other hand, the Mutapa was able to contain Portuguese ambitions and used the arrangement to keep other possible enemies at bay. It was a marriage of convenience that demonstrates the Mutapa's use of diplomacy to keep the enemy at bay. The exchange of ambassadors or emissaries between the Mutapas and the Portuguese is discussed in some detail by Mudenge (1988: 143–54).

King Moshoeshoe I of Lesotho

NB: Sources on Moshoeshoe I for this chapter include Ngara (2012), Ngara (2013), Samson (1974), *UK Essays* (2021), Wikipedia (10 July 2012) 'Moshoeshoe' and oral history, especially as narrated by Bernice Teboho Ngara (Nee Motanyane).

A brief historical account

Moshoeshoe (pronounced Mushweshwe), the son of Mokhachane of the Bakoena Ba Mokoteli clan, was born in Leribe, Lesotho, in about 1786 and was given the name Lepoqo. He used to help his father in raids against other clans. His name was allegedly changed to Moshoeshoe after a successful raid in which he shaved the beards of an adversary called Ramonaheng. In 1820 at age thirty-four Moshoeshoe succeeded his father and then formed his own clan consisting of the Bakoena Ba Mokoteli and some members of his mother's clan, the Bafokeng.

Moshoeshoe and his followers first settled in Butha-Buthe and then moved on to Thaba Bosiu which became his stronghold. Clans running away from Shaka's wars called the Mfecane joined him and the Basotho nation was born. He fought some battles against the British, the Boers, Shaka's Zulus and Mzilikazi's Ndebeles and was successful in some of these. In 1854, the Orange Free State became an independent Boer Republic. In 1865, he lost a large portion of what is now Free State to the Boers. Following some of these defeats of the Basotho by the Boers, Moshoeshoe asked for British protection in 1868. He died in 1870, leaving Lesotho as a British protectorate. He is known to have been a great fighter as well as a diplomat in dealing with both the British and the Boers.

Moshoeshoe as a leader who protected and provided for his people

One of the things that strike one about Moshoeshoe is that he is known to have been a leader who was very good at protecting his people and providing for them. That he protected his people against external aggressors is evident from the way he fought against the Boers and the British and finally decided to seek British protectorate status. Moshoeshoe's care for his people went beyond protection against external aggressors. When there was famine in the region during the Mfecane (or Lifaqane) wars, Moshoeshoe is reported to have seen to it that food was provided for his people. It was because Moshoeshoe's people were provided for that Rakotswane and his group of cannibals (*malimo*) who had killed and eaten the king's grandfather, Peete, found themselves going to Thaba Bosiu in search of food.

The story goes that when Moshoeshoe's *matona* (ministers/councillors) recognized Rakotswane, they urged the king to kill these cannibals, as we have already learned. Instead of welcoming the idea of killing his grandfather's killers, Moshoeshoe persuaded his *matona* to prepare a feast for the cannibals, arguing that they had to be respected because they were his grandfather's grave and graves of the dead had to be respected. Because of this generosity and spirit of forgiveness and reconciliation, the cannibals were fed, integrated into the community and ceased behaving as cannibals.

Relations with ministers (matona)

An important aspect of Moshoshoe's leadership style was his policy of consulting his *matona/ministers*. When negotiating with an enemy or adversary he would sit on the same side as the enemy team facing his own team which would be on the other side. He would position himself in such a way that his team would see from his gestures whether he wanted them to agree with the enemy or not. In this way consultation with his councillors/ministers and elders would take place even during the process of serious negotiations with the enemy. This collective decision practice strengthened trust and loyalty between the king and the people's representatives. Moshoeshoe's leadership style here is evidence of the correctness of what Mike Boon (2007: 44) sees as characteristic features of traditional African leadership.

It would appear that the collective decision strategy was such a key feature of the king's leadership culture that as a result some maxims developed as part of the daily discourse of the Basotho. One of these says *Lentswe la Morena le haeloa lesaka* 'The word of the King (or the voice of the King) must have a kraal built round it'. Whatever the king says must be protected. What this means is that you do not expose the king. You have the responsibility of advising the king so that he does not say something wrong. If he says something that is not appropriate, you have to find a way of protecting him. It also suggests that the leader must not shoot from the hip. He should learn to be accountable by consulting his team.

Moshoeshoe's pervasive influence in the promotion of peace

A characteristic feature for which Moshoeshoe was known is that while he was a great warrior, he was a man of peace. It was because he was a lover of peace that instead of massacring the killers of his grandfather, he chose the route of forgiveness, reconciliation and generosity. This gesture had such an impact on the cannibals that they stopped eating humans. It is also said of him that after defeating an enemy army, he would send the defeated army a herd of cattle as a gift. It is reasonable to assume that after receiving such a gift, the enemy army would not regard Moshoeshoe as an enemy. In his interactions with the British, the Boers and Christian missionaries, he chose the way of peace whenever this was possible and in the interest of his people. We learn that he used to say, 'Peace is my sister' (*UK Essays* 2021). His wisdom as a man of peace was buttressed by skilful diplomacy. It was a mark of his wisdom that he was prepared to engage a White man, Eugene Casalis, as his advisor in matters of foreign relations and was also able to accommodate both Protestant and Catholic missionaries.

The way he is said to have dealt with the rivalry between Protestant and Catholic missionaries shows what a shrewd negotiator he was: This story from oral history tells us that the Protestants arrived in Mosheshoe's kingdom before the Catholics. When the Catholics came, the Protestants tried to influence the king not to allow the new arrivals to work in his country. The king then held a meeting with the two groups after sunset. When the meeting started it was completely dark with no kind of light in sight. He said to the missionaries, 'Do you see anything?'; the answer was 'No'. He then said to the Protestant missionaries, 'Did you say you are bringing light to my people?' They answered 'Yes'. At this point he asked for a light to be brought to the scene. 'Do you see better now?' he asked the Protestants. 'Yes, we see better', they answered. He then asked for another light to be brought to the scene. 'How do you see now?' the King asked the missionaries. 'We see much better!' was the response.

'Did you say you see better with two lights?' The missionaries answered, 'Yes, we see much better with two lights.' Then the king concluded, 'My people will see much better with two lights. I will therefore allow both Protestants and Catholics to work in my country.' Here was an unschooled king presenting a proposition to these educated missionaries whose logic they could not negate.

Moshoeshoe's love for peace was so pervasive that peace became part of the culture and discourse of the people of Lesotho. A number of greetings that refer to peace developed as part of the daily discourse of the people. In fact the word for peace, *Khotso* quickly became an alternative greeting to *Lumela* 'Hello'. *Khotso* is so valued that it became part of the national slogan of Lesotho: *Khotso, Pula, Nala!* 'Peace, Rain, Prosperity!' What this means is that if there is peace and enough rain, the people will surely have a bumper crop. If you begin by promoting peace and pray for rain, the people will have a good harvest and be well fed! There are a number of other expressions that show that Moshoeshoe's concern for peace was so pervasive that the concept of peace became a key element in the psyche of a traditional Mosotho.

Lessons from the combined wisdom of the two kingdoms

There are two categories of lessons that we can learn from the combined wisdom of the Mutapa Empire and the Kingdom of Lesotho under Moshoshoe I: The first type of lesson has to do with what the leaders of today can learn about leadership from the wisdom of these ancient rulers. Well-meaning leaders who wish to draw inspiration from their own traditions can learn much from their forebears. The second category of lesson is about a political theory that scholars or political theorists can develop from the practices of the leaders of these two kingdoms. Here we are seeking to generalize the practices of these two kingdoms to acquire a deeper understanding of factors that affect power relations between the ruler and the ruled. An understanding of the power relations in these two kingdoms can lead to a deeper understanding of what happens generally in situations where a people or society is conquered by a ruler from outside that society. We shall begin by examining what the political leaders of today can learn from the wisdom of the two kingdoms.

What today's political leaders can learn from the two kingdoms

In today's world, Africa is regarded as the least developed continent, and African leaders are associated with inability to rule – inability to develop democratic states where people can live in peace and harmony enjoying reasonable standards of living. The continent is known to be rich in resources and is yet unable to feed its own people, many of whom find themselves abandoning their own homes in order to go overseas where they can use their education and skills profitably in conditions of relative freedom and peace. The impression created to the rest of the world is that Africans are inherently incapable of ruling themselves. If there is a deficit of leadership in the world, Africa is a glaring example of that. The leadership of domination is indeed the prevailing mode of leadership on the continent today.

In this chapter we have presented researched information about two traditional African kingdoms which show that Africa has had leaders who were not highly educated in the modern sense but were able to lead their people in ways that even people from more developed continents could admire. The leadership practices of these leaders were very much in line with what is today called transformational leadership. The purpose of this section of the chapter is to present a synthesis in summary form of the positives that today's leaders can benefit from. One of the underlying principles here is that an understanding of what leadership is, combined with knowledge of traditional wisdom, can lead to better leadership practice.

The benefits of the philosophy of Ubuntu

The philosophy of *Ubuntu/Botho/Unhu/Utu* presents one of the most powerful explanations of the power relations that should exist between the leader and the led, between political leaders and the populace. What this means is that in the traditional societies discussed here what we call transformational leadership went hand in hand with responsible leadership. In other words, the ancestors of the people of Southern Africa bequeathed to them the idea that leaders are accountable to the community, to the people they lead. The leader exists in large measure for the purpose of promoting the interests of the people. The leader must therefore regard himself/herself as a steward who owes the position he/she holds to the people or the nation and must consequently be accountable to the people: *Morena ke morena ka batho* 'A king is a king on account of the people'; *kgosi ke kgosi ka sechaba* 'A king is a king on account of the nation'.

The leader must have a high sense of responsibility for what happens to the people. The Mutapa felt he had responsibility for his people – he had to *personally* endeavour to resolve their problems. This went to the extent that the people themselves felt that the king had the duty to protect them against thieves and malefactors (Mudenge 1988: 154). Moshoeshoe clearly had a very high sense of responsibility for the peace and security of his people and for ensuring they were well fed. What this suggests is that where students are taught about Leadership in Africa, they must be educated about the philosophy of *Ubuntu* and how it can inform leadership practice.

Managing the economy and people's needs

Whatever political ideology the ruling authorities embrace, and whatever power relations exist between the ruler and the ruled, a prime consideration is that the general population must feel that their needs are catered for: that they have shelter and clothing; that an environment is created in which they can work the land, feed themselves adequately and sell their produce; that they have access to education and healthcare facilities; that there are employment opportunities for those who can work; and so on. Here we can learn useful lessons from how the Mutapas developed the economy of the empire and how Moshoeshoe attracted people to his kingdom by providing food for and feeding his people. When their material needs are taken care of, the people are likely to go about minding their own business without being overly concerned about who occupies the corridors of power. Rather than envy those who occupy the corridors of power, the people are more likely to be loyal because they are satisfied that their needs are catered for and may feel that their expectation of genuine representation by the rulers has been met. Goran Therborn (1980: 93–112) posits that this sense of representation when the rulers are seen to be ruling on behalf of the people may produce a sense of *deference* – conceiving the present rulers to be specially suited, whether by reason of descent or because the rulers have made an important contribution. The sense of deference is enhanced where the leader has the quality of *sereti*, *isithunzi* or *chiremera* which we translated earlier as 'dignified presence'. In the case of Moshoeshoe, there was definitely a sense of deference because not only had he founded the nation of Lesotho and had *sereti* in good measure but he had also courageously defended the nation and seen to it that the people were provided for.

Maintenance of peace and stability

Success in farming can only occur under conditions of peace and security. A major threat to precolonial states was the possibility of attacks from hostile African ethnic groups. From the information given in the earlier sections of this chapter, it becomes clear that the leaders of the two kingdoms under discussion worked for peace. Granted that one cannot be certain that every Mutapa was a man of peace, what is clear is that the Mutapas succeeded for long periods of time to create a relatively peaceful environment for their people by skilfully managing relations with the Portuguese and possible hostile African ethnic groups. It was because there was relative peace that agriculture, gold mining, hunting and trade could flourish in the empire. It is also clear that while a great warrior, Moshoeshoe was a man of peace who went to the extent of seeking British protectorate status for Lesotho in order to protect the peace and stability of the nation. A clear sign of his love for peace is what became something like an ideology of peace in the daily discourse of the Basotho.

Forms of shared and democratic leadership

In Chapter 3 we discussed the concept of shared and distributed leadership. This approach was not at all foreign to the Mutapas and Moshoeshoe I. The Mutapa was by all accounts a very powerful ruler, but as Mudenge (1988:85) points out, 'In practice he was assisted by a number of courtiers and officers who exercised some of those powers.' Furthermore, "the routine matters of state at the court were dealt with by the Council (*Dare*) made up of the immediate advisors of the Mutapa'. Moshoeshoe practised interactive collaborative leadership. The equivalent of the Mutapa's *Dare* was the *Khotla* (Council). According to *UK Essays* (November 2018, August 2021), the senior councillors were assured they would never be punished for what they said at the *Khotla*. Moshoeshoe also had the practice of a public gathering (a *Pitso*) where people discussed matters of governance. In both these structures the members were free to advise him and to point out his mistakes. A form of interactive collaborative leadership is what he demonstrated in negotiations with a team of adversaries as explained earlier. In this regard, the king's team would do the active negotiating while he was busy making gestures to show whether he agreed or not. In this way, shared leadership in the form of interactive collaborative leadership was perfected.

Relations between the king and provincial leaders

The extent to which the central government has control over provincial matters is a key issue, more so in large states than in small ones. This is an issue of devolution of authority as opposed to centralized control of power. In a kingdom or empire like the Mutapa state, this boils down to the power of the king/queen over provincial governors. In a modern democracy, the equivalent is the relationship between the state president and premiers or provincial governors, as the case may be. The question that arises is the extent to which the central government should have control on provincial matters. As already explained, here we learn useful lessons from the Mutapa Empire where the king gave relative autonomy to provincial governors. It would appear that the provincial governors became more loyal when they saw that the leader of the central government recognized their authority and went to the extent of showing appreciation by sending them gifts. This created an environment in which there was mutual respect between central authority and provincial leaders. This is a pragmatic form of transformational leadership which was based on soft management of relationships which resulted in the king positively influencing the hearts and minds of his provincial leaders.

Balancing national interests against foreign interests

Among the challenges that African governments of our time have to meet is the need to balance national interests against foreign interests. From an ideological and international relations point of view, there are two major considerations: First, nations of the twenty-first century exist in a global village. There is no nation that can exist in complete isolation from others. On the other hand, developing nations have to be aware of the possible dangers of what has been called neo-colonialism – a new form of colonialism in terms of which the resources of smaller developing nations can be exploited for the benefits of more powerful nations at the expense of the smaller nations. What this suggests is that for smaller developing nations, international relations depend to a great extent on balancing national interests against the interests of foreign countries and finding a suitable balance. No foreign country will enter into a relationship with a developing nation where there is no gain for that foreign country.

In view of the above, it is reasonable to assume that the Mutapas of the fifteenth, sixteenth and seventeenth centuries did not really want to have a standing relationship with the Portuguese, but they had to reckon with the interests of the Portuguese and possible threats from other powers and ethnic groups, and so they agreed to enter into a pact in terms of which the Portuguese kept a garrison at the palace, ostensibly to protect the Mutapa. Whatever the motives of the Portuguese, the Mutapas went into what appears to have been a marriage of convenience which made Portugal an ally of the Kingdom of Mutapa in the face of possible threats from elsewhere. Similarly, Moshoeshoe was able to guarantee the survival of the state of Lesotho by seeking British protection and seeking a European advisor.

The power to serve and inspire

The best index for testing the extent to which the political leader is accepted by the masses and seen to genuinely represent their interests is the degree to which ordinary people show confidence in, as well as affection, admiration and reverence for, the leader. When, by reason of his/her competence, character and humanity, the leader inspires the general populace and is revered by ordinary men and women, then the leader has become a truly great leader who influences the people to follow him/her *voluntarily*. He/she fulfils the requirement for what Goran Therborn (1980: 96) calls 'obedience based on a *sense of representation*'.

We can infer that to some extent the best of the Mutapas were able to induce admiration, respect and deference in the hearts and minds of ordinary subjects when they held day-long audiences about seven times every month trying to solve the problems brought to them. On the one hand, it can be argued that this sounds like too much centralization of power in the king. On the other hand, this is a situation where the Mutapa appears to have practised the ideology of what Robert Greenleaf (1977) has called 'the servant first' type of leader rather than 'the leader first' type, the difference being that the servant first type of leader is motivated, not by the ambition to lead but by the desire to serve, whereas for the leader first type, service may be incidental to the ambition for power or wealth. The practice of the Mutapa in this regard was also a practical demonstration of the leader placing himself at the service of the people in the true spirit of *Ubuntu-/Utu*-based leadership. A qualification that needs to be made in this discussion is that since there is now no way of knowing what motivated those we have referred to as 'the best of the Mutapas' to behave the way they did, there is every possibility that while they may have started as 'the leader first' type, for a variety of reasons, they ended up behaving like 'the servant first' type. There is probably also no way of knowing that there was consistency in this behaviour.

By far the clearest example of inspirational leadership that this chapter has dealt with is that of Moshoeshoe I of Lesotho who developed a genuine collective leadership style and became a great inspiration to his subjects. As already noted, he was such an inspirational leader that his influence had a lasting effect on the psyche, culture and day-to-day discourse of ordinary Basotho. In the 1970s, about one hundred years after his death, you still heard the people of Lesotho using *peace* as a greeting word or parting slogan: *Khotso Ntate!* 'Greetings, Elder!', *Ha e ate!* 'May it (i.e. peace) be multiplied!' or *Ha e phapatoe!* 'Let it be given a pat on the back!'

Three general conclusions arising out of a study of the two kingdoms

From a study of the two kingdoms, it is possible to make three general conclusions: two political conclusions and a set of lessons for educational leaders. The first political conclusion is about *conditions for developing a stable state* for countries that are not big powers, while the second can be regarded as a theory on what may be called *reciprocity relationships* between the leader (or ruler) and the general populace. The third conclusion consists of a set of takeaways for educational leaders.

General conclusion 1: Conditions for developing a stable state

On the basis of this analysis of the two kingdoms, it is possible to posit that the development of a stable state depends in part on the following among other factors:

1. Cultivating good relations with at least one powerful state that protects the nation against foreign aggressors.
2. Cultivating cordial relations between the ruler (or central government) and provincial leaders.
3. Developing a successful economy in an environment of peace and stability.
4. Being seen to be a leader (or government) who serves the people and truly represents them.

General conclusion 2: Reciprocity relationships between ruler and ruled

This is about the give and take that creates trust and good relations between the ruler and the ruled. The assumption here is that in the case of the Mutapa state, and to some extent the Kingdom of Lesotho, some of the regions were vassal states – they had been conquered and incorporated into the bigger state. In the case of a modern democracy, we are talking about how a leader who has emerged as the winner and ruler in an authentic election relates to members of the opposition and wins their confidence. There is a two-way process or development – the process the ruled go through and the actions and behaviour of the ruler:

> ***The Ruled:*** Where the ruler has managed over time to win the ruled to his /her side, the latter go through stages that can be represented as follows:
>
> *Resistance > Submission > Obedience (voluntary) > Deference (given) > Adulation*
>
> ***The Ruler:*** On his /her part, the ruler would have gone through actions and processes that can be represented as follows:
>
> *Conquest > Subjection > Deference (earned) > Loyalty (earned) > Adulation*

In terms of this theory, the minimum that a well-meaning ruler should aim for is *Deference* – recognition and acceptance of the ruler as specially suited to rule. In the case of the Mutapas, there were at least two indicators of deference: (1) recognition by provincial leaders; and (2) the people brought their problems to him to solve. In the case of Moshoeshoe, the fact that clans voluntarily came to his kingdom to be ruled by him was an indication of deference accorded even before they became part of the kingdom.

A strong indicator for adulation (high-level respect and admiration) of the Mutapa is the fact that the people had so much confidence in the king they believed he would as a matter of course or duty protect them from thieves and malefactors. A Portuguese writer was quoted as saying, 'They say that houses are built with doors for fear of malefactors, from whom it is the king's duty to protect his people, and above all the poor' (1988: 154). As for Moshoeshoe, there was clear evidence of adulation by the people. We have already referred to the maxim *Lentswe la morena le haeloa lesaka* 'The word of the king must have a kraal built round it'. Writers say by the late nineteenth century Moshoeshoe was so respected that the people referred to him as *Morena e moholo, morena oa Basotho* 'The Great King, the King of the Sotho People' (Wikipedia 10 July 2012).

In our time, the leaders one can identify as having received such adulation on the African continent are Mwalimu Julius Nyerere of Tanzania and Madiba of South Africa. Of Nelson Mandela, Martin Kalungu-Banda (2006: 70) quotes a professor of anthropology as saying,

Mandela now really is one of the best-known names in the world. The fact that his name comes second only to Coca-Cola, whose many years of successful marketing have given it the recognition that it has in the world, speaks for itself on how Mandela has become a world icon of struggle, forgiveness and sheer dedication to making the world a better place for all.

General conclusion 3: Takeaways for educational leaders

Educational leaders may think that the study of the two kingdoms is all about politics and government and nothing about education. The fact of the matter is that educationalists, and educational leaders in particular, ought to be able to make transferrals between one domain and another, to learn lessons about educational leaders from the practice of good state or government leaders. By transferring the good practices of these political leaders to the education sphere or domain, we can learn a number of lessons, including the following:

1. Applying the principles of *Ubuntu* in the running of institutions in respect of humanness, meaning issues like human rights, gender equality and justice for all – staff and students.
2. Hard work: Consider the Mutapa working on holidays and Moshoeshoe striving to build a new nation. One new vice chancellor jokingly said, 'What does the vice-chancellor do from eight o'clock to five o'clock?' This is a true story that shocked this writer and made him wonder how the vice chancellor had managed to impress the selection committee when he thought a university vice chancellor's hours of work are only from eight to five.
3. Working relationships between the academic leader/education leader and other senior officials. Is there something to learn from Moshoeshoe's interactive collaborative leadership and the Mutapa's use of *Dare* (the senior councillors' interactive discussion forum for dealing with important matters of state)? The university is traditionally a place where collegial leadership is practised. How can the principles of interactive collaborative leadership be used to enhance the collective decision-making process in the university?
4. In the *Khotla* and *Pitso* Moshoeshoe's councillors and other leaders did not only deal with important matters of state but were also able to advise or even criticize the king. What forum can the school principal or vice chancellor use to give other senior officials (including senior students) the opportunity to advise the head of the organization? Such a forum could be used to avert the possibility of extreme managerialism which can result in the sidelining of fellow senior staff and student structures.
5. The Mutapa developed a relatively strong economy and that was important for the empire's relations with other countries, including European and Far

Eastern countries. The economy of the university is in part determined by a strong research and academic culture. Just as the Mutapa state was able to attract trade with far-away countries, a university that has a strong research and overall academic culture will be able to attract cooperation with other institutions, and in that way promote internationalization.

6. Diplomacy is a useful strategy and tool for educational institutions. There is sometimes a case for fighting to preserve that which is educationally sound, but doing so diplomatically in relation to government and other authorities.
7. Learning to lead and inspire: The leader who is a person of integrity, who knows her/his job, is professional and respects other employees; who fights for the best academic conditions and the rights of the staff and students, and promotes a culture of academic freedom and autonomy in higher education, will win the admiration of the university or school community. Part of the deference, respect and loyalty earned by King Moshoeshoe and the Mutapas was a result of their good performance combined with respect for other leaders.

These and other principles and practices can inspire astute educational leaders to start thinking about innovative ways of improving the leadership and management of their institutions with a view to transforming the cultures of those institutions.

6

Educating people to serve: Servant leadership

TUNING IN EXERCISE

The president who pushed the principal's car

We start by narrating an anecdote in which we are taken to East Africa, to the Republic of Tanzania in the early 1970s. A well-known and successful man is driving his beautiful Mercedes Benz along a gravel road. He is well known partly because not many in the country can afford that kind of car. He comes to a swampy spot and the car skids. Wearing a spotlessly white shirt and a black tie, he gets out of the car frustrated, puts both hands in his trouser pockets and looks at the beautiful car in utter misery. Just then, a jeep pulls up driven by a man in a safari suit. The driver is wearing sunglasses and is accompanied by two other men.

'What's the matter, my friend?' asks the new arrival.

'I'm stuck here', answers the driver of the beautiful car, his hands in his pockets and his beautiful tie curling over his potbelly.

The safari suit man, with the help of his two colleagues, starts cutting down tree branches. They remove some mud from under the car and replace the mud with branches and leaves. He then turns to the owner of the car and says, 'If you get into the car now and start the engine, we will push you from the back.' In no time the engine starts and roars, and the car moves, splattering mud onto the safari suit man's suit, hair and sunglasses. The driver drives on to firmer ground, leaves the engine idling and comes back to the safari suit man. He takes out his business card and a wad of money. 'I'm the principal of Morogoro College. Here is my card and a small token of gratitude for your kind service.'

'Thank you for your card, Sir', says the other man, wiping his spectacles with his handkerchief. 'I will certainly contact you when I come to Morogoro; but my colleagues and I won't accept the money. We only did what we had to do for a fellow Tanzanian and a fellow human being.'

'But what's your name?'

'My name is Julius Nyerere, and these are my colleagues, Zamani and Joseph.'

It is only at this point that the principal of Morogoro College realizes that the man whose safari suit is now splattered with mud is the president of the Republic of Tanzania, the person who holds the highest office in the land.

Questions

1. What does this story tell us about the attitude of the president to manual work?
2. Compare and contrast the behaviour of the president in this story with the behaviour of Mr Nkosi the principal in Chapter 4. Which of the two conducts himself as a boss, and who behaves as someone who provides a service?
3. Who is likely to be admired more by those who witness the behaviour: Mr Nkosi the principal or Julius Nyerere the president? Give an explanation for your answer.
4. Is there anything to say about the president's behaviour in relation to the philosophy of *Ubuntu*?

Robert Greenleaf and the need to change society

Now read the following story that Greenleaf took from Herman Hesse's *Journey to the East*:

> In this story we see a band of men on a mythical journey ... The central figure is Leo, who accompanies the party as the *servant* who does their menial chores, but who also sustains them with his spirit and his song. He is a person of extraordinary presence. All goes well until Leo disappears. Then the group falls into disarray and the journey is abandoned. They cannot make it without the servant Leo. The narrator, one of the party, after some years of wandering, finds Leo and is taken into the Order that had sponsored the journey. There he discovers that Leo, whom he had known first as *servant*, was in fact the titular head of the Order, its guiding spirit, a great and noble *leader*. (Greenleaf 1977: 21)

Robert Greenleaf says it was his reading of this story which inspired him to conceive of the idea of servant leadership.

But first, who was Robert Greenleaf? Robert Greenleaf is the founder of the modern Servant Leadership Movement and of the Greenleaf Center for Servant Leadership, which is perhaps the greatest authority on the subject of servant leadership. Greenleaf worked for many years at American Telephone and Telegraphs (AT&T), the world's largest telecommunications company where he worked in a number of capacities introducing many innovations. In 1964 he retired from AT&T and started his career as writer, teacher and consultant.

Greenleaf was passionate about the need to change society through servant leadership; and to him servant leaders are both individuals and institutions (organizations). His book, *Servant Leadership: A Journey into the Nature of Legitimate Power & Greatness* (1977), has had enormous impact on thinking about leadership. He was convinced that 'the only way to change a society (or just make it go) is to produce people, enough people, who will change it (or make it go)' (Greenleaf 1977: 60). People must be prepared to lead and this must be first priority. He challenges us to think about who is responsible for the current state of affairs when society is not moving forward to a better future through servant leadership. Who is holding back the movement of society to a better future? Who is the enemy? Is it bad people? Is it stupid people? Is it the 'system'? Is it reactionaries?

We tend to settle at being critics, pointing fingers at what the politicians in power are doing wrong. We consider ourselves to be the innocent people, victims of injustice and of the mismanagement of our economies by the people in power, by those we would like to call 'the enemy'. Greenleaf wants us to reflect more on who is the enemy? Albert Einstein is quoted as having said, 'The world is a dangerous place to live, not because of the people who are evil, but because of the people who won't do anything about it.' In answering the question who is the enemy, Greenleaf says this: 'The real enemy is fuzzy thinking on the part of good, intelligent, vital people, and their failure to lead, and to follow servants as leaders' (1977: 58). He then emphatically summarizes his response to the question who is the enemy? 'In short, the enemy is strong natural servants who have the potential to lead but do not lead, or who choose to follow a nonservant' (59).

Greenleaf has thrown down the gauntlet. He is challenging us to be servant leaders or to follow servant leaders. But what is servant leadership?

Who is a servant leader?

In answering the question 'Who is the servant leader?', Greenleaf starts by contrasting two kinds of leaders – the servant-first kind of leader and the leader-first kind of leader. The servant-first and the leader-first types are two extremes with different shadings and blends between them. He explains, 'The servant-leader is servant first – as Leo was portrayed. It begins with the natural feeling that one wants to serve, to serve first ... That person is sharply different from one who is leader first, perhaps because of the need to assuage an unusual power drive or to acquire material possessions.'

Greenleaf goes on to explain the difference between the two in terms of the effect on the people led:

> The difference manifests itself in the care taken by the servant first to make sure that other people's highest priority needs are being served. The best test, and difficult to administer is this: Do those served grow as servants? Do they, while being served, become healthier, wiser, freer, more autonomous, more likely themselves to become servants? And what is the effect on the least privileged in society? Will they benefit, or at least not be further deprived? (Greenleaf 1977: 27)

In view of the above, it is therefore appropriate to define servant leadership as follows: 'Servant leadership is a philosophy and set of practices that enriches the lives of individuals, builds better organisations and ultimately creates a more just and caring world' (Greenleaf Center for Servant Leadership).

Servant leadership as propounded by Robert Greenleaf is said to apply to all faiths and to people who do not confess any faith, and this is how it should be taken. The point to note, however, is that while he may not have read the relevant passages of the Bible when he first formulated the concept of servant leadership, Greenleaf should be the first to admit that there are striking similarities between his philosophy of leadership and the teachings of Jesus on leadership. As far as I know, Jesus seems to have been the first thinker to associate the idea of leadership with the status of a servant. There are a number of passages in which Jesus teaches about servant leadership. For the purpose of showing the similarity between his teaching and Greenleaf's philosophy, we shall quote one such passage:

> You know that those who are regarded as rulers of the Gentiles lord it over them, and their high officials exercise authority over them. Not so with you. Instead, whoever wants to be great among you must be your servant, and whoever wants to be first, must be slave of all. For even the Son of Man did not come to be served but to serve, and to give his life as a ransom for many. (New International Version, Mark 10.42-45)

This observation is not in any way intended to be a derogatory comment and should not in any way reduce the enormous contribution that Robert Greenleaf has made to our understanding of the true meaning of leadership. The purpose is to put the origins of the idea of servant leadership in its proper perspective.

Some characteristics of a servant leader

Since Robert Greenleaf actively publicized the concept of servant leadership, presenting talks, publishing papers and ultimately his famous book referred to above (Greenleaf 1977), there has been a movement of scholars who support the concept, and other authors have published books which have further clarified the idea. Among these authors we should include Ron Boehme. In comparing the leadership of domination with servant leadership, Boehme (1989: 56–62) has said that the leadership of domination operates to a great extent by fear, force, manipulation and control, while servant leadership operates out of motives of love and is based on pillars of truth, righteousness and justice. In this chapter we are looking at servant leadership from a purely generic, non-religious perspective. To have a deeper understanding of this approach to leadership, it is necessary to identify the characteristics of a servant leader. From a generic (general) leadership point of view, the following are some of the key characteristics that have been identified:

1. First, for the servant leader, leadership is secondary to service. Service comes first and leadership second, and the exercise of power in the sense of making a show of it becomes unnecessary. The servant leader puts others first. Service of others becomes more important than position and the exercise of authority. Like Leo, the servant leader is not motivated by the expectation of a reward and does not have to prove to everybody that he/she is the boss.
2. Second, servant leadership comes from the heart. It is not just another clever way of getting support from the followers. Servant leaders have a personal conviction about issues of character, honesty, integrity, morality, ethical behaviour and respect for fellow human beings. Many leaders will do in private what they do not do in public because what matters is that one should not be seen or caught doing something that the public disapproves of. This idea is aptly captured in a Sesotho saying whose English translation is 'A thief is one who has been caught'. As long as nobody has caught you stealing, you are not a thief. On the contrary, a true servant leader does not normally do something in his/her private life that he/she would not do in public. In this way servant leadership becomes a way of life which applies to all situations – to the political or business environment, the family or the church. In this regard, the servant leader will do what is right no matter what – regardless of the circumstances – because he/she believes in upholding the value of integrity.
3. The servant leader recognizes human potential and acts to bring out the best in people. As human beings we have a responsibility to help each other to be better people, to be more human, to make the best of our talents in the service

of humanity and the betterment of society. The power that the servant leader has to grow an organization partly lies in the ability to make others realize their potential to make their organization a better organization. It is the power to energize the team in the service of their organization.
4. The servant leader seeks to empower other leaders and other people, not to control them. Many leaders fear competition from other leaders. A leader who believes in the leadership of domination will surround himself/herself with less capable people because he/she fears to be overshadowed by more competent people. The true servant leader, even if he/she naturally fears competition, will facilitate the development of other leaders and strive to remove any obstacles that may impede their growth as leaders. He/she knows that leadership is not about self but about the people and the organization.
5. The servant leader adopts the stewardship view of leadership. Many self-serving leaders have a distorted view of their responsibility. Some will not want to relinquish the positions they hold, while others will see their responsibility only in terms of the duration of their contract. On the contrary, the servant leader adopts the stewardship view of leadership which enables him/her to understand that he/she is not only accountable to the present generation but also to past generations and, more importantly, to future generations. To past generations because the power he/she currently enjoys drives in part from the struggles and achievements of those who have gone before us who had a vision of what the nation should be; and to future generations because the present generation should not deprive future generations of what we currently enjoy. Instead, we and our leaders should preserve the wealth, natural environment and heritage we have inherited and strive to create more wealth so that the unborn can enjoy what we currently enjoy in even greater abundance. The idea of preserving the environment in the face of global warming is based on this principle: we who live today have a duty to preserve the environment for future generations.

It is true that some companies are owned by certain individuals. However, correctly understood, the leadership of a country, company, church or institution is generally a stewardship position. The leader does not own the country, company, church or institution concerned. The leader was appointed or elected to ensure that both the organization (or country) and the people succeed and prosper and to see to it that the interests, freedoms and rights of the people are protected. The leader who fails to do this has no justification for wanting to continue in office. On the other hand, the leader who understands the stewardship view of leadership will know that there will come a time when he/she has to give way to new leaders.

6. The servant leader gets fulfilment from serving the whole community and from serving humanity. The ultimate goal of the servant leader is not just to serve a particular organization, political party or religion. He/she will dedicate himself/herself to the service of a particular political party, church or organization because that is what he/she has been specifically appointed to do; but in his/her greater scheme of things the ultimate question is: Of what service is the particular church, political party or private sector organization to the community in which it is located, to the nation as a whole, and indeed to humanity?

Servant leadership and other types of leadership

It should be clear to the reader that servant leadership and the leadership of domination are very different approaches. The leadership of domination is closely related to autocratic or dictatorial leadership, although these two are not necessarily synonymous. Someone who practices the leadership of domination may in principle not approve of overt dictatorial leadership. On the other hand, a dictator is most likely to practice the leadership of domination.

The servant leader's primary motive in leading is to serve people. Consequently, the servant leader will listen to the people in order to cater for their needs. In seeking to serve people, the servant leader has to guard against the possibility of becoming a populist leader who wants to please the followers even in cases where pleasing the people is not in the best interests of the organization or entity concerned. The servant leader has to be tough enough to resist unwise suggestions coming from the people. He/she may sometimes be forced to take decisions that may disappoint followers if following the dictates of followers entails betraying his/her own principles. Equally, the servant leader must avoid becoming a doormat who allows everybody to walk all over him/her.

The genuine servant leader will be guided by the virtues of integrity, truthfulness and honesty and will do what is right no matter what. The servant leader therefore upholds the highest principles of democratic leadership in that he/she is not only guided by the requirement to abide by the law but takes decisions out of a firm conviction of what is right, just, fair and necessary.

There are areas of convergence between servant leadership and *Ubuntu*-based leadership. We saw in the previous chapter how the Mutapa would spend the whole day striving to solve the problems brought to him by the people at the expense of his own rest. When the people were having a holiday, he was busy solving their problems. Similarly, Moshoeshoe I inspired his subjects to be loyal and to embrace the king's values because he showed that he was committed to provide for his people and to protect them. This suggests that there is a close affinity between a leader who genuinely embraces the values of *Ubuntu/Utu* and a leader who is motivated by the principles of servant leadership.

Part III

Education for personal development and leadership

7

Discovering one's purpose in life

TUNING IN EXERCISE

The farm boy and the famous statesman

We begin with a story the writer learned in Pretoria from an Evangelical friend, the late Bishop James Tshenkeng:

> In the 1880s, a distinguished member of the British Parliament was travelling from England to Scotland to give a speech. On his way his carriage became hopelessly stuck in the thick mud of a rural road. A young Scottish farm boy suddenly appeared on the scene with a team of large draft horses. He quickly had the carriage out of its dilemma and ready to resume the journey. The gentleman insisted on paying the young man, but the lad refused saying that he was just being a good neighbour, and neighbours help each other when there is a problem.
> 'Are you sure I can't pay you for your time and effort?' the gentleman asked.
> 'Thank you, Sir, but it was the least I could do. It was a privilege to help such an important person as yourself', the boy replied.
> 'What do you want to be when you grow up?' the man asked.
> 'I'd like to be a doctor, but I doubt it will happen since my family does not have the money for such education.'
> 'Then I'll help you to become a doctor', the man said.
> Nearly fifty years later, another famous English statesman lay dangerously close to death due to pneumonia. Winston Churchill had become ill while attending a war time conference, and Britain desperately needed his leadership as Adolf Hitler threatened the destiny of the British nation. Churchill miraculously recovered because his physician gave him an injection of a new wonder drug called penicillin. Penicillin had been recently discovered by a brilliant medical doctor called Alexander Fleming.

Questions

1. What does the young boy in this story have in common with Julius Nyerere as portrayed in the anecdote at the beginning of Chapter 6?
2. What leadership ideology do these two (the Scottish boy and Nyerere) represent?
3. What do you know about penicillin and when was it discovered?

Discovering your purpose in life

Let us put the story of Dr Alexander Fleming aside for a while and talk about us – you and me, the reader and author of this book: There are many things we do not know about ourselves. With a little bit of study about biology and physiology we get to know something about how our bodies work. There is also something spiritual that many of us do not know about themselves. Many go about as if asleep or in a dream because they do not know the very reason for their existence. Life can become meaningless for some people because they do not know themselves, they do not know the *Why* of their lives; and if you do not know your Why, you do not know who you are! Life can become a meaningless cycle of working, eating, sleeping; sometimes enjoying the pleasures one can get in this life and getting satisfaction from that; very often suffering a lot without any understanding of who they are. I, the author, have watched the behaviour of chickens, road runners in particular. Their life seems to consist of three things: eating, exercising and resting (or sleeping) – not much beyond that. If we are not careful, we human beings can behave like chickens –working, eating, sleeping, enjoying some pleasures and suffering. What do I mean?

The point is that the life of a human being has significance beyond our daily routines. The life of a human being has a *Why*, a reason for existence. In other words, each and every one of us was created for a purpose. This is what distinguishes us from other earthly creatures. Some of us were created to do great things, but some to do something modest, something that does not necessarily turn us into soapy stars, or great singers or soccer players, or presidents of countries or chief executive officers of great companies. But the fact of the matter is this: There are over seven billion people in the world today, and yet each one of us has something significant to do for the world; each one of us has a unique mission. Each one of us has the obligation to leave the world a better place than he or she found it. That is the challenge: to find our purpose in life, however modest it may be. The challenge is to discover that purpose and fulfil it. This is what gives significance to our lives.

Many of us get side tracked and follow careers we were not meant to follow because we think the main purpose of life is to earn a lot of money. As a result, a large percentage of us are in the wrong jobs, either because our country's economy does not provide everybody with the jobs they want or because we have put money as our first priority. Some may be earning a lot of money but be thoroughly unhappy because they are in the wrong jobs. Let me hasten to add that money is important for all of us. Anyone who suggests that money is not important is a liar because there is nothing we can do without money. Even religious people who take the vow of poverty will still need to have money to survive! The question is: Are we in our jobs simply to earn money, or have we discovered our calling and our unique mission and are earning money while fulfilling our mission in life? Let me say it again: The challenge is to discover our calling, our mission in life, because when we discover our *mission* in life and work towards achieving it, we will get fulfilment in what we do.

There is some clarification that needs to be made here: A personal mission and a vocation are the same, but different. One is called to a vocation such as teaching, religious life, medicine or political life. But one is called to a vocation with many others. There are many who are called to be teachers; many called to work as scientists; many called to religious life or even to the same religious congregation, but within that vocation one is likely to find a special calling, which can be called a calling within a calling. That is one's unique mission. In many cases, one is first called to a vocation along with others and then finds something of particular interest within that vocation, or even outside it. For example, one can be called to religious life but have a strong passion for scientific or medical research – as a religious person. In *Man's Search for Meaning* (1985: 131), the great psychiatrist Viktor E. Frankl has said, 'Everyone has his own specific vocation or mission in life to carry out a concrete assignment which demands fulfilment.' Thus one's mission is not just a vision – it is an assignment that one should complete. Each one of us has been given a life and that life demands that we fulfil the purpose for which it was given to us.

When some people think of their purpose in life they think only in terms of themselves: to be famous people; to be rich and powerful; to be admired by all who see them. In *The Purpose Driven Life*, Rick Warren has a very important message for such people and for all of us:

> The search for the purpose of life has puzzled people for thousands of years. That's because we typically begin at the wrong starting point – ourselves ... But focusing on ourselves will never reveal our life's purpose. (Warren 2002: 17)

Warren says to find out what your purpose in life is you must start with God. 'But, I don't believe in God', you might say. What I can say to that is this: To those who believe in God there are three dimensions to one's purpose of life: two external dimensions and one internal. First, there is the Creator who determines one's reason for existence, one's purpose; and second, there is humanity that one must serve in order to find fulfilment in life; and finally there is the self – the sense of personal satisfaction that one has achieved what one has been yearning to achieve. To those who do not believe in a Superior Being outside human life, there are at least two dimensions – humanity that must be served and the self. There is no doubt that in any situation where one has achieved something, there is a sense of personal satisfaction even if the achievement has to do with acts of service to other people.

What this discussion leads to is that whether one believes in God or not, focussing only on the self can never give one real satisfaction, as such an attitude can result in egotistical or selfish ambitions and desires which have no consideration for the welfare of others. One can go about raping and making young girls pregnant to satisfy one's sexual desire; or someone can be a serial killer, getting away without being caught; or someone can use all sorts of corrupt means to enhance his/her wealth at the expense of other people. One can even ride roughshod over other people to get to the pinnacle of power. Such victories can give temporary satisfaction but cannot result in lasting happiness and peace of mind. Real happiness and satisfaction comes from doing good to fellow human beings and making life better for others as well as for oneself. It is in serving God and other people that we find real fulfilment. Searching for one's purpose in life therefore entails having a sense of personal satisfaction as a result of doing something that is good for others and that is in line with what those who believe in a Creator will see as the will of God for them.

The question that you may ask is how do I discover my purpose in life? Stephen Covey, the author of *The 7 Habits of Highly Effective People*, gives this advice: Begin with the end in mind. Now, what is to begin with the end in mind? This is how Covey puts it: 'To begin with the end in mind is to start with a clear understanding of your destination. It means to know where you're so that you better understand where you are now and so that the steps you take are always in the right direction' (Covey 1989: 98). In simpler terms we can say you should ask yourself: When I retire from active life, what do I want people to remember me by? Or, when I die, what should people say about me? What do I want to achieve for my family, for my institution, for my church and for my nation?

One person who began with the end in mind is the young Scottish boy whose story is narrated at the beginning of this chapter. The young man had a purpose, even as a small boy. His ambition was to be a doctor, but as it turned out, he did not want to be just a doctor who earns money that way. He wanted to be one of the best researchers so as to serve his country and other nations. The young man became Dr Alexander Fleming. The man who sent him to medical school was Sir Randolph Churchill who was Prime Minister Winston Churchill's father. Because Alexander Fleming started with the end in mind, because he discovered his purpose in life, Sir Randolph Churchill helped him to fulfil that purpose by sending him to medical school. Because his purpose was to serve humanity as a doctor, he not only helped to save Britain from the threat of Hitler by finding the drug that saved the British prime minister but also served the whole world because penicillin, the drug he discovered, has saved the lives of millions of people around the world.

Born in 1881 at his parents' farm in Scotland, Alexander died in 1955 at age seventy-three. By the time he died, he had had an illustrious life. What made him famous was not personal wealth or political power but achievements resulting from work that served humanity. Among his numerous achievements were the following:

- Appointed Fellow of the Royal College of Surgeons (FRCS) (1909)
- Discovered and named Penicillin (1928)
- Appointed Fellow of the Royal Society (FRS) (1943)
- Was Knighted Sir Alexander Fleming (1944)
- Won Nobel Prize in Physiology or Medicine (1945)
- Served as a member of the Pontifical Academy of Sciences (the Vatican)
- Long after his death (1999) was named by *Time Magazine* as one of one hundred most important people.

Fleming began with the end in mind, and from a very young age he had learned the importance of selfless service to other people. This is what struck Sir Randolph Churchill. If the young boy had accepted money for his service, he would probably not have been able to train as a doctor. Thus service of others often brings benefits to oneself.

Alexander Fleming had a passion for medicine and medical research. Similarly, each one of us who desires to have a purpose-driven life will have a passion for something; a passion to do something positive. This is one of the ways in which you discover your purpose in life. Examine your life, your interests, and see what you have a passion for. You may have several areas of interest. You may love sport; you may like watching soapies; you may like jogging in the morning. But there will be that one thing which is not just a hobby or a pastime – that thing you want to pursue with your life and make it an important part of your career. Look for it inside of you and you will find it. Your role as a leader will be in relation to that thing for which you have a passion.

The search may take time, but if you seriously want to have a purposeful life, you will find it. And when you have discovered that which gives significance to your life, you will find that, under normal circumstances, you also have talents, gifts or skills that facilitate your ability to fulfil your purpose in life. However, if you discover your passion, your mission in life, and then realize that you have shortcomings that militate against your ability to execute your mission, do something to remove the barrier, to bridge the gap between where you are and what you want to achieve.

Developing a personal mission statement

Every country has a constitution; and nowadays every business or organization has a mission statement. A constitution states the country's laws and rules as well as the rights and duties of all who live in it. An organization's mission statement is a guiding statement which helps the organization to stay aligned to its values and the purpose for which it was established. Unfortunately, many leaders are not aware of the importance of a personal mission statement. However, many successful chief executive officers now have personal mission statements.

If you seriously want to be a leader in a sphere of life or leadership domain, you are well advised to develop your own personal mission statement. Your personal mission statement incorporates your beliefs and values, what you consider to be your purpose in life and the principles that guide you as you make decisions, as you carry out your duties and as you grow as a leader. It is some kind of compass that guides your life. In this regard, a personal mission statement is to an individual what a constitution is to a country.

The question that naturally arises is how to develop a personal mission statement. Nowadays there are websites that one can visit to see examples of personal missions statements and to get tips on how to develop one. Two such websites are:

https://www.andyandrews.com/personal-mission-statement/
https://fastcompany.com/3026791/personal-mission-statements-of-5-famous-ceos-and-why-you-should-write-one-too

The first website leads you to an article by Andy Andrews, 'The Ultimate Guide to Writing Your Own Personal Mission Statement'. In the second website there is an article titled 'Personal Mission Statements of 5 Famous CEOs (And Why You Should Write One Too)'. Andy Andrews gives his own personal mission statement as an example. One of the five famous CEOs cited in the second article is Oprah Winfrey.

A personal mission statement can be fairly long – as long as a paragraph, may be – or it can be very short. Some short ones can be just one phrase such as the following: 'To be one of the best creative writers of my time'. The problem I see with such a short mission statement is that it may sound like a slogan that does not strike the reader as something that has depth; something that the writer has spent time to reflect upon. For our purpose in this chapter, I will give three examples that you may use to think about your own:

1. 'My mission is to help others live the lives they would if they only knew how' (Andy Andrews).
2. 'To be a teacher. And to be known for inspiring my students to be more than they thought they could be' (Oprah Winfrey).
3. 'My mission is to do the will of the ONE who gave me this life, by, among other things:
   - Striving to be a true disciple and witness of Jesus
   - Conscientizing others about the importance of a purpose driven life, and

- Inspiring them to lead productive lives that are guided by the values of integrity, democracy and servant leadership' (My own).

A personal mission statement is not cast in stone. You can keep on modifying it as you develop as a leader and as you get new insights about your life.

8

Personal mastery, self-awareness and leadership qualities and habits

TUNING IN EXERCISE

The two gardens

'No fruits without roots'

There were two neighbours who were friends. They lived in a suburb in which they each had enough land for a small vegetable garden. They decided to grow vegetables on their small plots. As friends they decided to buy the same seeds which they sowed at the same time. The seeds germinated at the same time, but shortly after germination differences began to show. The vegetables in one of the gardens were doing very well, but in the other garden the seedlings began to wilt and die. In a little more than a month, the one friend was beginning to eat vegetables from her garden and was generous enough to give some to the one whose seedlings had wilted and died.

The two had a mutual friend who was known to be a very successful farmer. The woman whose seedlings had wilted and died called the farmer to come and explain the mystery. The plots were next to each other – only separated by a fence. Why was it that her vegetables wilted and died while her friend's did so well? The farmer came and applied a very simple test. She took a strong stick and pushed it down the soil of the garden that had failed to produce vegetables. The stick could not go very far down. It nearly broke. She then went to the other friend's garden and pushed the stick down, using the same force as she had done in the other garden. The whole stick went down into the soil.

'There is the answer to your question', the farmer told the other two women. 'One of you dug very deep into the ground. This is what I see in this garden. In the other garden, the digging was very shallow. In this garden, the seedlings had roots that went deep into the soil. In the other garden the roots had nowhere to go; the soil was as hard as rock; the roots could not penetrate into the hard soil; so they wilted and died.' By way of conclusion, she went on to say, 'No roots, no fruits. You cannot get fruits where there are no roots.'

Questions

1. Discuss the relevance of this story to leadership development?
2. Look up the words 'habit' and 'discipline' as they apply to leadership development, and compare their meanings.
3. Are the words 'efficiency' and 'effectiveness' synonymous, or do they have different meanings? Explain.

The disciplines, practices and qualities that shape the leader

Now that you are aware of the importance of leading a purpose-driven life, and now that you are clear about the importance of a personal mission, you are probably also aware of the sphere of life in which you are going to exercise your leadership abilities. You may actually already have a position of authority and are regarded by others as a leader. To enhance your growth as an effective leader, you also need to develop the disciplines, practices, qualities and habits that shape you as a leader so that they become part of your life as someone who leads others. In this chapter we are going to deal with four related issues: two principles that help developing leaders to know more about themselves and to understand themselves better; and then qualities and habits that shape leaders. The first two are the principles of *Personal Mastery* and *Self-awareness*, while the other two are *Leadership Qualities* and *Leadership Habits*.

Personal mastery

Let us begin by reflecting more on the story of the two friends. The story tells us there are no fruits without roots. Applied to leadership, your fruits come in the form of your ability to lead others and the recognition that others give you as a leader. Your fruits are the satisfaction you derive from leading others with competence and your ability to bring about positive change in organizations and in other people. For you to maintain that ability and that recognition by others; for you to improve your capacity to lead, you must have roots; you must be like a tree that bears fruit because it has deep roots. To have those deep roots you must continue improving your capacity to lead, and this in part entails developing the capacity for *Personal Mastery*. Personal Mastery may be called a habit, but it is really a *discipline*. It is a discipline that goes hand in hand with your discovery of your purpose in life. It helps you to continually remind yourself about your mission in life and about what is important for you to be able to pursue that mission relentlessly without being side tracked by other desires, concerns or preoccupations. What, then, is personal mastery?

I once heard a senior government official giving the example of a warthog as a creature that sometimes does things without knowing why it is doing what it is doing. He said a warthog can start running and then runs furiously in a certain direction. At some point it just stops: It no longer knows why it is running and where it is running to. This kind of behaviour is not entirely alien to human beings. We may not behave in as dramatic a way as the warthog does, but there are times when our behaviour can be basically similar. Someone in a job may get so used to doing something he/she has to do on a daily basis that the job becomes just a routine – the same thing done day in and day out that in the end the original purpose or motive is lost.

One of the very first things a Catholic priest says when celebrating Mass is "The Lord be with you!" To that the congregation answers, "And also with you!" Now on this day there was this priest who had just been ordained. He started by fiddling with the mike as he could feel that there was no sound. He then said, 'There is something wrong with this mike', whereupon the congregation answered loudly and in unison, 'And also with you!' The response to the prayerful greeting had become such a ritual that the congregation did not listen carefully to what the priest was saying and so responded in the way they were used to.

As the term implies, personal mastery has to do with competence, but it means a lot more than just mastering a trade, a profession or a craft. It has to do with the way one approaches one's life, one's profession and one's mission. It is a discipline of personal growth and learning. When it has become a discipline that guides one's approach to things, it then sharpens one's competence and one's skill. In *The Fifth Discipline* (1990: 141–5) Peter Senge explains that when it becomes a discipline, personal mastery becomes an activity that is integrated into our lives. The activity is based on two key principles or what Senge calls 'underlying movements'. These are:

- The practice of continually clarifying what is important to us. We may be side tracked by focusing so much on our problems or on the pleasurable things of life that we forget what our purpose, our mission, is. Thus personal mastery is 'a process of continually focusing and refocusing on what one truly wants, one's vision'.

- The practice of continually learning how to see current reality clearly. We must see the present situation as it is – do not deceive yourself by saying things are OK when you know they are not. In other words, do not hide your head in the sand like an ostrich.

Related to these two principles is a third activity: the juxtaposition of future vision (what we want) and a clear picture of the current reality. This juxtaposition generates 'creative tension' – a force that brings together the current reality and our future vision. The challenge is to generate and sustain creative tension. You must therefore continually make yourself aware of the gap between current reality (where you are) and future vision (where you want to be), and develop attitudes and strategies for bridging the gap. You want to be an effective leader and you know your present weaknesses; you have a mission that you want to achieve, and you know, or should know, what prevents you from achieving that mission. You should therefore strive to develop attitudes and strategies that enable you to achieve that mission.

Characteristics of people with high levels of personal mastery

Now, what does having personal mastery entail? People with high levels of personal mastery have the following characteristics, among others:

1. They have a special sense of purpose. It has been said, 'For such a person, a vision is a calling rather than simply a good idea.'
2. People with high levels of personal mastery live in a continual learning mode to improve themselves.
3. People with high levels of personal mastery have a strong sense of commitment, and they take initiative.
4. They have a very high sense of self-awareness.

Self-awareness

One of the most important requirements of true leadership is self-awareness: the capacity to know one's purpose and understand one's potential, strengths and weaknesses as a leader. To be a true and solid leader, one must live a purpose-driven life as was the case with Martin Luther King Jr. In *The 7 Habits of Highly Effective People*, Stephen Covey explains at length that the second of the seven habits is 'Begin with the end in mind' (Covey 1989: 95–144). Explained briefly, beginning with the end in mind means if you want to be a leader, you should start with a clear understanding of your destination and sense of purpose. Ask yourself: What is the ultimate purpose of my life? What do I want to achieve in my life? What contribution do I want to make to my country, organization, church or nation?

What this means is leadership requires one to develop a personal mission based on one's beliefs, values and goals in relation to one's purpose in life. It is the leader who cherishes the sense of a personal mission and vision who is able to develop an inspiring vision for whatever organization or institution he/she is working for. Chris Lowney has correctly said: 'Only the person who knows what he or she wants can pursue it energetically and inspire others to do so' (Lowney 2003: 27–8). Once you have a clear idea of where you want to go and what you want to achieve, you can assess your own suitability for the mission: your strengths, weaknesses, potential, character and even your qualifications. You can decide what steps you need to take to prepare yourself for your mission.

Awareness of one's shortcomings suggests acceptance of the need to continue learning, continue developing and improving oneself. Every leader, like every human, has weaknesses, blind spots and shortcomings to overcome, as well as strengths to optimize. Overcoming weaknesses and optimizing strengths demand continuing to examine ways to improve – and that entails having time for reflection and being honest with oneself about blind spots and limitations standing in the way of one's ability to execute. Ancient Greek philosopher Socrates made a statement as relevant then as it is today: 'The unexamined life is not worth living.' As Anthony De Mello would say, many of us are 'asleep'. What we need to do is 'Wake up!' by becoming self-aware. He calls the discipline of self-awareness a 'bug' (De Mello 1992: 38): 'The moment you get bitten by the bug of awareness. Oh, it's so delightful! It's the most delightful thing in the world; the most important, the most delightful.' He goes on to add, 'There's nothing so important in the world as awakening. Nothing!' When you get bitten by the bug, you begin to learn and unlearn. You unlearn truths about yourself and the world. You know your true self better and you understand the world better.

You may be aware of leaders in politics and other spheres of life who start well, appear to be promising at the beginning of their careers and are universally admired. Somewhere along the line something happens. They end up as failures or as leaders who disappoint their followers. One contributing factor is they become comfortable in their positions and forget about the need for reflection and learning, what the Japanese call *hansei*, meaning 'self-reflection', as we shall see in a later chapter. Some even forget they are mere humans as they are obsessed with the flattery of sycophants deceiving them with information feeding their egos and shielding them from reality. By forgetting the principle of reflection and continuous learning, these leaders have abandoned their guiding compass when leadership becomes difficult. As circumstances change and new challenges arise, they resort to tactics and gimmicks, taking decisions based on expediency rather than on well-considered principles and strategies. Such decisions may lead the organization or country to rack and ruin, and the leader may fail to finish well. In some cases they end in disgrace.

An important consideration in leadership is that circumstances and conditions keep changing, and one must adjust and learn how to cope with new challenges. Consequently, self-awareness should always be complemented by awareness of the changing environment, so one can make the necessary adjustments taking into account the realities of the situation. Yet, in seeking to adjust, one should never forget the guiding principle: one's mission and purpose in life and one's principles and values.

Self-awareness and the Johari Window

Self-awareness is such an important aspect of personal growth that we need to elaborate more on it by discussing the Johari Window, a technique that helps people to better understand their relationships with themselves and with others. The Johari Window was created in 1955 by two psychologists, Joseph Luft and Harrington Ingham. The name Johari is derived from a combination of the psychologists' first names, Joseph and Harrington.

The Johari Window consists of four quadrants (also referred to as 'rooms'). The first quadrant is called the *Arena* (or Open Area); the second is the *Blind Spot* (or Blind Area); the third is the *Façade* (or Hidden Area); and the fourth is called *Unknown* (or Unknown Area). The basic principle here is that there are aspects of our lives or character that are known to us which other people may not know about; there are areas of our lives that may be known to others which we may not be aware of. There are also aspects of our lives that are known to us that we may not want others to know about; and finally there are certain things about us that are unknown to both ourselves and others.

In brief the four quadrants can be explained as follows:

1. Arena (Open or Free Space): Known to self and known to others
2. Blind Spot: Known to others but not known to self
3. Façade (Hidden Area): Known to self but hidden or unknown to others
4. Unknown Area: Unknown to self and unknown to others.

The original Johari Window can be found on the internet. For the purpose of this book we will represent the four quadrants diagrammatically as follows (see Figure 4):

Joseph Luft and Harrington Ingham developed this technique by listing fifty-five adjectives that describe an individual and asking the individual and fellow workmates or other people who know the subject to choose the adjectives that apply to the individual. Those adjectives that were chosen by both the individual and the group were put in the *Arena*. Those that were selected by the group and not by the

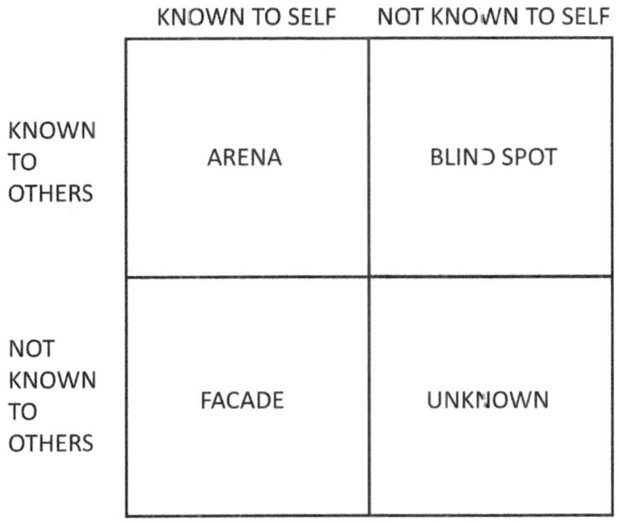

	KNOWN TO SELF	NOT KNOWN TO SELF
KNOWN TO OTHERS	ARENA	BLIND SPOT
NOT KNOWN TO OTHERS	FACADE	UNKNOWN

Figure 4 A modified Johari Window model – for illustration purposes only

subject were put in the *Blind Spot*. Those that were selected by the subject and not by the group were put in the *Façade*. Those that were selected by neither the group nor the subject were put in the *Unknown Area*.

Now, what is the significance of all this for personal leadership development? As indicated above, you may not always be aware of some of your negative behaviour which other people are aware of. It is good for you to know about such behaviour so that you can improve your communication and relationships with others. It is important to know our blind spots in particular. It is good to know the things we do that are hurtful to others. It is also good to know the positive things about ourselves that are acknowledged by others. The ideal is to enlarge the Arena or the Open Space. From my perspective as the author, this can be done in at least two ways: first, by moving the Blind Spot to Open Space. Listening to what others know about you can help in this regard. For example, some people may have a bad odour which they are not aware of but other people may be aware of. If you were such a person with a bad odour, it would be an advantage for you to know so that you can do something about it.

The other way is to move the Facade to Open Space. There may be things that you want to hide from others because they get you embarrassed or may disadvantage you in some way. It is up to you to make a judgement about the pros and cons of revealing something negative about yourself to others and to take the most appropriate action. There are, however, circumstances in which concealing something can ultimately have a negative outcome for you. Let's say you have an illness which you do not want to disclose, but you are working for a company that requires disclosure. That illness becomes part of your Façade, your Hidden Area. Let's say the illness affects your performance at work. It may very well happen that your company may eventually find out from other sources such as previous employers that you have the illness. If this happens, your company may accuse you of dishonesty and your fellow employees may not trust you either. On the other hand, if you disclose the illness and you tell the company what you are doing to overcome the limitations that the illness imposes on you, you may be regarded as an honest person; and when occasionally the illness negatively affects your performance, the authorities will know that you were honest enough to disclose the problem. Some employers may not be sympathetic, of course, but honesty and integrity are likely to be of benefit to you in the final analysis.

Some observations on Personal Mastery and Self-awareness

By way of concluding this part of the chapter, we can say Personal Mastery is about knowing your purpose in life and understanding your beliefs, your strengths and your weaknesses. Thus self-awareness is a key aspect of Personal Mastery as it enhances the process of self-understanding. This understanding of yourself enhances your ability to strive towards perfection in all you do. When you know your purpose in life, your mission, and you have adopted the discipline of Personal Mastery which sets you on the path of continuous improvement, you can then aspire to be what Robin Sharma (2010) calls a FMOB, meaning 'the First, the Most, the Only and the Best!'. Leadership qualities and habits will enhance your ability to become a FMOB.

Leadership qualities

When you have developed the disciplines of Personal Mastery and Self-awareness, you are ready to go to higher levels: You need to develop leadership qualities and habits. You need to be aware of what qualities you need to have in order to be an effective leader and you need to develop habits that turn you into a leader who does not slide back into the life of non-leaders or positional leaders, namely people who are leaders in name by the positions they hold and not true leaders by way of deeds. You may be aware of some of the great leaders of the world or people who have played admirable leadership roles in your country or region. These people had or have certain leadership characteristics and those characteristics were buttressed by habits they developed in order to continue playing their roles effectively as leaders.

We will learn more about leadership qualities in Part IV where we deal with organizational leadership. In this chapter we shall briefly examine a few key qualities as examples:

1. Vision, purpose and communication
2. Ability to influence
3. Professionalism
4. Character and ethical conduct
5. Courage, confidence and the capacity to execute

Vision, purpose and communication

We will learn more about vision in the part on organizational leadership. For now it is enough to point out the following: To be a leader you must have a clear idea of what you want to achieve for your institution, company or country. In other words, the first requirement of a leader appointed to lead an organization is to have a vision and a sense of purpose. If you are appointed to lead a school, university or college, you must be able to dream about the kind of future you want to see. You must dream and then, together with others, actively undertake the task of creating the desired future. For a leader the future does not just happen. The future is not something we wait for. The future is created. It has been said the best way to create a future is to create it. But to create that future with others you must have the power to both influence your followers and to communicate your vision. You must also have a great sense of purpose. A good example of a traditional leader with a sense of purpose is Moshoeshoe I of Lesotho. Moshoeshoe was motivated by his purpose of creating a new nation of the Basotho and whatever he did – in fighting wars, in welcoming strangers into his kingdom, in forming a relationship with the British and so on – was part of his vision and his purpose of creating an independent state for the Sotho people. He was a purpose-driven person.

In more modern times, we have the example of Martin Luther King Jr, who was a leader of the Civil Rights Movement of the 1950s and 1960s in America. In his 'I have a dream' speech, King painted a picture of a future America where children of former slaves and former slave owners would sit and eat together as brothers and sisters. Even the state of Mississippi where injustice and oppression were as palpable as its desert heat would be transformed into 'an oasis of freedom and justice'. He had a dream in which his four children would not be judged by the colour of their skin 'but by the content of their character'. In this liberated America there would be no Black or White, Jew or Gentile, Protestant or Catholic; but these various groups would join hands and together sing the song that freed slaves once sang: 'Free at last! Free at last! Thank God Almighty, we are free at last!' (see King Jr 1963).

King had this vision when African Americans were segregated in ways probably unimaginable to African American children today – with little or no civil rights and no voting rights, among other injustices. He developed a vision of an integrated America where people were treated equally regardless of colour, race or creed. He did not just dream, but as a leader of the Civil Rights Movement he acted on the dream by leading boycotts, marches and other activities and by communicating his vision effectively in the speeches he delivered, as exemplified by the 'I have a dream' speech. He and his followers were guided by the principle of non-violence in a country where the state security systems used brutal force to try and control the popular movement of African American people.

Segregation still exists in America today and the country has not yet achieved the full vision that Martin Luther King Jr fought for, but through his indefatigable leadership, he influenced the passing of the Civil Rights Act and the Voting Rights for African Americans. He also paid the highest price for his vision and convictions when he was assassinated in 1968. A fascinating aspect of Martin Luther King Jr's victory is this: When he was assassinated, Barack Obama was a seven-year-old child, who, just over forty years later, became the forty-fourth president of the United States in 2009. Obama was the son of a Black African from Kenya and a White American woman, but from 2009 to 2017, he and his wife Michelle Obama, the first Black First Lady of America, together with their two daughters, occupied the White House. The American voters judged Obama, not by the colour of his skin but by the content of his character, as Martin Luther King Jr had predicted.

Ability to influence

A key leadership quality is ability to influence. If you think of any great leader, you find they are people who have influenced others. Great leaders have moved others to do extraordinary things. They have inspired others, changed lives and given them a sense of purpose. Consider Mahatma Gandhi, Jesus Christ, the Prophet Mohammed, Martin Luther King Jr, Nelson Mandela and Mother Teresa – any great leader – and their quality of influence comes to the fore. At the Lead and Inspire School we used to say, 'The mark of true leadership is the power to lead and inspire!' American leadership guru John Maxwell believes, 'The true measure of leadership is influence – nothing more, nothing less.' He calls this the Law of Influence.

Nelson Mandela's influence was felt globally when he was alive. The man who had persuaded the African National Congress (ANC) to form a military wing to win the struggle for freedom was the same person who preached reconciliation when South Africa's new dispensation became a reality in 1994. The *Umkhondo we Sizwe* (Spear of the Nation) fighters laid down their arms. By the time Mandela (fondly known as Madiba) retired from office long before his death, he had become a legend respected and listened to by all – presidents, singers, sports people of all colours, religious leaders, politicians, White people, Black people, great people and humble people. When Madiba spoke, everyone listened, even when his message was simple and ordinary. Nelson Mandela was a man of tremendous influence.

Mother Teresa was a small Catholic nun, but she too became a legend in her lifetime. When she spoke all listened, including people who did not share her religious beliefs – presidents, prime ministers, the Pope, Catholics, Protestants, Hindus and others. Yet, she not only influenced people in positions of authority: The young women who first joined her Missionaries of Charity congregation were not attracted by worldly pleasures or benefits but by the extraordinary example of dedication to the poorest of the poor. So influential was Mother Teresa that many members of the Hindu faith who had originally opposed her because of her religious beliefs began to think she was an incarnation of Hindu deities such as the Goddess Kali Ma. So powerful was her influence, it is reported someone (Malcolm Muggeridge) once asked, 'Mother, from where do your sisters get a vocation or inspiration or inducement to join your convent and to do these sorts of services without reservation or reluctance or hesitation?' (Mundakel 1998/2001: 97).

There are two sides to influence: it can be positive influence; it can be bad influence. Nelson Mandela and Mother Teresa became living legends by doing good. They each left a footprint on this world because people saw the good things they did, and in that way they left the world a better place than they found it. Education is one of the areas of leadership where good influence is essential as the leader is involved in people development, in shaping people's lives.

Professionalism

In this book, educational leaders refer to both those in executive management in a university and the academics who have distinguished themselves in teaching and research and can play a leadership role in curriculum development and transformation. In a school you have the principal and other management staff as well as teachers who do an excellent job of helping learners to learn effectively. Professionalism is a leadership quality that is essential for both categories of personnel. Defining professionalism in Bush et al. (2019: 119) David Middlewood has said, 'When we say that someone has carried out a task "professionally" we imply that it has been done very thoroughly, highly competently, and in a morally correct manner.' In our scheme of things in this chapter, we imply the following, among other things: For vice chancellors, members of the university executive and deans of faculties or colleges we refer to the way they treat staff and students competently, fairly and justly. The same applies to school principals and excellent teachers. We imply they do not have a group of friends to whom they give favours at the expense of others; and that they do not turn the institution, school, college or faculty into a structure that furthers the political interests of a political party or political individual but are running the institution according to its policy and mandate as articulated in the Education Act or Statute and in accordance with its mission and vision. For academic teachers and school teachers we also refer to how they perform their duties according to their contract and how they deal with students and staff under them fairly and without undue favour. For both groups we also refer to the avoidance of corrupt practices which seem to be creeping into the life of many universities according to some articles published by the University World News (see, e.g., University World News: 27 June 2020, 19 November 2019).

Where the university has been turned into a veritable business operation with research being valued more for the income it generates than for the extension of knowledge for human development, professionalism for academics might in part mean focusing more on the teaching and learning requirements of students than on research output. This might be a controversial point as it might be understood to be suggesting adopting a rebellious spirit on the part of the teaching staff. The point here is one of the qualities of leadership is the ability to influence. The suggestion is as leaders who are dedicated to the nature and function of a university or school, academics and school teachers have a responsibility to influence those in higher offices to ensure the institution has a mission and a vision arrived at after questions such as the following have been addressed in a collegial fashion: With regard to a university, the following questions apply: What is the mission and vision of the particular university? What is the role of both teaching and research in achieving the mission of the university? What is the role of the university in educating government leaders about the purpose and place of the university in society? In an earlier chapter we learned about the *Ubuntu* philosophy and King Moshoeshoe I of Lesotho's approach to interactive collaborative leadership. Later we shall refer to African traditional leadership practices based on concepts that refer to interactive collaborative discussion groups such as *Umhlangano* (Zulu), *Khotla* (Sotho) and *Dare* (Shona).

David Middlewood (Bush et al. 2019: 128) has commented that in schools, post-compulsory schools and universities, 'colleagues working collaboratively is seen as a process which is both effective in its capacity to solve problems and as evidence of support for professionalism'. University leaders could use the approach of the traditional practices referred to above for purposes of resolving the problems facing their institutions and bringing about greater understanding between various groups. This would be one way of promoting professionalism in higher education.

Character and ethical conduct

Related to professionalism is ethical conduct. This entails avoidance of fraud, cheating and sexual abuse of students in exchange for favours, among other forms of corruption. Corruption in higher education has become so prevalent that a book has been written about it (Denisova-Schmidt 2020). In this book cases of corruption are cited from a wide selection of countries, including the most developed Western countries. At an international conference held in Accra, Ghana, in 2017, Professor Goolam Mohamedbhai, former secretary general of the Association of African Universities, read a paper titled, 'Fraud and Corruption in Higher Education: Why,

How and What Role for Leadership'. Mohamedbhai's paper lists various forms of corruption at meso level in higher education, including the following:

- Admission of students: fake documents, corrupt foreign recruiters and agents, bribery of admission officers
- Fraud in internal financial management of higher education institution (HEI)
- Nepotism and favouritism in appointment and promotion of faculty
- Sexual harassment by faculty
- Cheating at examinations, plagiarism in PhD theses and faking of research results

The regions and countries from which he sourced the evidence included the following: Australia, Russia, China, India and Africa. Denisova's book includes a much wider group of countries. Mohamedbhai suggests some ways in which educational leaders can combat corruption in HEIs and concludes with the following statement: 'The guiding principle in fighting corruption should be that higher education is neither a business nor an industry, but a public good impregnated with values.'

To be able to fight corruption and behave ethically, the educational leader must be a person of character. To earn people's trust as a leader, you must be a person of character. John Maxwell (2007: 64) has said: 'Character makes trust possible. And trust makes leadership possible.' He calls this the Law of Solid Ground, suggesting that without trust between leader and followers, the former's capacity to lead is built on shaky ground – it has no foundation. Now character is built on the principles of integrity, accountability, honesty and respectability. People respect someone who is honest and truthful, morally upright, respects others and is not showy and snobbish. Among the Basotho of Lesotho, the quality of being respectable is expressed in terms of the concept of *sereti* or 'shadow'. Someone who is respected is said to have a shadow. The Zulu equivalent is *isithunzi*, also meaning shadow, while the Shona word is *chiremera*, meaning 'weightiness'. All three words mean 'dignified presence'. To be a person of *sereti* is something you earn through your behaviour and conduct. It is not necessarily a matter of the position you hold, because you might have a high position and still be devoid of this quality. Having a dignified presence is a combination of positive qualities such as integrity, moral uprightness, wisdom, influence and respectability. One of Mandela's indisputable characteristics was he possessed *sereti*. He was not pompous, showy or boastful; he was friendly and approachable. He was revered – not feared, but revered.

As a person of character you are also able to be a *role model*. The leader must embody what they stand for and walk the talk. The Chinese have a saying this writer learned from John Adair (2003: 61): 'Not the cry but the flight of the wild duck leads the flock to fly and to follow.' This means the leader must lead by example – be committed to the vision, the mission, values and goals of the organization and demonstrate a high degree of consistency between the story he/she seeks to communicate and his/her behaviour. The leader's ethics become paramount. John Maxwell (2007: 170) has formulated what he calls the Law of Buy-In, stating, 'The leader finds the dream and then the people. The people find the leader and then the dream.' This means people will not follow you just because you have a good cause or vision. Having a vision (or dream) is absolutely essential because without it you have nothing to sell. However, the people support the cause, buy into the vision, because they trust you personally and have confidence in you as an honest, reliable and dependable leader. They identify with you before they identify with the vision. In this way you can be a trusted and admired role model.

Courage, confidence and the capacity to execute

Other qualities a leader needs to develop are the following:

- *Courage*: Courage is the quality to do something dangerous or something that others may disapprove of when, on the other hand, the leader is convinced it is of great value. It often involves the boldness to take a risk without being reckless. Bonnie Hagemann and his co-authors (2017: 52) have warned against boldness that amounts to recklessness: 'We respect leaders who make a bold decision that puts their own job at risk; we do not respect leaders who make reckless decisions that put everyone's job at risk.'
- *Confidence*: Leadership is like salesmanship in which you are selling two products: your vision and yourself. You cannot sell the one without the other. Remember: The leader finds the dream and then the people. The people find the leader and then the dream. If you want people to follow you, the first person to convince, your *very first customer* is: YOURSELF! You cannot convince others to follow you when you cannot convince yourself you are worthy to be called a leader.
- *Capacity for execution*: We shall discuss this quality fully in Part IV: Here suffice it to say: Execution is about getting things done. Many beautiful strategic plans fail at the stage of execution because the leader is incapable of ensuring that things are done.

Leadership habits

For a sportsperson to participate in their sporting activity, they must practice. You cannot win a marathon unless you persist in practicing. The same is true of leadership – you need to develop certain principles and practices into habits. Take the two key principles of Personal Mastery, for example:

- The practice of continually clarifying what is important to us
- The practice of continually learning how to see current reality clearly

Personal Mastery is a discipline, but it also becomes a habit in that these practices are repeated; the leader continually or repeatedly goes back to them in order to make Personal Mastery a reality in his or her life. The same can be said of Self-awareness – the capacity to know one's purpose in life and understand one's potential, strengths and weaknesses. This entails constant self-reflection – hence reflection becomes a habit equivalent to the Japanese *Hansei* 'self-reflection'. Chris Lowney (2003: 28) has correctly said, 'Self-awareness is never a finished product.' In the book just referred to, *Heroic Leadership: Best Practices from a 450-Year-Old Company That Changed the World*, Lowney has expounded on the four leadership principles that made the Society of Jesus a successful company by reason of the Jesuits incorporating them into their daily lives: Self-awareness, Ingenuity, Love and Heroism. Some may doubt whether it is appropriate to categorize some of these as 'habits'; but the point is they became a way of life that every Jesuit had to continually reflect and act on.

There are, however, certain specific habits that have been developed by leadership development specialists which are meant to apply to every leader, regardless of their ideology or religious affiliation. Surfing on the internet one can find the article '9 Leadership Habits That Anyone Can Master' by Peter Economy. The following are listed and explained in the article as leadership habits:

1. Show enthusiasm.
2. Be approachable.
3. Have a sense of purpose.
4. Be generous with praise.
5. Communicate effectively.
6. Be brave.
7. Be humble.
8. Be respectful.
9. Be your true self.

A publication that has had an enormous impact on people's conception of leadership habits is Stephen Covey's *The 7 Habits of Highly Effective People* (1989). This publication was followed later by *The 8th Habit: From Effectiveness to Greatness* (2004). Covey's seven habits are the following:

Habit one: Be proactive.
Habit two: Begin with the end in mind.
Habit three: Put first things first.
Habit four: Think win/win.
Habit five: Seek first to understand, then to be understood.

Habit six: Synergise.
Habit seven: Sharpen the saw.

Covey's basic thesis is to change a situation we must first change ourselves by changing our perceptions. What we do depends on how we see things. If we want to succeed, we must change the way we see things. Relating this idea to the concern of this book, we can say if we want to be effective educational leaders who are going to have a positive impact on the world, we must begin by changing our own perceptions. *The 7 Habits of Highly Effective People* (and its sequel also) is an important book that I would encourage developing leaders to read. What we intend to do in this chapter is to give an idea of Covey's thinking by commenting on the first three habits.

Habit one: Be proactive

Being proactive means taking responsibility. Covey says as humans we are responsible for our own lives. Plenty of what happens to us depends on our decisions. There are external factors, but how we respond to those factors depends on us. We can either be *proactive* or *reactive*. We can either take control of our lives or allow circumstances, conditions or other people to decide for us how we live. When what happens to us depends on other people's perceptions and paradigms, we are reactive. We allow external circumstances or the views of other people to *determine* how we should live.

Covey cites three types of *determinism*, what he calls social mirrors or social maps: *Genetic determinism* says if you have a defect such as an illness or physical inability, your ancestors did it to you. *Psychic determinism* says your parents did it to you. They treated you badly – that is why you are an angry person who cannot control his/her anger or that is why you are such a coward or timid person. You tend to remember how your parents treated you as a child. *Environmental determinism* says it is your boss, religious superior, colonialists or missionaries who did it to you. You believe you are conditioned to behave in a certain way and you are incapable of changing that behaviour because of these factors. Your response to what happens to you depends on these external stimuli. If you are inclined to behave in this way you are reactive and a victim of circumstances.

On the other hand, *proactive* people take responsibility for their lives. They are masters of their lives, not victims of circumstances. They are affected by external stimuli but choose how to respond, knowing they have the ability to change their situation for the better. Instead of blaming their parents or ancestors or bosses for the situation, they look for ways of resolving the problem confronting them. The principle here is you are your own liberator; do not allow other people to oppress you; do not allow a situation where bad things happen to you while you watch passively or hopelessly: do something about it. Act or be acted on!

Habit two: Begin with the end in mind

This habit was referred to in Chapter 7 in relation to discovering one's purpose in life. To begin with the end in mind is to begin with a clear understanding of where you are in relation to your desired destination. It requires of the learner leader to have an understanding of his/her purpose in life, personal mission and vision. Have a clear idea of your future vision and current reality, so you can plan your way to achieving your goal.

Begin with the end in mind is based on the principle that all things are created twice. There is a mental or first creation and then a physical creation. Covey gives the example of a house – it starts as a plan on paper that is eventually transformed into a physical building. To begin with the end in mind is about the kind of person you want to be. Create that person in your mind and work assiduously towards becoming that person. Visualize the leader you want to become and work hard towards it. As explained in Chapter 7, one of the ways of ensuring you become the leader you want to be is to develop a personal mission statement as your constitution and guiding principle keeping you on the straight and narrow.

The habit also applies to your daily routine. Do not begin your day without an idea of what you want to do and achieve. Plan your day before you start work and decide what you want to achieve – provided you make provision for flexibility in case something unexpected happens.

Habit three: Put first things first

This is about how to manage creating the person you have decided to become. It has to do with deciding on priorities and executing them. Covey uses the statement 'organise and execute around priorities' (1989: 49) as a guiding principle. You could think into matters falling into four categories of priorities:

- Urgent and important
- Not urgent, but important
- Urgent, but not important
- Not important and not urgent

Which do you attend to first? Time management becomes of the essence. You have to break down your activities in terms of such categories, sequence them and act accordingly. The processes you follow in ensuring the right sequence are analyse, prioritize and execute.

These three habits deal with what Covey calls private victories. They reinforce the discipline of personal mastery and have to do with what you must be to be able to lead others. Covey says, 'You can't be successful with other people if you haven't paid the price of success with yourself' (186). You cannot have the fruits without the roots.

To lead others, you must be the person you want others to be. Be the change you want to see in others. Habits four, five and six are about our relationship with others. They deal with what Covey calls public victories.

General conclusion

By way of general conclusion, it is appropriate to see Personal Mastery as a process of continuous improvement. Self-awareness enriches the process by acting as an assessment tool regarding your potential and your strengths and weaknesses. Leadership qualities are about the kind of leader you strive to be: Are you a leader who has a vision; who can impact others; who can inspire by having an exemplary character and *sereti*? Are you a professional and ethical leader, courageous in doing what is right and in executing decisions and possessing of confidence that inspires others to follow and implement the vision of the organization? Habits complement self-awareness: Whereas self-awareness serves as an assessment tool and a mirror that enables you to see more clearly where your strengths and weaknesses are and what potential you have for leadership, habits are ways of strengthening the self-improvement process of Personal Mastery and help to strengthen and solidify your good qualities as a leader.

9

Educational leadership and the development of intelligences

TUNING IN EXERCISE

Thabo the wizard

Everybody said Thabo was 'a wizard'. Everybody in the region was familiar with Thabo's academic wizardry. As a primary school child he did both grade 6 and grade 7 in one year. An official from the Ministry of Education was so impressed when he visited Thabo's school that he said the boy was wasting his time in grade 6 and promoted him to grade 7. At secondary and high school he got As in all his subjects.

As a university student he majored in Accounting. On completing his degree, he was employed by the Ministry of Finance where he was quickly promoted to the rank of director. His colleagues noticed that Thabo had a problem which became obvious when one day he slapped a female subordinate so hard with the back of his hand that she nearly lost her eye sight. Thabo was given summary dismissal for the offence. Soon after this he was often seen in beer halls quarrelling with fellow drunkards. His pastor managed to get him enrolled for an anger management course.

Questions

1. Thabo was obviously an intelligent person. What is his kind of intelligence called?
2. What was missing in his character as an intelligent person?
3. Someone made the following statement: 'Being academically bright is not necessarily an indication of full intelligence.' Do you agree or not? Explain your answer.

Human intelligences

Human intelligence, a very complex subject, has been defined by Roberto Colom et al. (2010) as follows: 'Intelligence can be defined as a general mental ability for reasoning, problem solving, and learning.' The same authors go on to make the point that 'intelligence integrates cognitive functions such as perception, attention, memory, language or planning'. Much has been written about intelligence, and it is not the intention here to try and discuss the subject in detail. Traditionally we have tended to think in terms of only one intelligence – the mental intelligence or intelligence quotient (IQ). There is general agreement now that human beings possess more than one intelligence. Here we shall refer to three sets of publications as examples of the numerous publications that have seen the light of day on this important subject. We begin with Howard Gardner, Professor of Education at Harvard University, who, in 1983, developed the theory of multiple intelligences which relates to a person's unique capabilities. This has led to the discussion of what some scholars refer to as Gardner's nine intelligences, while others say the professor identified eight intelligences. The nine are:

1. Naturalist (understanding nature and living things)
2. Musical (discerning sounds)
3. Logical-Mathematical (quantifying things)
4. Existential (tackling questions about life)
5. Interpersonal (ability to sense people's feelings and emotions)
6. Bodily-Kinaesthetic (coordinating mind and body)
7. Linguistic ((ability to find the right word to express what you mean)
8. Intrapersonal (understanding oneself)
9. Spatial (visualising the world in 3D).

Another key figure in the discipline is Robert Sternberg who in 1985 published *Beyond IQ: A Triarchic Theory of Human Intelligence*. Sternberg suggests there are three forms of intelligence:

- Componential (or Analytical)
- Experiential (or Creative)
- Practical (or Contextual)

Sternberg also argues that behaviour must be viewed within the context of a particular culture. Thus a behaviour that is highly regarded in one culture may not be so highly regarded in another. A publication which seems to go beyond Sternberg in terms of the relationship between culture and intelligence is *The Bell Curve: Intelligence and Class Structure in American Life* (1994) by Richard J. Herrnstein and Charles Murray. Their findings seemed to point to links between social class, race and IQ scores. Part of the argument is that people can be differently gifted: someone who is gifted in one area may not be gifted in another area.

The purpose of opening this chapter with these comments is to make the following points:

- Any simple definition of 'human intelligence' is inadequate because the subject is complex and is continually evolving.
- There is a wide variety of mental abilities such as those identified by Gardner, and others such as the ability to learn quickly, the ability to solve problems, the ability to communicate effectively and so on.
- The definition of intelligence seems to depend on prevailing social values on the one hand and the advance of scientific ideas on the other.
- A dimension which probably needs to be brought into the discussion of our understanding of human intelligence is indigenous knowledge systems and indigenous ways of knowing.

Our interest in this chapter is on multiple intelligences as they relate to leadership. More importantly, the leadership student and practitioner should be aware of the fallacy of judging people's abilities on the basis of only one form of intelligence – the mental intelligence or IQ. A publication that has received much attention in this regard is Robert J. Sternberg's 'WICS' article, 'A model of educational leadership: wisdom, intelligence, and creativity' (2005). In this article Sternberg argues that an effective educational leader must have three attributes – wisdom, intelligence and creativity – synthesized, that is, all three working in harmony with each other, hence WICS. This is an important article for educational leaders and students of educational leadership to refer to. Going beyond the attributes identified by Sternberg is the work of Joel Garcia (2012) who talks about the four intelligences of a leader. These are wisdom, character, social and spiritual wisdom. These four are in addition to IQ, or what Garcia calls 'mental capacity'. Garcia argues cogently about the importance of these 'intelligences' for a leader. While what he says about the need for a leader to have these characteristics is for this writer not open to question, a difficulty may arise in some people's minds about whether a characteristic such as 'character' can, by itself, be defined as an 'intelligence'. Character is surely a dimension of spiritual intelligence (SQ or SI) – as is explained later in this chapter.

This brings us to a school of thought on which much of this chapter is based. Among the proponents of this school of thought is Stephen R. Covey who explains the concept in some detail in appendix 1 of *The 8th Habit* (2004). While there have been further developments since the publication of *The 8th Habit*, a leader or developing leader will do well to pay attention to the four intelligences identified by Covey and other specialists and strive to develop them. These four intelligences are essential for your development as a leader and as a healthy and competent human being. The four intelligences are

1. Physical Intelligence
2. Mental Intelligence
3. Emotional Intelligence
4. Spiritual Intelligence

In this chapter we give a very brief explanation of each one of these. In an article entitled 'How to Develop Stephen Covey's 4 Intelligences' (2017) Layton Cox makes special mention of the fact that Stephen Covey's explanation of the four intelligences encompasses all four dimensions of a human being – body, mind, heart and spirit. It is therefore a relatively simple but comprehensive approach to what constitutes human intelligence.

Physical intelligence

There is an old Latin saying *mens sana in corpore sano* 'a healthy mind in a healthy body'. We might think that the body has nothing to do with intelligence, but that is a fallacy. You do need a healthy body to be able to function well in all that you do. For your mind to work well, you must be physically fit. For you to be able to competently and successfully lead others, you need physical fitness. What, then, is physical intelligence (PQ)? Modifying Layton Cox's definition slightly we can define PQ as '*the extent of* our ability to maintain and develop our physical body'.

Following Stephen Covey and like-minded thinkers, we can say that maintaining and developing the physical body requires three things: wise nutrition, consistent exercise and proper rest.

Appropriate nutrition is of the utmost importance for the maintenance of a healthy body. We can easily do a lot of harm to ourselves if we are in the habit of eating what we like eating: red meat, fatty foods and a lot of sugar. Red meat and fatty foods can give rise to cholesterol which may not be good for the heart. Sugar can cause diabetes and similar ailments. A diet which consists of low-fat foods, white meat, fruits, green vegetables and plenty of drinking water (particularly purified water) is good for the health. Some people force themselves to eat certain kinds of foods when those food items are not good for them. If, for example, you regularly experience heartburn after eating bread, you should consider eating something else in place of bread. Some people react to wheat products, some to the lactose in cow milk. People who experience problems with these food items should go for alternatives such as wheat-free foods and lactose-free milk. It may well be a good idea for you to see a homeopathic doctor to advise you on the most appropriate diet for you. Abstaining from food items you like can be difficult – it requires discipline. Once you have gotten into the habit of abstaining from such delicacies, you will realize the sacrifice is worthwhile.

In addition to a good diet, the body needs regular exercise: Some people go to the gym, some do aerobic exercises, some get involved in sports and so on. There are some relatively cheap ways of exercising. You can get into the habit of going for a sprint every morning and having a shower at the end of it. Walking long distances is a very good, inexpensive and relatively relaxed method of exercising the body. Manual work can also be very good – you exercise while doing something productive. The body will also need to rest. After you have worked and exercised, you need to give your body a good rest. This includes giving yourself enough time to sleep. This is where chickens, particularly road runners, can be a good example to humans: They eat, exercise and rest. The important thing to remember is that whichever method or methods of exercising you choose will be effective if you do the exercises regularly. The exercise must become a habit.

Mental intelligence

Following Layton Cox, I have defined mental intelligence as '*the extent of* our ability to analyse, reason, think abstractly, use language, visualize and comprehend with our mind'. Intelligence and ability have in the past been based on IQ only. In some cases some extremely intelligent people have failed to demonstrate that they are as competent as they are mentally intelligent. Furthermore, some people who were average performers at school, have turned out to be very good performers in the workplace. This is an indication that mental intelligence alone is not an adequate measure of competence, and that there is more to human capability than mental intelligence. This also points to the usefulness of Howard Gardner's research referred to earlier.

With regard to the continuous improvement of mental intelligence, there is no doubt that you master an idea, a body of knowledge or a skill when you have learned it or practised it repeatedly. Speaking as the author of this book, I recall what an elder brother of mine once said to me when I was very young: 'Young man, if you want to know something, learn it; if you can't learn it, teach it; if you can't teach it, write about it.' At the time he said this to me, I thought it was just a clever and fascinating statement, but when I reflected on it as a more mature person, I began to understand that this was a very profound statement because it explains different ways of learning: You cannot teach what you do not know; consequently in order to teach something you need to learn more so that you can master it to the extent of being able to teach it to others. If on top of teaching the subject you go to the extent of writing about it, you are raising your level of mastering it to the extent of being regarded as an expert or specialist in the field concerned. Stephen Covey makes the point that it is only by doing, by applying, that we can internalize knowledge and skills (Covey 2004: 343). The expression 'practice makes perfect' is spot on. In order to keep abreast of developments in knowledge and technology, we must become lifelong learners.

There are reasons why we should be lifelong learners: The quantum of knowledge keeps on increasing, and technology continuously changes the way we do things. You cannot continue to depend on the knowledge you acquired at school or university – that is a recipe for disaster as such knowledge can easily become obsolete. Ways of knowing keep on changing and you need to keep on changing with the times and with the dictates of technology. I recently learned a saying: 'You must change with technology, otherwise technology will change you.' Among us are born before computers (BBCs) who have had no choice but to learn how to use computers because one can no longer cope without the use of a computer.

There is yet another reason why we should continue to sharpen our minds: A human being is a unity of body, mind, heart and spirit. These four depend on each other for survival. For example, if the mind is neglected, the body suffers. In this regard, it has been observed that some people quickly deteriorate or even die soon after retirement. Two things seem to be happening in such cases: First, a retired person can cease to have a purpose for living; and second, he/she neglects exercising the mind. It is therefore important to know that when you retire you should not only have something that motivates you to continue enjoying life and facing its challenges, but that you should also keep your mind active by engaging in intellectual activities such as reading, writing and research.

Emotional intelligence

Emotional intelligence (EQ, also abbreviated EI) has been briefly defined as 'the ability to identify and manage one's own emotions as well as the emotions of others'. It includes the ability to control oneself in an emotionally charged situation and the capacity to read emotions in other people. EI is important for one's development in character and for one's social and professional relationships. For a leader, the capacity to control oneself when one is provoked, offended or disappointed is extremely important, just as it is necessary for one to maintain one's cool when mediating between quarrelling and angry individuals. A leader who is in the habit of losing his/her temper in the workplace and in negotiations with potential partners or clients can easily lose the respect of subordinates and can be a liability to his/her organization. The story of Thabo narrated at the beginning of this chapter vividly illustrates what can happen to a leader whose IQ is very high but is not emotionally intelligent.

Empirical studies have been conducted that show the importance of EI for leaders. Here we cite two examples: Downey et al. (2006) carried out a study on the relationship between leadership, EI and intuition among senior female managers with the aim of measuring EI in workplace environments. The findings were as follows: 'The results indicated that female managers displaying transformational leadership (TL) behaviours were more likely to display higher levels of EI and intuition than female managers displaying less transformational leadership behaviours.' This suggests a correlation between EI and TL. In another paper, Molly Mathew and K. S. Gupta (2015) attempted to draw a conceptual framework between TL and EI. The researchers developed the conceptual framework after empirically examining three hundred leaders from different industries. The assumption is that transformational leaders are smart with their feelings and they are capable of driving the emotions of their subordinates in the right direction.

A question that arises is if EI is such a key aspect of leadership, how do we recognize it in leaders? What are some of its characteristics? In *The 8th Habit* (2004) Stephen Covey says there are five commonly accepted components of EI. These are:

- Self-awareness – knowing your purpose in life; knowing your strengths and weaknesses and the ability to reflect on your life and personality
- Personal Motivation – that which excites you; your vision, your goals and values
- Self-Regulation – the ability to control and guide yourself as you pursue your vision and goals and desires
- Empathy – the ability to feel for others, to understand how others feel about things and how they are affected by events and situations
- Social and Communication Skills – your interpersonal relationships; how you relate to other people and how you communicate with them

In what is regarded as a groundbreaking book, *Primal Leadership: Unleashing the Power of Emotional Intelligence* (2013), Daniel Goleman and his co-authors focus on four domains of EI. These are:

- Self-awareness
- Self-Management
- Social Awareness
- Relationship Management

These four domains are equivalent to four of the components mentioned in Covey's book. The difference is that Goleman and his co-authors do not seem to highlight Personal Motivation. However, their book has apparently had a big impact in that it has made business leaders and managers realize the importance of EI in business. Some companies are now interested in EI in the processes of hiring and promoting employees.

EI has become so important that in some countries, such as America, there are now programmes in what is called Social and Emotional Learning (SEL) which teaches young children how to recognize their emotions and to know how these emotions lead them to act in certain ways. Among other things, SEL is said to help children to improve their self-awareness and confidence, and to even do better in academic performance, as some of the literature on our reading list for this chapter explains.

Practising and aspiring leaders are well advised to get some understanding of EQ. Psychologists and other specialists talk about the consequences of neglecting developing EI. You would do well to read the works of Stephen Covey, Daniel Goleman and other specialists in EQ. What we would like to point out in this chapter, in addition to what is said in the opening paragraph of this section, is the following: People who lack EI can easily behave in an unbecoming way, as is exemplified in the case of Thabo whose story is narrated at the beginning of this chapter. Thabo had extremely high IQ but very low EQ and, consequently, he was unable to control himself in a fit of anger. You may be very angry with your subordinate and be tempted to slap them or use another form of physical violence, or even just shout at them, but the negative consequences on you could be huge. Such an action can cost you a job or a promotion.

Lack of EI can harm your relations with others. You easily become angry; you can experience trauma; you may even become unnecessarily tearful. As a leader, that hampers your ability to manage others in emotionally charged situations. High levels of EQ or EI help you to maintain your dignity and calmness in situations where there is conflict between you and others. Your capacity for self-awareness should come in handy here. Be conscious of how you relate to other people, how you speak to others and how you react to situations and to unpleasant experiences. Be aware of all your negative behaviours and learn to regulate yourself and to grow as a leader who has a dignified presence, a leader who has *sereti*. As a leader you should also learn to recognize followers or subordinates who have low levels of EQ and find ways of helping them to grow in EI.

Spiritual intelligence

Stephen R. Covey suggests three ways to develop SI: 'first, *integrity* – being true to one's values, convictions and conscience, and having a connection with the Infinite; second, *meaning* – having a sense of contribution to causes; and third *voice* – aligning our work with our unique talents or gifts, and our sense of calling' (Covey 2004: 348–51).

As the author of this book I would put it this way: 'I suggest three ways to develop spiritual intelligence: First, *Identity* – discovering *who* you are and *whose* you are; second, discovering your *Purpose in Life* (your Calling); third, *Character and Values* – aligning your work, your behaviour/conduct, and your gifts with your Purpose and your understanding of the values and requirements of Him/Her to whom you belong – in other words, becoming a person of integrity and a role model.'

Discovering who you are entails having a sense of self-awareness – getting to know your talents, your weaknesses, your interests and so on. For those who believe in a Superior Being, discovering whose you are entails first of all knowing that there is a Creator (the Infinite) who made this wonderful universe with all its fascinating systems and mysteries; and knowing that you were created by the Creator and for a purpose. Discovering your purpose goes beyond just having a vocation or a professional career. It goes beyond just having a passion for something, the desire to achieve something in life. It means you understand that you were created for a purpose, that you have a mission in life.

Character and values are of the essence in leadership. It is not enough to know what your purpose in life or calling is. As you respond to your calling, you should also respond in how you behave and conduct yourself before others. In this regard, it is appropriate to remember Ron Boehme's profound statement: 'This is true greatness: knowing your calling and developing the character to fulfil it' (Boehme 1989: 71).

We noted in Chapter 8 how, in *The 21 Irrefutable Laws of Leadership* (2007: 58–9), John Maxwell says, 'Character makes trust possible. And trust makes leadership possible.' People trust you when you have these qualities, and they will be willing to follow you. Integrity is about being consistent, whole, keeping promises and doing the right thing no matter what. The purpose of highlighting these qualities is to explain that spiritual intelligence can be said to have two dimensions: First, it is about connecting with the Infinite, the Creator; and second, it is about developing righteous character – comprising integrity, accountability and honesty.

Part IV

Education for transformational organizational leadership

10

Vision and organizational leadership

Case study: Climbing the misty mountain

There were three teams competing to get to the top of a mountain. We shall call them Team A, Team B and Team C. Each team had a leader, and each decided to commence the climbing from a particular vantage point. On the day the competition was to commence, it was misty at the bottom of the mountain.

TEAM A: Team A was composed of five men. When the time to commence the climbing came, the team leader told his fellow team members, 'Let's go guys. We all know about mountain climbing. The important thing is to be strong and brave so that we can win this competition.' So they set out, each man to himself without a clear idea or guidance about how they were to get to the top of the mountain. There was no coordinated plan and nothing specific to motivate every member of the team except for the fact that they wanted to win the competition. As the mist thickened and visibility became very poor, the team members began to give up the fight, and soon they found themselves struggling to find their way back to the bottom of the mountain.

TEAM B: Team B was made up of three men and two women, with the leader being one of the men. At the commencement time, the team leader told his teammates, 'I have told you how to get to the top; let's get going and maintain our team spirit so that we can win this race.' As they went up, the mist became so thick, the team members could not see where they were going. Not long after they set out, two members of the team, one man and one woman, slipped one after the other and went down the gorge. The remaining members could hear the two wailing as they went down and perished, never to be seen again. The climb was abandoned as the remaining three members struggled to find their way back to the foot of the mountain.

TEAM C: Team C was comprised of three men and two women, with one of the women being the team leader. As the time for the commencement of the race approached, the team leader said to her teammates,

'My instincts tell me we cannot get to the top of the mountain in this mist. In the literature that we have read, we have learned that there are times when the mist is so bad that visibility is very, very poor, and there are times when the mist clears and visibility greatly improves. My suggestion, therefore, is that we commence the climb with the other teams, but stop shortly after the commencement to study the terrain further and to strategize on how best to get to the top.'

Accordingly, on the first day the team did not go very far. So bad was the weather and so thick the mist that the team spent the night not very far from the foot of the mountain. Then mid-morning on the second day, the conditions improved, and the team started the climb in earnest. Night came and the team rested. Early the following morning, it was misty again. They were now halfway up the mountain. But they waited until late mid-morning when the mist had cleared. On the morning of the fourth day the team reached the mountain top – all alive and well!

Tuning in Exercise

1. Can you think of an incident when you found yourself in a situation where you felt lost, either because you did not know where you were going; or you were in complete darkness; or you were in a misty or foggy place; or you just did not know what you were supposed to do because someone had not clarified the task to you. How did you feel, and how did you resolve your dilemma?
2. Discuss what lessons we can derive about organizational leadership from the mountain climbing story.

A lesson from Scripture

Three versions of the Bible translate Prov. 29:18 as follows:

New Revised Standard Version (NRSV): Where there is no prophecy, the people cast off restraint, but happy are those who keep the law.
New International Version (NIV): Where there is no revelation, people cast off restraint; but blessed is the one who heeds wisdom's instruction.
The New Jerusalem Bible (NJB): Where there is no vision the people get out of hand; happy are they who keep the law.
Significance: Whether you call it prophecy or revelation or vision, the absence of this key feature has dire consequences – the people lose any manner of discipline, order or peaceful behaviour. We know from experience that in

situations where there is no shared vision, people tend to resort to violence, theft and criminal activity.

Vision

Discussion exercise

What three elements are usually used to describe the identity of an organization or institution?

They are:

- Vision: A clear picture of a future positive state
- Mission: The *Why* of an organization; the purpose for its existence
- Goals: Those manageable targets which, when achieved, help the organization to achieve its desired future positive state

Simon Sinek (2009) has published a classic entitled *Start with Why*. Sinek cogently argues that organizations that do well start with *Why?* The Why being the purpose, cause or belief that is the reason for their existence. In this regard, it would be appropriate to change the normal order given above and have the three elements in the following order:

- Mission: The Why of the organisation, the purpose for its existence
- Vision: A clear picture of the desired future state in support of the mission of the organization
- Goals: Short-term or near-term targets which, when achieved, enable the organization to achieve the desired future state

Now, what is a vision, and why is it important in organizational leadership? As indicated above, a vision is a desired future state. It provides the members of an organization or institution with a clear picture of what the entity wants to be. It makes those who work in the organization have clear understanding of where the organization is going. If it is couched in a compelling manner, the vision becomes a rallying point which motivates those who work in the organization to want to work for this desired future which is beneficial, not only to the organization as an abstract entity but to all who work for the organization. A vibrant vision provides the stakeholders with hope and optimism about their own lives.

Bonnie Hagemann et al. (2017: 20) have defined vision as follows: 'For us, the definition of a vision is this: a clear picture of a positive future state. For organizations, a vision articulates this view of a realistic, desirable and positive future state.'

What is important in an organization is that the vision should excite the staff. They should see themselves as characters playing their role in the effort to reach the desired future state. In some cases the excitement may not be limited to the staff only but may extend to those who are served by the organization such as parents of students and diners in hotel restaurants. The excitement of these stakeholders will reinforce the enthusiasm of the staff to work even harder for the desired future state. The following are examples of possible visions that could excite workers and other stakeholders:

Restaurant: 'To become a popular food outlet that cares for its staff and puts a smile on the face of every customer'.

University: 'To become a world-class research and teaching university which offers qualifications that make its graduates competent, competitive and marketable both nationally and internationally'.

Institute: 'To be an institute whose impact on leadership development is felt and recognized by both church and state throughout our region'.

Leadership Academy: 'To become an academy that inspires and empowers all who work and study in it to reach for the stars and become renowned leaders'.

The process of developing a compelling vision

Imagine that you are an incoming leader, a newly appointed CEO of an organization that is not performing well. You have been appointed to revive this organization – to put new life into it so that it can live up to its mission and mandate. Where and how do you begin? If you follow the steps outlined below, you should be able to achieve your goal.

Step 1: A preliminary analysis of the current reality

Our assumption here is that when you were appointed, you had developed some ideas about what positive changes you were going to bring to the organization. You must have been able to convince the interviewing panel or appointments board that you were going to bring great value to the organization because you had gathered some information about the entity. You now want to buttress your ideas by doing some on-the-spot investigation so as to be more assured that your views are valid and can stand the test of time.

At this stage, it would be to your advantage to do a small discreet investigation to acquire a better understanding of the environment and the factors that may be influencing the organization to be a poor performer. Is it the existing culture? Is it economic or financial issues affecting the performance of the workforce? and so on. Carry out informal interviews with some of the staff to get a rough impression of what the staff think about their organization and their own conditions of work. Are they happy and satisfied? Are they looking forward to a brighter future?

Step 2: Creating the vision

Now begin the process of creating and formulating the vision: What kind of future do you see for the organization and its employees? What image of the organization do you want its external stakeholders to have? Visualize its ideal future state and dream dreams about the kind of entity it is going to be. Craft a vision statement which captures in a compelling and inspiring manner your picture of this ideal future state. Make sure that while it is compelling and inspiring, the vision is realistic and achievable. Consider some of the risks and impediments in the way of achieving the vision, and think of means and ways of addressing those risks and impediments.

Step 3: Testing before promulgating

Some leadership authorities say it is one thing to create a vision and quite another to get buy-in. For this and other reasons, it is strategic to share your vision with your senior managers before you publicize it. Let them discuss it freely. Let them examine and comment on both the general vision and your proposed vision statement. They may wish to make some amendments here and there, and if those amendments make the vision even more compelling, allow them to feel that they have made a contribution to the creation of their organization's vision. By the time it goes to the general staff, it is a shared vision and one that is easier to market.

Step 4: Communicating the vision

When you and your senior colleagues are happy about the future vision, communicate it powerfully and in a persuasive and inspiring manner to the generality of the staff. Let them feel that it is a convincing and compelling vision.

Get a hint from the traditional African storyteller. When we were young, the stories, *ngano* in Shona, were told at night and during that time of the year between harvesting and the next planting season, when there was a lot of time to relax and sleep. The storyteller involved the audience by making her listeners participate in the standard recitation at the beginning and then inviting them to sing at strategic points of the narration. Members of the audience were not just listeners and spectators – they were participants. Similarly, the leader of a modern organization should see herself/himself as a storyteller with a story to tell, but with a difference: Her story is a story with a present and a future with members of the organization as characters in the story. What on earth is meant by that?

First, a dull story told in a dull manner can only send people dozing and dreaming; and by the time they wake up, the lousy story is over and they have no clue what it was all about. Yes, the vision or story must be related to a definite purpose, and that purpose must be something the people can relate to such as a liberation struggle from conditions of colonial oppression or the drive to liberate people from employment conditions which they find uninspiring and oppressive. It should not be just the leader's story. The people should be able to see themselves in the story. They should see their present, which is undesirable, and their own future, which promises to be glorious. It is part of the challenge of the leader to develop a consciousness in the people; to create awareness of the present undesirable state of affairs; and to paint a realistic and desirable future so that the people can see it, and see themselves creating it and making it real.

Step 5: Publicizing and marketing the vision

Now that the vision has been embraced by the people; now that they own it, it is time to publicize it by means of banners, pamphlets and other means. But wait, the process of transforming the organization does not end here – there is still planning and more to be done!

11

Strategy as the road map to the desired state

The need for a strategy and a plan

During the course of your research on organizational leadership, you might meet this statement: 'Failing to plan is planning to fail.' To transform an organization, you need to do more than develop a compelling vision. You have to device a systematic method of achieving the desired future state that is encapsulated in the vision. One of the things you must do is to develop a strategy by means of planning.

Understanding strategy

One way of having a good understanding of a word is to know its *etymology* or its origins and historical development. We learn from John Adair (2003) that *strategy* comes from two Greek words, *stratos* – meaning an army spread out or a large body of people; and *egy*, meaning to lead. A senior army commander came to be called a *strategos*, meaning leader of the army or military general (Adair 2003: 7). *Strategia* meant the art of being a commander-in-chief, that is, a high-level leader.

With this military origin of the word 'strategy', John Adair came to believe in what he called 'the three levels of leadership', which are:

Team: The leader of some ten to twenty people with a defined task
Operational: The leader of one of the main parts of the organization
Strategic: The leader of a whole organization (Adair 2003: 81)

A strategic leader in these terms is the leader of a whole organization with other leaders below her/him. Since *strategia* referred to the art of being a leader-in-chief, says John Adair, 'Strategy is simply the thinking appropriate to someone at that level of leadership responsibility, and it embraces far more than military operations or marketing strategy. It is the product of an individual mind, not the output of a corporate staff at head office' (ibid.: 170).

In view of the above, John Adair makes a distinction between strategic *thinking* and strategic *planning*. The former is thinking appropriate to a strategic leader, that is, the leader of an organization, while the latter is a corporate process involving other members of the senior management of the organization, led by the strategic leader who should, by that fact, be a strategic *thinker* – hence strategic thinking leads to strategic planning (ibid.: 198).

A strategy is a means to an end. Strategic planning is consequently a process that is intended to help the organization to achieve its desired future state, its vision. It is not the end but a means to an end.

The Three-Circle Model

Before we delve into strategic planning, we need to deal with what John Adair calls 'the three elements of need', leading to the 'Three-Circle Model'. In any situation where there is a need to achieve a task by a group, there are three important considerations:

- The need to achieve the task
- The need to maintain the team and keep it together
- The needs of the individual members of the team

It is the role of the leader to see to it that these needs are taken care of. Adair explains this in terms of three interlocking circles as shown in Figure 5.

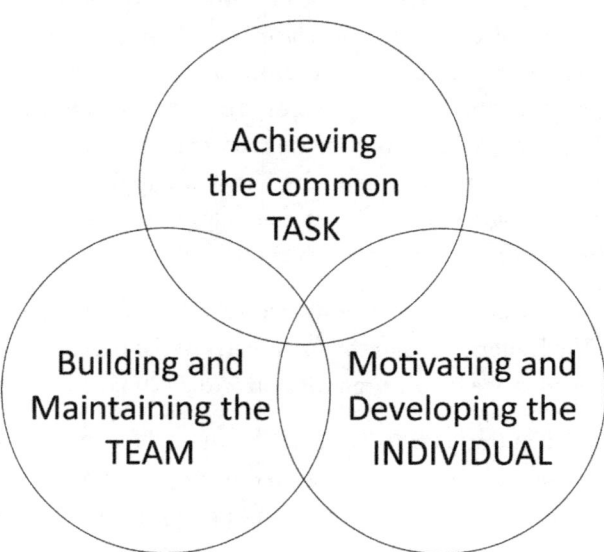

Figure 5 The broad functions of strategic leadership (John Adair 2018).

Leadership functions

The above leads to the functions of the leader. As explained in Chapter 3, Adair summarizes the functions of a leader as follows:

- Planning: seeking available information; defining group tasks, purposes and goals; and so on
- Initiating: e.g., explaining why the plan is necessary; allocating tasks; and setting standards
- Controlling: e.g., maintaining group standards; keeping discussion relevant; and so on
- Supporting: e.g., encouraging team/individuals; creating team spirit; and so on
- Informing: e.g., clarifying task; giving new information; and so on
- Evaluating: e.g., testing the proposed solution; evaluating team performance; and so on

Building the strategic plan

A strategic plan is a roadmap which shows the organization how it will get where it wants to go. What is given here is just a snapshot view of what a strategic plan is and what is involved in developing it.

An important aspect of strategic planning is analysis. This is a more in-depth analysis than the preliminary investigation of an incoming CEO referred to in Chapter 10. It is not an individual process but an organizational process in the form of a systematic and thorough analysis of both its internal dynamics and external environment (Ngara 1995: 157).

What has become the basic approach to strategic planning is said to have been the brainchild of Professor Kenneth Andrews of Harvard Business School (Adair 2003: 168–9). He published a book titled *The Concept of Corporate Strategy* (1971). He proposed what is called the SWOT analysis, that is, an analysis of the strengths, weaknesses, opportunities and threats of an organization. It is necessary to have a clear idea of these elements in order to be able to make strategic decisions about where the organization is and where it should go. Professor Andrews also drew attention to the importance of scanning the environment from the perspective of the political, economic, social and technological (PEST) factors which impact on the organization.

In view of the above, a strategic plan should ask questions about the following and related factors:

Questions aimed at getting to know your organization better

- What are our strengths as an organization, and what are our weaknesses?
- How does the political and economic environment affect our business and our performance?
- What opportunities exist in the environment we operate in which we could take advantage of?
- Are there any threats to our existence?
- Who are our competitors?
- Of our competitors, who are doing well and who are not doing well?
- Why are some organizations/companies in the same business doing better than us, and why are we not doing as well as those organizations/companies?
- What technologies are the successful companies employing, and how are we doing in regard to those technologies?
- What social factors could be impacting on our performance?
- Is our organizational culture appropriate for the environment in which we operate?
- Who are our stakeholders, and what do they expect from us?
- In short, why are we where we are?

Questions aimed at helping the organization to go forward

You have defined your vision as explained in Chapter 10. You have now analysed the organization in relation to environmental and other factors. The organization has in a sense looked at itself in a mirror and seen itself for what it is. You now need to develop the strategy for moving forward, for achieving the desired future state. Ask the following and similar questions:

- What is our vision?
- Where are we now in relation to where we want to go?
- How do we get there?
- What steps must we take in order to achieve our vision?
- What are the barriers to achieving our desired future state, and how do we overcome them?

In answer to these questions, you must develop goals and an operating plan.

Setting goals

The strategy of an organization is the methodology that is used to achieve the desired end. As explained earlier, a strategy is a means to an end. The end in question can be defined as 'the goal'. Leo Isaac defines a goal as follows: 'A goal is a specific target, an end result or something to be desired. It is a major step in achieving the vision of the organisation' (Leo Isaac.com).

The standard practice in modern times is to set what are called SMART goals. This is an acronym which is used to mean the following:

- S – *Specific* Your goals must not be vague but clear and concise.
- M – *Measurable*: Not necessarily measurable in terms of figures and percentages, but the goals must be such as to enable you to measure the progress made.
- A – *Achievable*: They must be realistic in the sense that with the time and resources you have, you are able to attain them.
- R – *Relevant*: They must be relevant to your overall plan or to the vision of your organization.
- T – *Timely*: The goals must have a time frame or target time within which they are to be achieved.

Example: The story of Linda

Linda was the daughter of a domestic worker in a high-density township. Her mother was using her earnings as a domestic worker and other initiatives to send Linda to school. Linda had friends in low-density suburbs where each child had a bedroom to herself or himself.

At the beginning of her last year of high school, Linda became clear about the profession she wanted to follow in life – she wanted to be a lawyer. Through career guidance, she got to know that it would take her four years to qualify as a lawyer, and that there would be a period of attachment to a law firm. Linda set herself the following goals:

Overall Goal: To buy a house for my mother and myself within six years.

- *Goal 1*: To work hard during my last year of high school so as to qualify for admission to university and law school.
- *Goal 2*: To work hard and consistently as an undergraduate student so as to ensure a good pass on completing the degree.
- *Goal 3*: To be such an industrious and pleasant worker during the period of attachment that the firm I will be attached to will recommend me for future employment.

Goal 4: To apply for a mortgage bond so as to buy a house within the first six months as a full-time employee.

Linda passed with an upper second class degree. The firm she had been attached to as a student offered her full-time employment with a good salary. She found out that before she could buy a house, she had to accumulate enough money for a deposit. Eight months after she started working and less than six full years after she set herself these goals, Linda and her mother moved into a three-bedroom house in a low-density suburb. She had a bedroom to herself; her mother had a bedroom to herself; and there was a guest bedroom. Linda had set herself SMART goals and she achieved them.

Milestones

Goals can be couched in terms of *milestones* as follows:

- Short term (or near term): 0–2 years
- Medium term (2–5 years)
- Long term (5+ years)

Linda's goals in terms of milestones were as follows:

Overall Goal: Long term

> *Goal 1*: Short term
> *Goal 2 and Goal 3*: Medium term
> *Goal 4*: Long term

12

Execution as the key to the actual destination

We begin with three statements:

Statement 1: Between conception and creation, a shadow may fall.
Statement 2: Between the Land of Slavery and the Land of Milk and Honey, there was the Sea.
Statement 3: Between the door and the inside of the house, there is the key.

The gap between the Land of Slavery and the Land of Milk and Honey

The Israelites went out of Egypt, ready for battle, confident that they were leaving slavery behind them. But alas! There was a big barrier, the Red Sea. Then the LORD said to Moses, 'Raise the staff and stretch out your hand over the sea to divide the water so that the Israelites can go through the sea on dry ground' (Exod.14:16). Moses did likewise. And again the LORD said to Moses, 'Stretch out your hand over the sea so that the waters may flow back over the Egyptians and their chariots and horsemen' (Exod. 14:26). And again Moses did likewise.

The Red Sea was the barrier, the gap between freedom and slavery. God did something practical with his executing hand, using the hand of Moses, to ensure that the Israelites were saved from Pharaoh's army and freed from slavery. One young boy wanted to understand in concrete terms what happened here. His explanation was that God constructed a bridge over the sea for the Israelites to cross. Once the Israelites were safely on the other side, God just broke the bridge, and 'the water covered the chariots and horsemen – the entire army of Pharaoh … Not one of them survived' (Exod.14:28).

The three sisters and the key to the house

There were three sisters: Veronica, Stella and Esther. They lived with their parents in a rented house. Both parents died in a car accident. The sisters had nowhere to live as the landlord chucked them out of the house. Veronica always had big ideas in her mind. She took her sisters to their uncle, their mother's brother. She pleaded with the uncle, 'Please Uncle, get us a house to live in, even if we have to pay rent for it.'

One day the uncle called the three sisters. He showed them an elevated place where there were a number of beautiful houses. He described the house without saying which one was the one he had acquired for them among the houses on the mountain. 'I will describe the house again', he said. 'It is a long walking distance from here. I want you to walk there, identify the house and get in. Once you have unlocked and opened the house, then you will know you have arrived at the correct destination. There is a bunch of keys hanging over there. Get the correct keys and begin your long walk to the house.'

Veronica had a photographic mind. When the uncle described the house, she was able to tell exactly what it looked like. The question was how to get there. Stella told her sisters, 'I have done Geography. I have a very good sense of direction. I'll plot the way and we will surely arrive at the correct house.' So the three sisters started on their trek to the mountain house which their uncle had organized for them. The third sister, Esther, apart from being the youngest, had a bad leg which made her hobble along as she walked. Veronica had her eyes on the house; Stella was guiding them with her good sense of direction; and Esher hobbled her way to the house, way behind the two sisters who all but forgot about her existence as one of them. The two were excited about their vision of the house and their mastery of the terrain as they made their way to their future home.

Veronica and Stella arrived at what they thought was the correct house. With great excitement and a sense of victory, they then tried to open the door of the house. They had a big bunch of keys. They tried one key after the other, and none could unlock the door. Eventually, tired and feeling neglected and abandoned by her sisters, Esther arrived. By the time she arrived, the two elder sisters were dejected and deflated. 'What is the problem sisters?' Esther asked, and they told her about the keys. 'Let me try this one', she said holding one single key. And indeed she opened the door.

'Where did you find the correct key?' the two elder sisters asked.

'I found it along the path you followed, not far from Uncle's house. You must have unintentionally dropped it.'

When the uncle came to see them later and was told about the problem with the key, he simply said, 'Veronica, Stella and Esther, you are three sisters, each with her own talents and role to play in your life together. There is none of you who should be ignored or forgotten by the others. You are equally important.'

Explanation: Beware of the gap nobody knows

'Between conception and creation, a shadow may fall.' This is a statement which echoes a line in T. S. Eliot's poem, 'The Hollow Men', which for copyright reasons we cannot reproduce here. The message is essentially this: It is not enough to have a great idea, because the idea could fizzle out into nothing. You can have a great plan about what you intend to do, but you are likely to find hurdles and impediments on the way. There are likely to be risks you are going to face, and you need to act decisively to obviate those risks. You may create a great vision and put in place a wonderful strategic plan, but the vision and the plan may gather dust on people's shelves unless practical action is taken to ensure that all concerned put their hands to the plough and turn the vision and the plan into reality. We are all familiar with great visions and plans that produce no tangible results.

In leadership literature there is a new term, *the gap nobody knows*. Bossidy and Charan have defined it this way: 'The gap nobody knows is the gap between what the company's leaders want to achieve and the ability of their organization to achieve it' (Bossidy & Charan 2011: 19). The question that arises is: How do you close the gap? The answer is: through *execution*, which can be defined as 'the discipline of implementing a plan through the practice of rigorously following strategies aimed at getting things done'. It is by rigorously applying the discipline of execution that an organization can bring about real change. Bossidy and Charan have again said, 'Execution has to be a part of a company's strategy and its goals. It is *the missing link between aspirations and results*' (ibid., italics mine).

Execution is the force that removes the shadow between conception and creation, meaning between idea and reality. It is the metaphorical bridge between the Land of Slavery and the Land of Milk and Honey. It is the key that opens the door to the inside of the house. Just as there were three sisters who needed one another in the story, there are also three elements needed to bring about the transformation of an organization, to effect change in the process of change management. We can call the three elements 'the VSE Factor', meaning 'Vision, Strategy and Execution' – metaphorically the Viola, Stella and Esher Factor (VSE). The key to translating the dream and the road map into reality is the discipline of Execution. Execution is the Esther in the story without whom Veronica and Stella cannot enter the house.

The key elements of execution

We have partly defined execution above as 'the discipline of implementing a plan through the practice of rigorously following strategies aimed at getting things done'. What, then, constitutes the discipline of execution? What are its component parts? Some authorities talk in terms of 'Building Blocks to Execution' (see Bossidy & Charan 2011). That is a very good and powerful way of describing what execution is and what elements it is constituted of. Another way is to refer to the 'Building Blocks' as simply *elements* of execution. In this regard we can identify the following key elements:

- The leader's strategic operational behaviours
- Strategies for shaping organizational culture
- The people process
- The operational plan

The leader's strategic operational behaviours

It has been said that there is a difference between *leading* an organization and *presiding over* an organization. The one who presides over her/his organisation is not actively involved in the day-to-day running of the entity. He/she leaves it to operational leaders to do all the work, believing that by so doing he/she is empowering them. Here the leader becomes a passive overseer. The one who leads is actively involved in supervising, guiding and monitoring without going to the extent of micromanaging. It is the latter type of leader who demonstrates what have been called 'the seven essential behaviours' of business leaders in companies that execute. Bossidy & Charan (2011) have identified the following:

- Know your people and your business
- Insist on realism
- Set clear goals and priorities
- Follow through
- Reward doers
- Expand people's capabilities
- Know yourself

What follows is a very brief summary of each item:

> *Know Your People and Your Business*: As a leader you should not only have knowledge of the kind of business you run. You should be familiar with what is going on in different departments/units. You should not only depend on reports given to you as these may be distorted or may conceal a lot of what is

going wrong on the ground. Be where the action is; do not be out of touch. We shall learn in the next part of the book that the Japanese call this leadership strategy 'Going to Gemba' – a more systematic and principled way of 'managing by walking about'.

Insist on Realism: This is being realistic, not only in terms of avoiding setting goals that are not achievable but also in terms of being honest about the strengths and weaknesses of the organization. Do not put your head in the sand like an ostrich but confront the problems of the organization head on and insist on others doing the same. You and your staff should be honest and realistic about how your organization is performing relative to other organizations in the same business.

Set Clear Goals and Priorities: Do not set too many goals. Focus on three to four, at most five goals that are clearly articulated. These should be SMART goals that can be achieved with the available resources. When people focus on a few clear goals, they are likely to achieve them.

Follow Through: Failure to follow through is a major weakness in companies and organizations. A decision has been made, but it is not followed through to its logical conclusion. Things are left hanging in the air with no clear idea of who should do what and when. The discipline of execution requires that specific people be made accountable for every decision made and for every goal set.

Reward the Doers: There should be a distinction in rewards between performers and non-performers. Salary increases and bonuses should be based on performance. People should feel that compensation is commensurate with their efforts and results. In this way people are motivated to be results oriented.

Expand People's Capabilities: It is the leader's responsibility to empower those he/she works with through coaching, training and staff development. Empowering people this way makes them more productive and raises their own moral and sense of self-worth.

Know Yourself: Knowing yourself is a key strategic operational behaviour. It requires strength of character resulting from self-awareness and emotional fortitude. With emotional fortitude you are able to confront your own weaknesses; you are able to deal with poor performers and cope with conflicts and challenges in the workplace; and you become trustworthy.

Bossidy and Charan have identified what they call the four core qualities that make up emotional fortitude:

Authenticity: Being real, not fake, resulting in people trusting you and having confidence in you.

Self-awareness: Being aware of your own strengths and shortcomings and blind spots, this awareness giving you the strength to learn from your mistakes and the capacity to be a good judge of people, a good strategist and an effective operational leader.

Self-Mastery: The ability to take responsibility for your own actions and behaviours; the ability to take risks; and the ability to change and adapt to new situations and new ideas.

Humility: The ability to contain your ego; to acknowledge your mistakes and learn from them, leading to good decision-making.

Strategies for shaping organizational culture

Organizational culture or corporate culture includes the shared beliefs and values that influence people's behaviour in the organization concerned. In the academic world, for example, you may find institutions that are traditionally believed to have high standards. Some such institutions are truly high-quality institutions that produce graduates who are competent and competitive in the world of work. Some may merely thrive on the reputation they have traditionally acquired, continue to bask in the glory of that reputation and refuse to adapt to changing realities. An institution of this kind may produce graduates who are inferior in terms of skills and competences compared to the graduates of a newer institution that is sensitive to the changing environment and that reviews its programmes and approach to teaching and learning in relation to the changing world.

An academic leader who comes to the first type of institution and notices that there is a need for change may be resisted and may be told what he/she is trying to do is contrary to 'the way we do things here'. Similar attitudes and behaviours may also be found in the world of business. A CEO may be appointed to head a business where people are used to doing things in ways that are not very productive. The new CEO may find that salaries, bonuses and promotions are not linked to performance, for example. The company may not be doing well compared to other companies in the same business. There may be a purely subjective belief that the company is doing well when in reality that is not the case. Or the workforce may be resigned to the idea that their own organization is just not capable of performing at the level of its competitors.

In situations described above, there is a dire need for a change of culture, or to put it more appropriately, there is a need for *reshaping* the culture of the organization. There is now an understanding that, as far as corporate culture is concerned, organizations are like computers that have both hardware and software (see Bossidy & Charan 2011).

The hardware of an organization consists of formal processes, systems and structures. What has been called 'the social software' includes values, beliefs and norms of behaviour. The hardware may need changing, but where the greater change or the reshaping is paramount is in the social software. It is attitudes and beliefs that determine behaviour, and to change the behaviour for the better entails changing beliefs and attitudes.

Ways of reshaping culture

The ways of reshaping culture include the following:

a. The social software
   1. Communicating the future vision effectively and in an inspiring manner.
   2. Creating an awareness of the negative effects of the present culture.
   3. Cultivating an awareness of the need to change attitudes, beliefs and behaviours as a condition for attaining the future state.
   4. Creating forums for interrogating the existing corporate culture – giving the opportunity to the staff to compare the present culture with what could be a new desirable culture capable of facilitating the transformation to the desired future state. Workshops would be ideal methods of providing an opportunity to interrogate the organization's culture. Such workshops should be characterized by free and open debate, with staff being free to express their views without fear of reprisals. In the next part of the book, we shall learn about traditional African forums that can be used to deliberate on important organizational issues.
b. Hardware

On the hardware side, the following could be done:

1. Writing job descriptions for every post.
2. Introducing rigorous performance appraisals, with the CEO being actively involved and setting the standards for effective performance appraisals.

As leader, you should be an example of the culture you want to see in the organization. Mahatma Gandhi is quoted to have said, 'Be the change you want to see in others.' Bossidy and Charan (2011: 105–6) have made this important comment about culture change and its impact on business performance: 'You change the culture of a company by changing the behavior of its leaders. You measure the change in culture by measuring the change in the personal behavior of its leaders and the performance of the business.'

The people process

As is commonly said, an organization's people are its most important asset. It is by influencing followers that the leader can move an organization to higher levels of performance. The people process is about having the right people in the right place. It typically involves selecting, appraising and developing people.

- *Selecting*: This is a critical point. First, as leader you must be involved in the selection process. See to it that the advertisement for a post or for posts clarifies what kind of people you want. Do not allow a situation where an advert is designed to fit someone whom one of your officials (such as the head of human resources) would like to see in the position. Make sure the right people are shortlisted.

    The interview is a critical point in the selection process. It is at this stage that you must make sure you select a doer for each advertised position. Some candidates are very good at talking and may have impressive academic qualifications. But the important question for an organization that believes in execution is, 'How good is this person at getting things done?' (Bossidy & Charan 2011: 119). It is therefore important to check on the track record of the potential appointees. It is also important to assess whether the selected candidate demonstrates the capacity to perform in the specific job for which he/she has applied.

- *Appraising*: This process is referred to in the section on shaping culture. It should be a rigorous process in which the leader is personally involved. It is partly through performance appraisals that the leader can judge whether there are right people in the right place.
- *Developing*: A key element of the people process is developing your people. This can be done in a variety of ways: You can provide opportunities for staff development with deserving staff getting financial assistance and time off to improve their qualifications. Coaching on the job is very important. It helps people to improve while performing their functions. It also helps to give staff experience in different jobs or different stations. Providing exposure by way of attending conferences and workshops or attachment to other organizations is yet another way.

The point to make here is that leaders should turn their organizations into learning organizations so powerfully articulated in Peter Senge's *The Fifth Discipline* (1990). Senge quotes one O'Brien as saying that one of the fundamental tasks of managers (i.e. leaders) is 'providing the enabling conditions for people to lead the most enriching lives they can' (Senge 1990: 140). This takes us to the principles of personal leadership development, especially personal mastery, the discipline of personal growth and learning. People should be energized and made to feel the desire to learn more and to achieve more for the organization.

The operational plan

The operational plan (OP) is the fourth of the elements of execution we have identified. What is an OP? An OP (or an operations plan) can in part be defined as 'a manual that translates the strategic plan into concrete and practical activities that have a time frame and a budget, with the aim of achieving the organisation's goals'.

A strategic plan is a general guide that gives the direction the organization is taking and specifies the goals that must be achieved in order to get to the desired future state. It does not define day-to-day activities. The OP is more specific. It provides the linkages between the strategic plan, activities, people and budgets.

An OP should have the following characteristics, among others:

- It should be derived from the strategic plan.
- It should specify the activities that are going to be undertaken as well as the desired outcomes.
- It should specify who is going to work on which strategies/tasks.
- It should indicate the timelines within which the identified tasks should be completed.
- It should give the budget that is required to complete each task.
- It should normally be a plan for one year.

With the above done, a strategic plan ceases to be a mere document that can be forgotten on book shelves. It becomes a living document that helps the organization to move in the direction of achieving its desired future state.

Example of an operational plan

The OP outlined below is based on a real-life experience. However, the name of the organization, the dates and other details have been changed to make the OP a generic or general one that is applicable to developing countries in similar circumstances. The responsible organization is a quality assurance agency that is responsible for maintaining and improving quality in all higher education institutions in the country. There are roughly fifteen universities in the country, and the quality assurance agency, called the National Quality Assurance Agency (NQAA), notes that there are major differences in the quality of degrees and other qualifications awarded by the different universities or higher education institutions in the country. Among other things, the calculation of credits for programmes is based on different systems. One of the consequences of these disparities is that it is difficult for students to transfer from one university to another.

The NQAA develops a strategic plan, one of whose Key Performance Areas is 'Harmonisation of Higher Education' on a nationwide basis. The chief executive officer (CEO) is personally actively involved in leading the project assisted by the heads of the NQAA's departments (directors), the public relations officer (PRO) and her personal assistant (PA). The project involves working closely with the leaders of higher education institutions, and this means running workshops in hotels and other venues that provide suitable rooms and food. The CEO and her management team develops a budget of US$50,000 to cover the cost of running the workshops. Before the project can commence, the CEO carries out a research project which provides facts and figures about the state of fragmentation in the system and the implications for quality. This provides evidence of the need for harmonization.

One of the objectives of the project is for institutions to agree on a common approach to credit accumulation and transfer. This entails deciding whether to use the *credit hour* approach or the *notional study hours* approach. (These concepts are discussed in some detail in Part V.) Once there is agreement on which approach to adopt, there is now a need to develop a policy document with guidelines on how to implement the system. A team of experts in quality assurance from higher education institutions, called the technical committee, is tasked with the responsibility of developing the guidelines under the supervision of the CEO. Institutions will expect to have the opportunity to comment on the document and to suggest improvements before the document is adopted by all the stakeholders, including the Ministry of Higher Education. Once the new system is endorsed by all the stakeholders, there needs to be a special workshop for the implementers. This includes deans, faculty officers and others. It takes a whole year (throughout 2018) for higher education institutions to start implementing the new system.

NQAA operational plan 2018–19

Key result area: Harmonization of higher education

Strategies/Tasks	Time Frame	Responsible Person	Budget ($)
Research on fragmentation	Two months (by 28 February 2018)	CEO	2,000
Organize workshop on harmonization	Two months from completion of research (by 30 April 2018)	CEO and PRO	5,000
Run workshop to agree on harmonization approach	28–29 May 2018	CEO and directors	10,000
Develop document on credit accumulation	Thirty days (by 30 June 2018)	Technical committee	1,000
Run workshop on the proposed system	2–4 July 2018	CEO and directors	15,000

Strategies/Tasks	Time Frame	Responsible Person	Budget ($)
Invite comments from all institutions	Thirty days (by 8 August 2018)	CEO and PA	90
Run workshop for all stakeholders	One day (26 October 2018)	CEO and directors	7,000
Run workshop for deans and faculty officers	15 November 2018	Directors and CEO	5,000
Commence implementation	1 February 2019	Institutions	0.00
Total expenditure by the NQAA			**45,900**

Part V

Beyond the organizational context of educational leadership

13

Issues and principles of educational leadership

TUNING IN EXERCISE

Read the two stories below and answer the questions that follow:

Story 1: The sports trainer and the gifted student

This story is based on a true story that has been slightly modified. It is a story about Maggie, the gifted sports girl, and Mr Makiwa, the sports master at the University of Lesape. Maggie was still a high school girl but had been provisionally admitted to study for a degree at the University of Lesape, a public university in a newly independent African country. Maggie's parents were poor African peasants and were looking up to her for financial support when she completed her education. Mr Makiwa was leading the national team to Moscow in the former Soviet Union, which team included both university and high school students. Makiwa noticed how gifted Maggie was and made sure she was in the team that was going to Moscow. While the team was away in the Soviet Union, Mr Makiwa forced himself on her, arguing that she had made it to Russia because of his efforts. The rape left her pregnant and she was expelled from school, ending her dream of acquiring a university degree and shattering her parents' hopes.

Story 2: Monica, the university student

Monica was a student of Law at a public African university called City Heights University. There was so much competition for places in the university hostels that

Monica could not make it. She lived in an African township on the far side of the city. To get to the university she would board a crowded taxi (mini bus) to the city and another one from the city to the university. To get to lectures at eight o'clock in the morning, she would have to start travelling at five o'clock. At home she shared a bedroom with two younger sisters in a room where there was no space for a desk. In order to cope with her homework and the amount of reading required, she would work in the university library until eleven o'clock at night. She would very often get home after one o'clock in the morning. She had at most three hours of sleep per night.

Monica then heard of a family some thirty minutes' walk away from the university. She went to apply for boarding there. What she saw was shocking: The students slept in a big room where nine students were crowded together – she would be the tenth student. There were no beds, and each student had to bring her or his own bed. What shocked her more was that there were both boys and girls sleeping in the same room, using the same showers and toilets. Monica was in a dilemma: Which was better – to sleep at home where she had only three hours of sleep per night or to sleep in this dungeon where she could not avoid seeing boys and girls having sex in the presence of fellow students?

Questions on the first story: Maggie and Mr Makiwa

1. What does the story reveal about Mr Makiwa's morals?
2. Have you heard about or do you know about any officer or academic in your country who is known to have behaved in a similar way?
3. What does the incident say about Mr Makiwa's professional training?
4. What would you say about Mr Makiwa's behaviour in relation to the philosophy of *Ubuntu?*

Questions on the second story: Monica, the university student

1. Are you aware of any students who find themselves in circumstances similar to Monica's?
2. What is the responsibility of institutions like City Heights University to students in Monica's position?

3. What action could the university have taken to ensure students who were accommodated in private homes were offered appropriate conditions to live and study under?

Broader educational leadership issues

The previous three chapters focussed on organizational leadership in the generic or general sense, the education domain included. In this part of the book two approaches are taken: First, organizational leadership is focussed on a specific sphere of human life and activity – education. Second, within that sphere, educational leadership is broadened beyond considerations of organizations alone to incorporate issues that impact on education beyond the walls of a single institution. There is also a sense in which this part takes us back to the beginning of the book. Chapter 1 discusses what may be called the main purpose of an educational establishment – teaching and learning. In this chapter we focus on how to make the establishment achieve its mission – we focus on educational leadership in the sense of how to run an education institution, with special reference to a university. Before we proceed further, it is necessary to mention that a university is not only about teaching and learning. It should also include in its mission the functions of research, innovation and community service. These are referred to in the next chapter.

Educational leaders in the sense of those who have the responsibility of running higher education institutions (HEIs) should be aware of the various levels at which leadership is exercised; they should have good knowledge of the nature and functions of a university; the context in which HEIs operate; the factors that impact on the functions and operations of such institutions, including factors that impact on individual students; and should have the leadership qualities that enable one to succeed in running such an institution. In view of all this, this chapter will examine the following dimensions of the higher education domain:

- The macro, meso and micro levels of higher education leadership
- Issues of quality assurance management relative to academic freedom and autonomy
- What this author calls 'supra-macro level' factors, such as globalization, Covid-19 and internationalization
- The special context of institutions in Africa and other former colonies
- What institutions in Western countries can learn from non-traditional societies – with special reference to former colonies
- The implications for higher educational leaders in our time.

The macro, meso and micro levels of higher education leadership

The education system of a country can be viewed as an ecosystem involving the leadership and management of education at the macro (sociocultural and political level), the meso (the organizational level) and the micro (the personal level) levels. In her article on understanding Sustainable Development Goal 4 of the United Nations which is on education, Ellen Boeren (2019)focuses on micro-, meso- and macro-level perspectives as referring to (1) the role of individuals and their families (the micro level), (2) schools and education training institutions (the meso level) and (3) regulating governments (the macro level). Boeren says that in her 'comprehensive lifelong learning participation model' (2016) she indicated that participation can be theorized as an interplay between an individual's social and behavioural characteristics, the availability and structures of education and training providers and the role of supporting governments.

By the micro level in the sense given here we are talking of parents, children, young adults and adult learners as key players at this lowest level. The general observation is that children with highly educated parents are likely to participate in further education. Their parents are likely to afford a university education for them, and they are consequently likely to be employed in high-paid jobs. Universities that have highly qualified staff are able to cater for learners' needs; and that present clear and strong visions are likely to attract the best students. Accessibility to learners and their parents is also a factor in the extent to which an institution is likely to attract good students and the likelihood of the students to perform well and consequently to land high-paying jobs. We are referring here to students who are not able to get university accommodation. This reminds one of some institutions in urban centres in some African cities where students have to travel far to get home at night; the home environment is one where conditions for study are not good, forcing the student to work in the library until very late in a situation where transport facilities are not the best.

The scene just described above presents problems to education leaders at both the macro and meso levels. At the meso level the challenge is to provide an ideal learning and study environment for the students and to ensure there is a good transport system between the university and the residential areas of the students. For the government the challenge is to provide sufficient financial support to the university so that the university can in turn give the students the support they need. Ideally governments should also give scholarships, bursaries and loans to students. But there are big challenges for many African governments here. These range from poorly performing economies, competing budgetary requirements and depreciating currencies – all of which make it difficult for the governments to afford to give adequate support to HEIs and individual students. Furthermore, whereas from the 1940s to the 1970s university institutions were few and the number of students was low, now since the last quarter of the twentieth century, there has been massification of higher education and this makes it hard for governments to cope with the financial needs of institutions and students. To make matters worse there has been an ideological shift worldwide from the idea of the welfare state to the privatization of education. In the UK, the Margaret Thatcher administration started withdrawing financial support from British universities in the 1980s forcing them to be more resourceful and more self-reliant in generating income.

The points made in the immediately preceding paragraph pose a challenge, not only for the university as an organization but also for those individuals with the responsibility of leading HEIs. In this regard, there is a sense in which the micro level of educational leadership at HEIs can justifiably be conceived of as referring not only to individual students and their parents as explained above but also to an official such as the vice chancellor or dean who has the responsibility of leading an institution or a faculty or college in such an institution – and even to the chairperson or head of department. The issue is what are the leadership challenges for such an individual in this kind of environment? How can the individual exercise leadership successfully so as to have a positive impact at the meso level? This is a matter that relates to the changing character of the university which the higher educational leader should be aware of. An important part of this chapter is to show something of this changing character of the university.

Quality assurance practice as a challenge to academic freedom and autonomy

Writing about the university as 'a self-motivating and self-perpetuating institution' in a previous work (Ngara 1995: 15), this writer boldly proclaimed, 'There is however no gainsaying that a university worthy of the name charts its own direction, designs its own curriculum and determines the manner in which it promotes and maintains high academic standards and keeps itself true to its mission. In other words the university is its own policeman and has the duty to keep itself on its toes.' That was before I had the experience of leading a quality assurance agency and got to know how some institutions (particularly young universities) need guidance from outside the institution for them to maintain high academic standards. The sentiments expressed in these two sentences are correct, but it is unlikely that now in 2021 I would couch the idea in these words.

This statement was made in relation to a feature that was regarded as a key characteristic of a university: academic freedom and autonomy. The view has been for the university to properly perform its functions of teaching, research (and innovation) and community service (or public service), it should be free from control by governments, political parties, the private sector and multinational and international organizations. Universities in the former colonies inherited the tradition developed by Western universities in this regard and embraced it, although in Africa there were voices that pointed to the need for accountability to national governments for purposes of being relevant to national development. At a major workshop held in Accra in 1972 under the aegis of the Association of African Universities, academic freedom was defined as:

> the liberty of the university to determine course content and curricula, what to teach and how to teach; and it must embrace the liberty to do research, publish and disseminate knowledge freely without let or hindrance.

Significantly, the statement went on to add, 'This is a fundamental freedom which African universities must defend at all times' (Yesufu 1973: 45). In the next decade, 'autonomy' was defined by the World University Service (WUS1988) as follows:

> 'Autonomy' means the independence of institutions of higher education from the State and all other forces of society, to make decisions regarding its internal government, finance, administration, and to establish its policies of education, research, extension work and other related activities.

By the late 1980s governments, including African governments, were beginning to adopt principles and policies that modified this traditional concept of academic freedom and autonomy, meaning that policies at the macro level were beginning to determine the character of the university for the meso level. Among other things, governments were beginning to demand accountability from HEIs and to be involved in planning which involved conditions for the funding of universities and expecting certain levels of outputs in key areas such as Science, Technology, Engineering and Mathematics (STEM). An important development in this regard was the establishment of state-owned enterprises (SOEs) called quality assurance agencies. These enterprises began to perform the function I referred to above as that of policemen. In the face of massification with both public and private universities increasing in number, it was necessary to ensure acceptable quality was maintained by all universities. In some African countries these enterprises gave guidance to institutions by ensuring that programmes were of sufficient quality; lecturers were highly qualified; buildings, libraries and other facilities were adequate and of an acceptable standard; and so forth. Quality assurance was defined as 'fitness for purpose'. It was an holistic approach which was meant to ensure that academic institutions were accountable to the state, to students and to the community – and were further expected to aspire to meet international standards of quality.

Quality assurance and higher education integration

A development which promoted the need for quality assurance was the mobility of students and staff, especially in specific regions. In the European Union, for instance, it was realized that students came from countries with different standards and traditions. This resulted in the initiative called the Bologna Process in the European Higher Education Area. This organization brings together forty-nine countries with different traditions with a view to promoting structural reforms that help not only to improve quality but also to facilitate staff and student mobility as well as employability for students. These countries have agreed to adopt reforms that are based on common values such as freedom of expression, autonomy for institutions and free movement of staff and students. There are agreed standards and guidelines for quality assurance which were adopted by the ministers responsible for higher education in 2005.

In Africa there are initiatives at both continental and regional levels. In order to save space we will briefly refer to continental initiatives only. Among these are three initiatives aimed at harmonizing higher education in Africa:

1. *The Addis Ababa Convention*
   The first of these is the Addis Ababa Convention (UNESCO 2014) whose aims include, among other things:
   a. Defining and putting in place effective quality assurance and accreditation mechanisms at national, regional and continental level
   b. Facilitating the exchange and greater mobility of students, teachers and researchers of the continent and the African diaspora
2. *The Pan African Quality Assurance and Accreditation Framework (PAQAF)*
   The aims of PAQAF include:
   a. Development of a continental Qualifications Framework
   b. Promoting the African Quality Rating Mechanism (AQPRM) for institutional assessment
   c. Implementation of the Addis Ababa Convention
   d. Developing a system of credits (African Credit Accumulation and Transfer System)
   e. Creating a continental register for quality assurance agencies.
3. *The Harmonisation of African Higher Education Quality Assurance and Accreditation (HAQAA) Initiative*

So far two phases of the HAQAA initiative have been implemented:
a. According to the Africa-EU Partnership (2021), 'The HAQAA project phase one (HAQAA1 2015-2018) trained approximately 50 personnel from QAA agencies and universities across the continent, in order to support a "common QA language" and enhance bi-regional (EU-Africa) and intra-regional exchange in QA.' There was also a working group that developed the 'African Standards and Guidelines' in quality assurance.
b. HAQAA2 (2021) was intended to build on HAQAA1 by, among other things, upscaling and promoting the results via such methods as continental training for nationally elected QA professionals from higher education institutions on 'a common understanding of quality in Africa', generally supporting the PAQAF and so on. The idea of graduates of HAQAA becoming 'ambassadors' was promoted via a webinar that was held in 2021. (The Africa-EU Partnership (2021))

The information from the two regions, Europe and Africa, is given here as examples. Readers from other regions such as Latin America and Asia should be able to give examples of the developments that have taken place in those regions. What these examples show is that quality assurance in higher education has become an industry which educational leaders should not only be aware of but be sufficiently knowledgeable about in order to comply with its requirements. From a practical point of view what the higher educational leader should know, especially when operating as an academic, is how to design programmes and qualifications and how to calculate credits. As these are essential skills, we shall comment briefly on them below.

Educational leadership and quality assurance technical skills

From the perspective of quality assurance there are technical skills that the educational leader should be aware of and should be able to use in the designing of programmes. For instance one should be clear about the differences between a module (individual courses), a programme (a group of modules that together lead to a qualification) and a qualification which has been defined as 'any degree, diploma or other certificate issued by an accredited HEI attesting the successful completion of an approved higher education programme' (UNESCO, Addis Convention 2014). In other words, a programme is a structured course of study composed of modules or individual courses, some of which are compulsory, some of which are optional, with the possibility of some modules being taken from a department other than the one in which the student is registered. When the student has satisfactorily completed the programme thus constructed, then he or she can be awarded the relevant qualification, whether it is a Bachelor of Arts (BA), Master of Science (MSc), Diploma and so on. What is of critical importance for an educational leader from the perspective of quality assurance is the following:

- Determining competences that a university graduate should acquire
- Developing a credit accumulation and transfer system

The following information is partly informed by the contents of a paper that this writer developed for the HAQAA1 initiative with a group from the Southern African Development Community (Ngara 2017): A major consideration in designing courses for higher education students is employability. Are the graduates we produce in universities and colleges going to be employable? This is a problem for HEIs even in developed countries like America. Many of the graduates universities churn out are not sufficiently prepared to fit into their jobs on Day 1. The challenge is to produce graduates who are not only employable but can generate employment for themselves and others. To meet this requirement, graduates should be trained to master two key elements: *Knowledge* and *Competences* (*KCs*) that are required in the job market. In some cases competences are distinguished from *Skills* so that we are talking about *Knowledge*, *Skills* and *Competences* (*KSCs*). However, it is often difficult to make a distinction between competences and skills; and so for practical purposes we shall refer here to *KCs*.

Knowledge relates to what in quality assurance parlance is referred to as *minimum body of knowledge (MBK)*. The MBK of any discipline is what is agreed by specialists in the field should be the minimum that a programme should cover in order for that programme to be regarded as one that is equivalent to similar programmes in reputable institutions. One has come across a situation where students who have done very well at one university have applied for postgraduate studies at another university. When tested at this new university they have been found not to have covered enough material for them to be awarded an undergraduate degree at this new university. What this means is that there can be discrepancies in quality in the same country or region. Consequently, MBKs are *curriculum benchmarks* which ensure there is comparability of standards between institutions in the same country and between countries and regions. Agreement on MBKs helps to enhance quality and to facilitate the harmonization of higher education in a region.

For the purpose of promoting the employability of graduates, it is advisable to think of competences that are required in the workplace, competences such as the following which one can find listed in internet articles:

- Ability to work in a team (teamwork)
- A sense of responsibility
- Communication skills
- Organizational skills

- Problem-solving skills
- Sufficient knowledge of the area of specialization
- Quick thinking – ability to think on your toes and so on

As explained in Chapter 1, the Tuning Africa Project (see Onana et al. 2014: 64–5) identified eighteen generic competences for African graduates, including the following:

1. Ability for conceptual thinking, analysis and synthesis
2. Professionalism, ethical values and commitment to Ubuntu (respect for the well-being and dignity of fellow human beings)
3. Capacity for critical evaluation and self-awareness
4. Ability to translate knowledge into practice
5. Objective decision-making and practical cost-effective problem solving
6. Capacity to use innovative and appropriate technologies

An important practice to promote the employability of graduate is to have attachment arrangements between universities and industry. This could even extend to areas that are not traditionally regarded as areas for which students need attachment experience to be awarded the qualifications in question. The mere experience of being in a work environment, even if the student is not paid for her/his service, is beneficial. In professional fields such as Engineering, Law, Medicine and others, the relevant professional bodies should ideally be involved in determining MBKs and the general content of the programmes in question.

The development of a credit accumulation and transfer system

An important skill for an educational leader in higher education is ability to develop, or to at least be able to work with, a credit accumulation and transfer system (CATS). Credit accumulation refers to the adding up of credits earned by a student. Credits may be accumulated from the same programme or from different programmes, or even from different institutions if they are regarded by the awarding institution as relevant to the programme in question and contributing to the achievement of the relevant qualification. The Credit Accumulation Transfer System of a nation or region has been defined by the South African Council on Higher Education (CHE 2013: 16) as 'the process whereby a student's achievements are recognised and contribute to further learning even if the student has not achieved a qualification'. In terms of this, any credits earned by a student can contribute to the completion of a qualification in the same institution or in a different institution in the same country or anywhere else in the world if there is mutual recognition of the value and relevance of the credits between the institutions concerned, and if there is a common understanding on credit weighting between the institutions. This is important for the process of internationalization that is addressed later in this chapter. For now, our task is to explain approaches to the calculation of credits. In this regard, we are obliged to explain that much of the information given below on credit weighting is based on the paper this author wrote in 2017 (Ngara 2017), together with a group of HAQAA participants from the Southern African Development Community (SADC). The writer is obliged by HAQAA to acknowledge this paper as follows:

> The paper was developed in the framework of the Harmonisation, Accreditation and Quality Assurance Initiative (HAQAA1) funded by the European Union, in partnership with the African Union, between 2015 and 2018. It was part of the work conducted for a continental African training course on a Common Language for Quality Assurance in Africa, which HAQAA1 executed. The opinions expressed reflect those of the author and not those of the African Union or European Union Commissions.

There are two approaches to credit weighting or the calculation of credits that are used in many parts of the world. These are *the Credit Hour Approach* and *the Notional Study Hours Approach*. Each approach is briefly described below:

1. *The credit hour approach*

    - The credit hour approach is based on the number of 'contact hours' per week and per semester. This should include any time the lecturer or professor spends with students such as lecture time and laboratory time.
    - A credit hour is normally based on the number of contact hours per week.
    - As there are normally fifteen weeks in a semester, a module that is allocated one (1) contact hour per week per semester is referred to as a 1-credit module. Similarly, a 3-credit module represents three hours of contact time per week for fifteen weeks; and a 4-credit module represents four hours of contact time per week for fifteen weeks.
    - It should be noted that in this approach the time for private study, research and the writing of assignments and examinations is not included in the calculation.

The credit hour approach is widely used in the United States where credits are usually referred to as 'credit hours'. A standard full-time load in the United States is said to be usually thirty credit hours per year. According to Alexander Pop (2016), in order to graduate with a degree, students must typically complete:

- 120–130 hours for a bachelor's degree
- 30–64 credit hours for a master's degree

2. *The notional study hours approach*

The basic principles of the notional study hours approach can be summarized as follows:

- Notional study hours (also known as 'learning hours') represent an estimate of the time spent by an average full time equivalent student to master a unit of learning.
- In countries such as South Africa, Zimbabwe and the UK (England Wales and Northern Ireland) it has been stipulated that ten notional study hours are worth one credit. The International Labour Organisation (ILO) has also used this approach in discussing credit accumulation and transfer systems (Tuck 2007).
- It is worth noting that in this approach the hours referred to here include all the learning activities of the student, inclusive of contact time (lecture time), private study, research, assignment writing and examinations.
- The following assumptions are made: The average student accumulates eight study hours per day, amounting to a forty-hour week. Undergraduate programmes are generally based on a thirty-week full-time academic year. At 40 hours per week this amounts to 1,200 hours per year.
- As ten notional study hours amount to one credit, a year's undergraduate programme is worth 120 credits. Master's and doctoral qualifications assume a forty-five-week full-time academic year, with the average student earning 180 credits per year.
- It is necessary to note that the 1,200 hours and 120 credits per year are the absolute minimums that must be met with institutions being free to go above these minima. The determining factor is whether students will be able to cope with the workload that results from the benchmarks used. In this regard, the maximum number of learning hours and credits stipulated by an institution must take this factor into account.

The examples below show how study hours and credits translate into qualifications. The study levels given are based on the Southern African Development Community (SADC) standards. The assumption is that for undergraduate programmes the average student works for a minimum of 1,200 hours per year, while the master's students puts in a minimum average of 1,800 hours of work per year. The more industrious students may spend more hours, while the less industrious students will put in fewer hours than the average on which the minimum number of hours and credits are based:

1. A one-year higher certificate (Level 5): 1,200 notional study hours = 120 credits
2. A three-year bachelor's degree (Level 7): 3,600 notional study hours = 360 credits

3. A four-year bachelor's degree (Level 8): 4,800 notional study hours = 480 credits
4. A two-year master's degree (Level 9): 3,600 notional study hours = 360 credits

It is advisable for institutions in the same country and the same region to use the same approach, either the credit hour approach or the notional study hours approach. This facilitates the easy mobility of students from one institution to another. With regard to the notional study hours approach, it is also necessary for comparability purposes to agree on the elements to be included in the calculation of credits such as lectures, practical work, field work, self-directed learning, projects, assessments and so on. It should be pointed out, however, that for the purposes of internationalization and student mobility across different regions, it is possible to work out equivalences between different credit weighting systems. In the paper referred to above (Ngara 2017) the following equivalences were given as examples of comparability where ECTS refers to the European Credit Accumulation and Transfer System of the European Higher Education Area:

1 SADC Credit = 1 UK Credit
2 SADC Credits= 1 ECTS Credit
1.67 ECTS Credits=1.00 US Credit
Therefore 3.34 SADC Credits = 1 US Credit (or 3 SADC Credits = 1 US Credit)

The paper was proposing for the whole SADC region to adopt a system that had been accepted by South African universities and by Zimbabwe and other countries of the region. In this regard, the SADC system would be equivalent to the UK system (England, Wales and Northern Ireland – excluding Scotland); and where the SADC Credit Accumulation and Transfer System would require a minimum of 120 credits per year, the ECTS equivalent would be 60 credits per year, meaning that 2 SADC credits would be equal to 1 European Higher Education Area credit. The American equivalent would be calculated as shown above.

A final point that needs to be made in this section is that the experience of Covid-19 is likely to bring about some modifications to these calculations as self-study assumes a much greater role in the work of students than was previously the case.

Common factors affecting the operations of higher education institutions

Apart from quality assurance, there are other developments that affect the operations of all HEIs in the twenty-first century, regardless of whether they are located in the North or the South. These include globalization, the effects of Covid-19 and, to perhaps a less extent, the phenomenon of internationalization. The difference between the first two and the last of these is that globalization and Covid-19 are externally imposed, whereas internationalization is an initiative of HEIs themselves.

Globalization

Globalization in the twentieth century was facilitated by inventions such as the aeroplane, the computer and the internet. Travel became easier, communicating information between nations became much faster and the transportation of goods between countries became much faster. As has been cogently explained by writers such as Howard Stephenson (see Bush et al. 2019), globalization has been largely a factor of an aggressive form of international capitalism in which raw materials and low production costs combined with access to increasing consumer markets have been the key impulses. This partly meant easy acquisition of raw materials from developing countries with transnational corporations being the means through which raw materials were moved from developing to developed countries, making those countries poor producers of raw materials. At the same time bodies such as the International Monitory Fund and the World Bank and UNESCO were busy deciding for leaders of developing countries how to run their countries, while news agencies such as the CNN, the BBC, Al Jazeera and others, as well as TV and other gadgets, were busy shaping our views of the world. Consequently, globalization impacted the world on at least three fronts: economic, political and cultural. On the cultural front, young people growing up in the twentieth and twenty-first centuries have lost their national identity and are part of the new international community that consumes the same values and interests.

What does this have to do with higher education, one might ask? Everywhere, HEIs have been affected by global trends. For one thing, all HEIs are now subject to international rating. While this is a good thing from the perspective of quality assurance, the downside of it for African universities and others in developing countries is that they now struggle to be on the list of internationally recognized universities without paying sufficient attention to the local environment which should be their responsibility to improve. A development which militates against the traditional understanding of a university is the idea of running the university as a business. As pointed out earlier, the idea of a welfare state has been largely abandoned with HEIs expected to generate much of their own income like private business establishments. The idea is not bad provided the leaders are aware of ensuring that the university does not become just another business company but remains conscious of its obligations as an education institution dedicated to teaching, research, innovation and community or public service, and as one that is conscious of its obligation to develop the leaders of tomorrow who are guided by certain values that help to preserve the culture and traditions of the nation.

A development that is related to turning universities into businesses is managerialism. This normally starts at the macro level with government authorities imitating what they see happening in the rest of the world. There are cases when a government is genuinely concerned about mismanagement of public institutions and is therefore compelled to step in and introduce measures that ensure the institution concerned is properly led and managed. An example of this is the Government of South Africa. The South African Council on Higher Education (CHE) (2016: 127) reports, 'Since 2010 the Ministry appointed five assessors and four administrators to address a variety of governance and management problems at five universities; this took the tally of government interventions into higher education institutions between 1994 and 2014 to fourteen.' The same publication (ibid.: 133) points out, 'Managerialism produced two fundamental casualties in higher education decision-making: academics and students.' Academics get alienated and students become what this writer refers to as 'customers' of the university. This is ironic in that these two groups that are the very reason for the existence of the university become outsiders while those who are supposed to play the role of supporting the essential activities of teaching and learning essentially become 'the owners' of the university. It is reasonable to argue that this is the outcome of the fact that those who are appointed to run these institutions as well as their government officials have no training in the leadership of universities. This can result not only in poor leadership and management of HEIs but also in conflict between government officials and universities. As the CHE publication (ibid.: 135) further points out, 'Lastly, governance relations between the Minister and the higher education sector have been strained, particularly since the Higher Education Amendment of 2011 and the related threat of court action.'

Howard Stevenson (ibid.: 284) has said, 'I have argued thus far that globalisation, or the process of globalisation, has had a very significant impact on education and therefore on those who have the responsibility of leading educational institutions.' What this means is that the process of globalization on higher education needs to be interrogated. We need to consider what are the advantages and disadvantages of globalization for the future citizens of the world. As educators, we have the responsibility of educating the world about the impact of globalization, whether good or bad.

The effects of Covid-19 on education

Covid-19 has been called 'the leveller'. There is no continent, no race, no social class and no gender that has not been affected. Both developed and developing countries have been affected. For the first time human beings have realized they are all human – there is no group that is superior to another. In this pandemic we have become one global village of sick and frightened people. Those countries that have been least affected have done so largely because they quickly took the right steps at the right time. As far as the education sphere is concerned, we have all become aware of empty classrooms, empty student hostels and semesters that have been disrupted with institutions having to be cautious about when semesters can start, when classes can be held, when examinations can be written and so on.

But such is the human spirit that while Covid-19 has brought about all these and other challenges, some solutions have been found. Chief among these is online teaching and learning. Many universities and schools resorted to online teaching just as churches had to learn to conduct online services since large gatherings were no longer allowed. This author personally learned a lot about the extent to which digitalization became *the* approach to teaching and learning worldwide by attending the 2021 OBREAL-Global Webinar entitled 'OBREAL-Global in Focus 2021 – Charting the Course for South-South-North Cooperation and Beyond'. This series of programmes was followed by the April 2021 Annual Conference of Symbiosis International University and the Association of Indian Universities entitled 'Reimagining Internationalisation: Blended Education as a Catalyst'. Much of what is said in this section of this chapter was informed by the deliberations of these two international events.

Advantages of digitalization

First, it is necessary to state that Covid-19 had some positive effects on approaches to teaching and learning in higher education. Perhaps the most prominent of these are digitalization and internationalization of higher education. Among the advantages of digitalization and online teaching are the following:

1. Travel costs are reduced. A student in India or Africa can attend lectures by a professor in Ireland without having to travel to Ireland. What this also means is that the costs of university education are reduced. There is no need for the student to pay for travel costs and for boarding as he/she can learn from the comfort of his/her home.
2. Students have more access to materials prepared by more specialists than from their own professors or lecturers, some of whom may not be the best in the world. In this regard, digitalization has the advantage of making the best staff in a discipline available for students in different parts of the world.
3. The lecturer can reach more students virtually than through face-to-face teaching.
4. The exchange of best practices is made easier through digitalization. It also means that virtual exchange (VE) of staff is made possible without the need for travel.

5. Digitalization facilitates integration within regions such as Latin America, Southern Africa, India and the European Higher Education Area. The integration can even extend beyond particular regions. In this way digitalization facilitates the creation of synergies and consequently promotes the internationalization of higher education.
6. The virtual approach makes it possible for academics to cooperate effectively across countries, regions and continents. The offering of virtual settings has broken down boundaries. Internationalization is operating at regional levels such as South America and between regions such as South America and Europe.

In view of the above and for other reasons, it is not surprising that the majority of the participants in the programmes referred to above seemed to be of the view that digitalization is essential; and that virtual settings and internationalization of the curriculum are here to stay – even post-Covid-19.

Challenges and disadvantages

While the advantages of online teaching and digitalization are real and should not be ignored by any higher educational leader, there are some challenges that should be noted. There are challenges for the higher education system and for lecturers and students.

Challenges for institutions: For the university as a system there are some challenges that may be resolved over time; but for now these are the challenges:

1. Depending on the regulations of the particular university, there is a likelihood now that a student who is studying from home and has access to materials from various universities in the world can collect modules and credits from different institutions in different parts of the world. What is the effect of this collection of credits and modules on quality? Is the degree of such a student equal in quality to a degree programme taken at a particular university with a senior academic advising on the combination of modules?
2. How does the university compile the modules and courses from different institutions using different credit accumulation systems into a normal qualification?
3. What does the university do with the buildings (classrooms and hostels) that now stand empty?

Challenges for professors/lecturers: There are some challenges for university teachers the world over. The following are some of them:

1. Most academics were trained to teach face to face: Online teaching may be threatening to those who are not yet used to it. This threat may be overcome over time, but initially it could be a concern for many.

2. There is the fear of being replaced by machines. We are used to projecting ourselves as particular persons when teaching, and so the handing over our knowledge to machines may be threatening to some of us.
3. Digitalization is sometimes introduced by the leaders and managers of institutions (the bureaucrats), and this may come about as part of the managerial approach to the running of education institutions. Some academics may feel alienated by this and develop a negative attitude to digitalization.

Challenges for students: Many students who are savvy at the use of technology may rejoice at the virtual approach to learning. There are obvious advantages such as reduced fees as well as reduced travel costs and time. For adult students with families, these and other factors may be real attractions. There are some challenges and disadvantages, however. The following are some of them:

1. The university is not only a place of learning. It is also a place of socialization, not only for students in residence but even for those who commute from home to university throughout the week. A student meets fellow students, participates in various social and sporting activities and has the university library available to them throughout the day. Some even meet future marriage partners at university. With online teaching and digitalization the socialization and other dimensions of university life are missing.
2. Part of learning takes place when students exchange ideas – and this is partly why group work is regarded as important in the pedagogy presented in this book. A student studying alone at home is deprived of this advantage.
3. Some of the participants in the OBREAL-Global programme referred to above noted that student participation becomes less in virtual contact. This is also related to the absence of eye-to-eye contact between lecturer and students. The absence of this eye-to-eye contact reduces the desire to participate on the part of some students.
4. At least one participant from Ireland reported how he noted grief on the part of international students who had gone to Ireland expecting to meet fellow students from Ireland and mixing with Irish people in 2020 but found themselves isolated because of Covid-19.
5. Some participants in the OBREAL-Global programme expressed the view that employability can be a problem for a student educated virtually.
6. Some students, and this is true of some African students known to this writer, come from homes that are crowded – where there is not much space for private learning. For such students, the advantage of a good learning environment in a university is lost.

Some proposed solutions

So far in this chapter we have mostly dealt with the challenges to the university as a global institution. Little has been said about the specific challenges that face African universities and other universities from some former colonies in other parts of the world. These need to be given particular attention as they operate in an environment that is significantly different from similar institutions in places like Europe, America, Australia and China. This will be done in the next part of this chapter. For the university as a global institution the following and other solutions were proposed by the participants at the two events referred to above:

1. Considering that digitalization will be with us post-Covid-19, the overall solution is to have blended education, with some modules presented by way of digitalization and others on the basis of face-to-face teaching and learning. Each institution will have to decide the proportion of each mode, but in the view of this writer, ideally 50 per cent of the courses or modules should be taught face to face when Covid-19 is behind us. In this way students will benefit from the advantages of each of the two modes.
2. There is a need for institutions to have responsibility for skilling and reskilling staff. Because most staff in our era were trained to teach face to face and digitalisation has been imposed upon us as an emergency measure in many institutions, there is a need for universities to budget for the reskilling of staff. This is where the establishment of university teaching and learning centres in HEIs becomes a necessity. These centres are necessary partly because many academics have not been trained to teach. The acquisition of a PhD or even master's degree in a particular area of specialization is regarded as the qualification for one to teach students at degree level, but knowledge of a subject is not necessarily a guarantee that one can teach the subject well. The other reason why reskilling is necessary is the need for lifelong learning. We live in a fast-changing world; and if we are to remain effective in our respective fields of operation, we must accept the need to continue learning and updating our knowledge and ways of doing things.
3. As far as students are concerned, the practice of attachments to industry is now more necessary than ever. There seems to be a disjuncture between what employers need and the education that universities generally provide. To bridge this gap, students should as far as possible be exposed to working environments before they complete their degree studies. A good practice that was practised at the former University of Natal (now the University of KwaZulu-Natal) was to have some part-time lecturers from industry in Engineering and related fields. This gives students the opportunity for exposure to lecturers who are not just theoreticians but also speak from real experience of what industry needs.

As CEO of the Zimbabwe Council for Higher Education this writer brought together academics and representatives of the captains of industry with a view to developing a systematic approach to university–industry relationships. The idea was that not only would the representatives of industry inform the design of curricula but that the attachments of students to industry would be done in a systematic way. Unfortunately the economy of that country does not presently allow a vibrant approach to industry attachments. Covid-19 makes the situation worse, but this is an approach that institutions could pursue post-Covid-19.

4. One solution this author has learnt from Indian specialists is that while the teaching of courses could be online, the examinations should be based on the contact approach.

Some special challenges to universities in former colonies – with special reference to sub-Saharan Africa

While the challenges explained in the previous section apply generally to all HEIs, there are certain challenges for institutions located in former colonies. The challenges may not be exactly the same everywhere. For example, India seems to have developed a system that is in some ways superior to the systems of certain regions. There is also reason to suggest that the higher education system of a country like Egypt is in some ways superior to the systems of many sub-Saharan African countries. Furthermore some of South Africa's universities regularly perform better on the international scale than the universities in the majority of other sub-Saharan African countries. Be that as it may, while universities like the University of Cape Town, Stellenbosch University, the University of KwaZulu-Natal and the University of Pretoria are better resourced and perform better in the area of research, they share some of the problems that universities in sub-Saharan Africa face. Among other things, both students and some African academics have questioned the character of the South African university that was shaped not only by the colonial legacy but also by the apartheid system which created a differentiated system along racial and tribal lines with some English-language universities, some Afrikaans-language universities and special institutions for Indians, Coloureds, and different African ethnic groups such as the Zulu, the Xhosa, the Sotho, Tswana and so on.

The main argument raised in the immediately preceding paragraph has to do with the issue of the context of the university and the context of education generally. Educationists are beginning to be aware of the need to see educational leadership in the context of the particular group of schools or universities. Thus part IV of Bush et al. (2019) is dedicated to educational leadership and context. As indicated in earlier chapters of this book, this author published a book entitled *The African University and Its Mission* (Ngara 1995) in which an attempt was made to sensitize those who run HEIs to be aware of the need to develop a university tradition that was sensitive to the needs of African countries and students. The problem here is that traditionally there has essentially been one epistemology developed in the West and consequently the accepted conventions governing the content and organization of knowledge in African institutions of higher education were based wholly on the Western tradition. The reason for this is partly the origins of the African university which is narrated in Ajayi et al. (1996).

In British sub-Saharan Africa, a good number of the prominent colleges such as Ibadan, Khartoum University College, Makerere and the University College of Rhodesia and Nyasaland (now the University of Zimbabwe) were colleges of the University of London while Fourah Bay in Sierra Leone was affiliated to the University of Durham. In order to maintain good standards, the staff of the University of London Special Relationships Colleges were to approach London with proposals for adapting London external degree syllabuses; the examination papers as well as the scripts and so on were vetted by London. The authors of *The African Experience with Higher Education* go on to say while there was theoretically an adaptation process, 'in practice, the emphasis was on transplantation, not adaptation' (see Ajayi et al. 1996: 55–6). As for the French and Belgians, there was no need to think about adaptation: 'The emphasis was not on the possibility of adaptation but on the provision of higher education identical in quality and content with that provided in France or Belgium' (ibid.: 56). The problem here was while all this could have been well meant, the colonial universities were intended to train an elite that was eventually meant to replace the colonial masters in exploiting the people; the curricula were narrow and unrelated to the culture and lives of the people; and the institutions were veritable ivory towers. As for South Africa, Africans were originally not admitted into the well-established universities such as Cape Town, the University of the Witwatersrand (Wits) and Natal, let alone in Afrikaans-language universities, but were restricted to Bantustan university colleges of UNISA such as the then University College of Zululand for Zulu people (now the University of Zululand) and the University College of the North for the Sotho-Tsonga and Venda (now the University of Limpopo). Even Fort Hare, the pride of the African people which was created before the apartheid system, was reserved for the Xhosa and Sotho of Ciskei (Ajayi et al. 1996: 71–2). The English-language universities such as Cape Town, Natal and Wits started admitting Blacks in a segregated fashion (ibid.). All these institutions were controlled by Whites and were therefore removed from the true traditions and culture of the African people.

In the independent African countries, some universities began to introduce innovations that were intended to reflect African realities such as the following:

1. Putting Africa at the centre in such subjects as literature and history
2. Setting up strong departments of African languages
3. Including Development Studies as a discipline
4. Including oral traditions in the teaching of literature
5. Including Ancient Egypt as part of African history
6. Including Ancient Egyptian literature in literature syllabuses
7. Changing the structure and content of the English syllabus to include not only African literature but the literature of the diaspora, as well as British literature and some European and Chinese literature
8. Including creative writing, drama and media studies as areas of specialization

There were some innovations in the areas of governance and leadership as well, and these are efforts that some South African universities could learn from. However, if the African university wants to seriously engage in decoloniality, the process of undoing colonialism, neo-colonialism and underdevelopment, it needs to do more serious work. This writer has learnt something from some of the successful Eastern countries such as Japan and China. For instance, the development of China from a backward nation to the new China whose economy is perhaps the second in the world was based on Marxism or socialism, but the Communist Party of China made sure it was socialism with Chinese characteristics. Similarly, there is nothing wrong in Africa developing the idea of a university from Europe, but the concept should have been like the Chinese model – the idea of the African university as an institution with African characteristics. What this means is that the African university should be one that reflects its African context by being a socially responsible institution that shows its relationship to African culture and its concern for solving African problems. The following are examples of how this could be done:

1. African indigenous knowledge systems should be a prominent part of the epistemology, and African universities should be the specialists on Africa.
2. Philosophies like the *Utu/Ubuntu* philosophy should inform the culture and practice of the university.
3. Leadership is a big issue on the continent because of the failure of many politicians to lead their countries to genuine independence and freedom. Consequently, not only should Leadership be an important discipline, but examples like the Mutapas and Moshoeshoe I should be used to develop good leaders for tomorrow.
4. Furthermore, the principles of *Ubuntu* which emphasize the importance of the group or community over the individual could be used in reward systems

such as the recognition of excellence in research. Group research could be encouraged and promoted rather than the present practice that puts so much emphasis on individuals. It is reasonable to argue that the present reward system in African universities is fully in support of the Western individualistic approach to life summarized in Latin by the French philosopher, Rene Descartes (1596–1650), who coined the expression *Cogito ergo sum* 'I think therefore I am'. As explained in Chapter 5, this is the very opposite of the philosophy of *Utu/Ubuntu* as expressed in the statement *Umuntu ngumuntu ngabantu*, which in Zulu means 'A person is a person because of other people', and is succinctly expressed by the Shona expression *Ndiri nokuti tiri* 'I am because we are'. The emphasis here is on the recognition that a human being is a social being who cannot survive on his or her own. The African university should ideally promote this idea of community and plurality in its reward system.

5. In the areas of governance and leadership, the vice chancellor, the faculty or college dean and the chairperson of department or head of school could be guided by the shared leadership style of Moshoeshoe I and by traditional practices such as *Umhlangano* (Zulu), *Khotla* (Sotho) and *Dare* (Shona), all of which emphasize the importance of discussion groups, resulting in interactive collaborative leadership.

An important point we are making here is that the African university as the top academic institution of African countries should not only play a leading and significant role in developing a new crop of African leaders of tomorrow but should also strive to shape a unique African academic culture and project itself as the specialist in things African. This would be an attraction to Western and other academics desirous of knowing the African approach to knowledge, education and leadership. As things stand at the moment, there may not be much that attracts students and academics from other continents to come to many sub-Saharan African countries (except, perhaps, for countries like South Africa, Kenya, Rwanda and a few others). A further drawback is that many African universities are poorly funded and do not have the resources that one is likely to find in a Western university or the best of universities in places like India and South America.

In view of the picture painted above, the worldwide factors discussed earlier are likely to bring further problems for the majority of African HEIs. With regard to Covid-19, Mohamedbhai (University World News, 9 April 2020) has pointed out that granted it is true that while the crisis has provided all HEIs with the opportunity to improve and maximize their ICT operations, the majority of universities in Africa 'do not have the capacity to fully deliver whole programmes online'. Globalization is likely to be another form of neo-colonialism with all the ideas being shaped from the West. Internationalization could also see African learners merely consuming the knowledge and ideas developed in the West. This further aggravates the development of an African middle class that is divorced from African traditions, values and realities.

An important consideration, as already indicated, is that the African university should not only play a key role in developing the African leaders of tomorrow and in shaping a unique African academic culture but should be a driver of economic innovation and the specialist in the production and implementation of knowledge relating to Africa. Unfortunately, as Eric Fredua-Kwarteng (University World News, 1 May 2021) has pointed out, in part quoting Mohamedbhai and other researchers, the quantity and quality of doctoral degree holders in Africa is low, due to such factors as inadequate funding, poor supervision, a poor research environment and even poor master's degree programmes. This negatively affects the research capacity of many African universities with the exception of top South African universities such as the University of Cape Town, the University of Witwatersrand, Stellenbosch University and the University of KwaZulu-Natal. But even these top universities are operating within a wholly Western paradigm and have not yet embarked on a transformative agenda to create an institution which is uniquely African and can effectively speak to African realities. Consequently Hoppers and Richards (2011: 89) have found it necessary and appropriate to state, 'In both knowledge production and high-level human resource production, the university in Africa has not been cognizant of any need for (or prepared for) rethinking the basic software and hardware of its system.'

Conclusion

What this chapter has shown is the following: First, while nationally higher education is affected by policies and practices at the macro level, there are also influences from outside the particular country, which I call 'supra-macro' factors or influences. In former colonies the university is strongly influenced by the former colonial powers. Globally two major factors have impacted higher education everywhere: globalization and Covid-19. The more recent factor, Covid-19, has had a major impact on the nature of the university and on approaches to teaching and learning. This was unplanned but was imposed upon education institutions by the pandemic which took the whole world by storm. Globalization, which has been with us with greater effect since the beginning of the twentieth century, has brought about a situation in terms of which the individual identities of countries and cultures, and consequently of institutions, have been eroded, with the whole world being shaped by technology, news agencies and the internet, with the effect of rapidly reducing distances between countries and continents. A global culture is emerging which favours all who have been educated to cope with the skill of handling technology and communicating in the English language. These can work in most parts of the world because for them the world has indeed become a global village. From an African perspective this global culture is not a neutral culture. Catherine Odora Hoppers and Howard Richards (2011: 7) have succinctly put it this way: 'In late 20th century parlance, the West is constituted as the "international community."' Covid-19 has dramatically accelerated the globalization process by facilitating digitalization and online teaching, and consequently making the world even smaller. I believe it is John Wesley who is supposed to have declared, 'The whole world is my parish.' Today the university professor can truthfully declare, 'The whole world is my classroom.' This has meant collaboration between institutions in far distant countries, regions and continents has become possible. However, these developments have brought about problems for institutions, lecturers and students, as has been explained.

The epistemology that dominates the world is based on experiences, ideas and philosophies of the West. This means the universities in former colonies, and in places like sub-Sharan Africa in particular, are producing graduates who suffer from the malaise of coloniality, who are Western in orientation, do not have enough knowledge of their own people's history and indigenous knowledge systems and consequently inadvertently participate in the erosion of their own people's good traditions and practices. Some of them who rise to political power become oppressors, as bad as, or at times even worse than, the former colonial rulers. A further problem is because of the poor economies in which they operate, many of the institutions become poor copycats of their Western counterparts, without enough resources to compete globally in knowledge production. Part of the reason for the poor performance of African institutions is because many of the best African minds ironically find themselves on the staff of Western universities because there is not enough freedom of expression in their own countries of birth.

A new awareness

While many of the products of the university in many former colonies suffer from the malaise of coloniality, there is now a new and rising awareness of the importance of indigenous knowledge systems as sources of knowledge, information and wisdom, not only for the people of Africa, Asia and non-European peoples of the American continent but also for Westerners. There is a rising awareness that the Western tradition alone is not enough to solve the problems of the world. There is a new realization that much can be learned by understanding the ideas and philosophies of Africans, Japanese, Chinese, Hopi and other non-Western ethnic groups. There is much that can be learned from these so-called 'non-traditional sources' about the world, about humanity, medicine, education, leadership and other areas of human endeavour. Earlier in this book we learned about the leadership principles of Isao Yoshino's Japanese principles as Toyota leader; we referred to Ngulube (2017) in which Rutendo Ngara (2017) discusses a dialogue between African, Chinese and Western medical systems; we can add to this another important collection of articles on indigenous knowledge systems (Hoppers 2002). Writing about indigenous knowledge intelligence (IKI) Alexander Maune (2017) in Ngulube (2017: 173–97) points out, 'The use of IKI systems has been considered by many to be *a*n alternative way that promotes development in poor rural communities in many parts of the world especially in developing nations.' By citing Israel I am by no means intending to get involved in the conflict between the state of Israel and its neighbours but to emphasize the importance of indigenous knowledge systems in development. Says Maune (ibid.: 174), 'Israel has been identified as a perfect example of a nation that has developed through the observance of its oral tradition, that is, the Talmud (Oral Torah).'

Once again by using the example of China, I am not necessarily suggesting that I agree with all its policies, but I wish to restate the point made earlier that China and Japan can be cited as nations that have not excluded ideas from the West in their development efforts but have ensured the incorporation of their traditions in their development strategies. In an earlier chapter, we cited the *New World Encyclopaedia* (2012) as saying knowledge of the Mutapa Empire, a traditional African society, built up through commerce more so than conquest, can help construct a balanced story of where, when and how human societies have flourished. This is knowledge that is useful, not only for Africans who should learn lessons from their own ancestors but also for all people of good will who wish to see the world developing in a balanced and non-exploitative manner.

Education institutions are the factories where the leaders of tomorrow are nurtured and developed. Unfortunately, those of us who are involved in the profession of education have not sufficiently taken upon ourselves the responsibility for educating society about the true purpose of education. We have not taken seriously the United Nations Sustainable Development Goal 4 which in part states, 'By 2030, ensure equal access for all women and men to affordable and quality technical, vocational and tertiary education, including university' (SDG 4.3). It could be argued that the policies and practices of education institutions are developed at the macro level, and educational leaders may not have the power to change such policies and practices. As Howard Stephenson and other scholars (Bush et al. 2019: 285) have pointed out, educational leaders occupy a 'contested space' in which they have the task of 'making sense' of the external environment as they lead institutions. A response to this is that a major quality of leadership is the ability to influence. What this means is that educational leaders must develop a clear vision of what the education system should be about and use their power as visionaries to influence those who sit in high offices to change their views. This leads to the issue of leadership training.

The need for training and for a new vision

If we take into account all the issues and themes analysed and discussed in this chapter, we should be able to see that there is a real need for those who are involved in university education to be trained in their trade. As already explained, it is no longer enough for a lecturer to acquire a degree in his or her area of specialization. The university teacher needs to be trained. As argued before, this should be an important function of university teaching and learning centres. But it is not only professors and lecturers who should be trained. Those who are responsible for running institutions and parts of institutions should also be trained. Vice chancellors, deputy vice chancellors, deans of faculties and even heads or chairpersons of department should be trained in how to play their leadership roles effectively and efficiently. There is also a new consideration: In view of the complexity of the mission of the university; in view of the need to build a new world based not just on one epistemology, one approach to knowledge, namely the Western epistemology; in view of the complications of globalization, Covid-19 and the necessity for internationalization; and in view of the realization that the world can learn much from different cultures, there is a compelling need to reconsider the content of a university degree and ways to present that content. It is the burden of the next two and closing chapters of this book to tackle these two issues.

14

Leadership development at meso level

Tuning in Exercise

Read the following story and answer the questions that follow:

Professor Sefale had taught at one of South Africa's Historically Black Institutions (HBIs) before he was forced to quit the country because of his involvement in liberation struggle politics. He went overseas where he specialized in Development Economics and Higher Education Studies and then worked for an international organization before the transition to democracy in South Africa. As 'Talks about Talks' began to progress after Nelson Mandela's release from prison, Professor Sefale was able to go back to South Africa where he was appointed vice chancellor of one of the HBIs. He was not an eloquent speaker, and in fact had a stammer in his speech. However, the new Black vice chancellor proved to be a very astute and competent leader. At first, the predominantly white staff of the university did not give him much respect, but less than one year into the job there were clear signs of a turnaround in the development of the university. Among other things, the institution's financial situation began to show signs of improvement. He had a fatherly but firm attitude towards students in terms of making sure they paid their fees while at the same time fighting for the poorest students to get financial aid. A dean of research was appointed to improve the research profile of the university, and some competent Black academics were appointed from both South Africa and independent African countries to replace White professors as heads of department. What was also interesting was that the vice chancellor made a point of having a coach who advised him on how to lead and manage. Soon after the change over to the democratic dispensation in the country, Professor Sefale was given a very high government position and had to resign as vice chancellor of the university.

After Professor Sefale's departure, Professor Tom Tau was appointed. In terms of his fame as an academic, Professor Tau had a far more prestigious reputation than Professor Sefale. For one thing, he had been Professor of Robotics and Informatics at a top American university. Not many Blacks on the whole continent could boast of such an achievement. True to his fame and reputation, Professor Tau was impressive during the interview. He had the gift of the garb and he painted a vision of the university which left the members of the Selection Committee agape with signs of wonder at this luminary who seemed to hail from a superior planet than Mother Earth. The student members of the committee were swept off their feet by this Black man's mastery of the English language and by his populist views on how he was going to relate to students. This was a vice chancellor whom Black people could be truly proud of, and by his interview performance, he overshadowed the fame the stammering Sefale had earned as a competent leader.

But not long after Professor Tau took up his position, it began to show he was not the person he had claimed to be. He continued with the tradition his predecessor had initiated of appointing Blacks to important positions, except that this time it was the vice chancellor's tribesmen and friends who were appointed. In appointing these he did not go through the consultation process that his predecessor had followed. As in other areas of university life, the choices were made dictatorially. He began a restructuring process of the institution – again without proper consultation. Council members began to complain that the vice chancellor was now taking over the responsibilities of the chairman of Council and even of the Council itself. He continued with his declared populist approach to the management of students – except that students were now experiencing more problems with financial aid. What was more, the Council began to raise issues about the financial status of the university and the way finances were managed. Students started demonstrating against the vice chancellor and what they referred to as 'his cronies'. Senior staff, both white and black, began to leave the university for other institutions. The situation was so bad the government appointed an assessor who recommended the appointment of an administrator to lead and manage the institution. At this point Professor Tom Tau resigned and returned to the United States to teach Robotics.

Questions

1. What does the performance of Professor Tom Tau as vice chancellor show about the interviewing process that is sometimes followed in the appointment of senior university personnel?
2. Do the two vice chancellors show something about the importance of training for people who hold senior positions?
3. With reference to the story of the two vice chancellors, comment on the difference between academic performance and leading a university.

Some international perspectives on the characteristics and development of senior university personnel

We begin with a snapshot view of vice chancellors and deans in the international community. First, an example of the roles and functions of the vice chancellor: On the internet, the vice chancellor of the University of Cambridge in the UK is described as 'the principal academic and administrative officer of the University'. The following are listed as some of the key tasks of the vice chancellor:

- Provide leadership, academic and administrative, to the whole university
- Represent the university externally, both within the UK and overseas
- Secure a financial base sufficient to allow the delivery of the university's mission, aims and objectives
- Carry out certain important ceremonial and civic duties

It is now a common practice in Europe, America and Africa to mount training programmes for vice chancellors and deans. Professor Paul Zaleza, vice chancellor of the United States International University – Africa (USIU), Nairobi, Kenya, is quoted as having given the following as the key roles of principals and deans in his opening speech at a leadership and management training programme for university principals and deans:

1. To manage the different sectors of the faculty (staff) effectively
2. To provide leadership by having a vision
3. Advocacy through connecting the top and lower management
4. To be the voice and face of the institution (RUFORUM Communication, 3 November, 2017)

There is now quite a lot of literature on deans. In terms of the functions of a dean and the characteristics that go with those functions, these are discussed in detail by, among other scholars, Margo B. Greicar (2009) and Oliver Seale (2015). Here we shall make special mention of the seven dimensions of dean leadership as identified by Heck et al. (2000). The dimensions are discussed in detail by Greicar (2009). We list them here with very brief explanations that show what are said to be the essential characteristics of a dean:

1. Vision and goal setting (the ability to articulate strategic goals for the unit, i.e. faculty or college)

2. Management of an academic affairs unit (the ability to manage the various aspects of the unit – including staff and funds – and to execute the duties with fairness and sound judgement)
3. Interpersonal relationships (the ability to handle staff and students with fairness and to deal with relationships outside the faculty/college)
4. Communication skills (this entails good communication with all concerned – staff, students and relevant officials outside the faculty)
5. Professional development, research and institutional endeavours (this includes the ability to perform one's academic functions and to promote a culture of research and other activities of the faculty such as community service and contact with professional and other relevant bodies)
6. Quality education in the unit (the ability to promote and maintain quality in the programmes of the faculty/college and in the appointment of staff and so on)
7. Support for institutional diversity (among other things, this has to do with managing diversity, advancing the employment of women, ensuring support for the needs of people with disability, promoting equal employment opportunities and so on)

The European Business Review (10 June 2020) lists the following as 'The Seven Essential Qualities in a Great Dean':

1. Leadership
2. Decision making
3. Empathy
4. Communication skills
5. Adaptability
6. Punctuality
7. Innovation

The article makes the valid point that academic deans serve both as academics and administrators. Consequently, 'A great dean empowers their students, sets a congenial environment, and ensures that their faculty and students have the required resources to succeed.'

The information given in this section of the chapter is very valuable. It is relevant for the training of vice chancellors and deans in both developed and developing countries. Some modifications may need to be made in a particular context, but it would be unfortunate for any university anywhere to ignore some of the information, in particular the seven dimensions of a dean identified by Heck et al. (2000). Furthermore, there is more wisdom that is offered by training organizations such as the German Academic Exchange Service (DAAD), the Institute of Leadership and

Management (ILM) in the UK, Higher Education South Africa (HESA), the Southern African Regional Universities Association (SARUA) and the Association of African Universities, among a host of others. The question that arises, then, is: What else can be said about the training of senior university personnel? What else does *Learning to Lead for Transformation* have to offer that is of value?

Proposed characteristics of some senior university personnel

This book presents an approach to the development of educational leaders that is based on a number of principles:

> First, a combination of two disciplines each of which is presented in some detail as a discipline: Leadership in its generic (general) sense and Educational Leadership.
> Second, an African perspective on leadership and learning is presented.
> Third, to the African perspective is added some insights from Japanese culture.

The concept of leadership characteristics and leadership development is informed by these principles.

For the reasons explained below in the section on *Programmes*, we shall outline the leadership characteristics and/or the training requirements of three levels of university leaders: the vice chancellor, the academic dean and the president of the Student Representative Council (SRC) together with his/her team, starting with the vice chancellor. What are the desirable characteristics of a vice chancellor that we would aim to develop with the programmes presented in this chapter?

Desirable characteristics of a vice chancellor

The following are *some* of the desirable characteristics of the leader of an academic institution:

1. The ideal vice chancellor is a person of vision as explained in Chapters 8 and 10. He/she has 'the ability to see in a way that compels others to pay attention' (Eskelin 2001: 39). He/she knows how to develop and communicate his/her dream of the desired future state of the institution.
2. A person of influence, who influences through both leading and learning, and can positively influence staff, students, government officials, the captains of industry and international organizations and institutions.

3. A role model who inspires others as a result of his/her integrity, courage, tenacity and commitment to the ideals of the organization and boldly pursues a course of action because he/she is convinced that even if the idea is unpopular, it is in the best interests of the organisation – but demonstrates boldness without being reckless.
4. A person of action who ensures the execution of all decisions taken.
5. A nationalist and an internationalist who is aware of and respects some of the key and wise traditions and practices of his/her people that do not violate his/her conscience but who also recognizes what is good in other cultures of the world and is prepared to make good use of those positive elements of foreign cultures for the benefit of his/her institution.
6. A strategist who is capable of reconciling apparently contradictory elements: the local and the international; the traditional and the modern; the autonomy of the university versus the need for accountability to the state and the community; the interests of students versus those of academics; the mission and academic pursuits of the university versus the requirements for efficiency and effectiveness.
7. A person skilled in the securing and managing of the finances of the university and is a scrupulous man or woman of integrity who does not tolerate corrupt practices in the management of the finances and the administration of the institution in such areas as student admission and the marking and grading of student assignments and examination scripts.
8. In terms of the leadership examples studied in this book, the vice chancellor is a Mutapa-Moshoeshoe-Isao Yoshino figure:
    a. As a Mutapa, the vice chancellor knows she must build a stable state which thrives economically at home and has international linkages with other countries which help to strengthen that economy. As a vice chancellor, she seeks international linkages partly based on what her institution can offer the international partners in terms of innovations and research into, and knowledge of, local traditions, indigenous knowledge systems and local development issues. As a Mutapa, she strives to protect the autonomy and independence of the university to the extent possible under modern governance arrangements, just as the Mutapa strove to protect the independence of the state against invasions by the Portuguese and other foreign powers. Like the Mutapa, she should be prepared to work while others are resting – working to solve the problems brought to her by the people. Like the Mutapa, she should be strategic enough to endear herself to the people (the general staff and students) and the provincial governors (such as the deans) so much so that the people build houses without doors because they have confidence in the protection of the ruler; so also the vice chancellor should endeavour to develop

a spirit of responsible freedom of speech among academics who have confidence in the vice chancellor's resolve to protect responsible freedom of expression.

b. As a Moshoeshoe, the vice chancellor should seek to solve the problems of the various groups in the university by holding *pitsos* (public gatherings) where the people are free to express their concerns and to advise their leader. As suggested in a recent paper (Ngara 2021) the vice chancellor could hold special *pitsos* (Sesotho) or *imbizos* (Zulu) for academic staff, for administrative staff, for workers and for students as well as a general *pitso*, and let the various members of the university feel free that what is said responsibly at a *pitso* or *imbizo* goes unpunished. Like Moshoeshoe the vice chancellor would do well to practice interactive collaborative leadership in terms of which relevant issues affecting the university are discussed with senior administrators, academics, workers and students at *pitsos* before they are brought to Senate and Council. As a Moshoeshoe the vice chancellor should strive to protect the identity and integrity of the university by forging strategic alliances in government circles and elsewhere, just as Moshoeshoe was prepared to seek the protection of the British in order to ensure the survival and independence of the nation of Lesotho.

c. As a Yoshino, the vice chancellor should respect indigenous culture and good traditions while prepared to learn from foreign cultures. And like Yoshino, the vice chancellor should respect his/her own language while eager to master useful foreign languages. As a Yoshino, the vice chancellor should learn to understand and act on 'the fabric concept', identifying the vertical warp (the dream that remains unchanged) and the horizontal weft threads (the experiences we encounter through the course of life which, when woven together with the warp threads, make us who we are). As a Yoshino the vice chancellor should practice the habit of *hansei*, the process of self-reflection and self-awareness which supports personal mastery, helps her/him to grow as a solid leader and facilitates her/his growth as a *sensei* (a wise leader) or a *Mwalimu* 'the teacher' as Julius Nyerere of Tanzania was popularly called. *Hansei* is 'purposeful, honest self-reflection' that 'can help us make better decisions and can allow us to lead ourselves and others more effectively' (Anderson 2020: 25).

As a Yoshino, the vice chancellor would do well to learn the foundational leadership principles of Toyota, three of which are the following:

Lesson 1: 'Communicate Purpose, Every Day and in Every Way' This creates the 'management by collective wisdom' that John Adair (2003: 211–12) recognized in Kunosuke Matsushita. 'Every day' does not have to be every single day in the case of a vice chancellor, and could be periodically.

Lesson 4: 'Go to See and Show You Care – Leadership Starts at the Gemba'

Go and see what is actually happening in the various workplaces. This is to some extent equivalent to what in the West has been called 'management by walking about' but as an elevated concept intended to make people feel they are important. As Yoshino states (Anderson 2020: 100), 'Going to Gemba makes people feel like they are important.' The vice chancellor could make it a point to occasionally visit a faculty dean, some heads of department, some lessons in progress and the student union.

Lesson 8: 'Set the Tone for the Culture You Want'

As explained in Chapter 11, changing organizational culture is a key aspect of transformation, and 'you change the culture of an organisation by changing the behaviour of its leaders' (Bossidy & Charan 2011: 105–6). According to Yoshino, the leader changes organizational culture by helping people to change. He narrates the fascinating story of how Toyota opted for a joint venture with General Motors (GM) in America and formed a company called New United Motor Manufacturing, Inc., abbreviated NUMMI. Now NUMMI sounds like 'new me'. This gave Toyota the opportunity to teach its own culture to American workers. It was an opportunity 'to inspire each person to improve and create a "new me"' with both employees and leaders striving to do their very best (Anderson 2020: 159–60). A partnership between an African university and a university based in Europe or America could result in a situation in which the university from the developed country could find itself learning and appreciating the humanizing culture of *Utu/Ubuntu*.

Related to the example just cited is an important Japanese principle which, together with 'Continuous Improvement', forms the two pillars of the 'Toyota Way'. This is the principle of 'Respect for People'. Respect for People in turn consists of two principles:

Respect: which leads to the building of mutual trust with people motivated to take responsibility.

Teamwork: which stimulates personal and professional growth and the maximizing of both individual and team performance. The beauty of this is that it resonates with the philosophy of *Ubuntu*. One of the principles of *Ubuntu* is respect for other human beings: One becomes their real self in relation to others, just as in the Japanese principle teamwork stimulates personal and professional growth: 'You become you because of we.' As explained earlier, there is a Shona expression which succinctly expresses the principle of *Ubuntu*: *Ndiri nokuti tiri* 'I am because we are'. You become a better performer in relation to others. By respecting others the vice chancellor sets the tone for staff and students of the university learning to respect one another.

Desirable characteristics of the academic dean

The ideal dean should have the characteristics or be able to meet the requirements set out below:

1. The characteristics outlined above, and especially the seven dimensions identified by Heck et al. (2000).
2. In terms of the philosophy of higher education presented in this book, the dean needs to have both a philosophy and strategy for the academic development of her/his faculty or college and an awareness of the challenges facing the university in the context of globalization, Covid-19, internationalization and the dissonance between the prevailing Western epistemology and the need to recognize IKS and the wisdom of the intelligences from the so-called 'non-traditional sources' which amount to a combination of some advanced Eastern countries and the cultures of the peoples of the developing countries in continents like Africa, Asia and the Middle East as well as groups in Australasia and the Americas such as the Hopi and the Maori.
3. The great dean is a leader with a vision that helps the faculty/college to develop a vision that is in line with, and advances, the institutional vision.
4. As an academic leader the dean should be aware of the teaching/learning philosophy advocated in this book and other relevant literature. He/she should facilitate in his/her faculty/college an awareness of the new teaching and learning challenges presented by Covid-19 and lead the faculty in developing a strategy for coping with them and maximizing on the opportunities presented by the challenges.
5. On the technical side, the dean should have knowledge of the technicalities related to the Credit Accumulation and Transfer System of her/his country or region and be able to facilitate the correct implementation of the system. In this regard, it is helpful to have a senior officer in the faculty (ideally a deputy dean) who is a specialist in the system and is knowledgeable enough to assist both staff and students in the implementation of the system. As faculty tutor (equivalent to deputy dean) in both Lesotho and Swaziland (Eswatini) this writer got to know how essential it was to have a senior person who could guide students in relation to the combination of modules and credits in a programme.
6. Following the Institutional Transformation workshop proposed in the next section, it would be ideal to have a faculty/college workshop aimed at ensuring the faculty plays its role effectively in the transformation process and in improving the quality of both the programmes and products (graduates) of the faculty, as well as the spirit of service to students.

Developing the ideal student leader

A university official whose training is not easy to handle is the president of the Students' Representative Council (SRC). Many universities do not even consider it important for her/him to be trained. There are also problems in running a leadership development programme for the president of the SRC. He/she is a popularly elected official. If he/she is seen being taken aside for training by either a university official or a specialist from outside the university, they could be seen to be taken aside in order for them to betray the students' cause. The best thing to do is to run a programme for the members of the SRC as a group. At times it may be necessary to include leaders of clubs and societies in the leadership development programme. This could be done by having special sessions to which committee members of clubs and societies are invited. A point to note here is that a university cannot expect to have a ready-made student leader with all the desirable characteristics, especially at undergraduate level. First, there is no likelihood of any student leader to have been sufficiently developed for leadership at high school level; and second, university authorities do not normally decide who is going to be a member of the SRC, as the election is done by the student body. It is therefore incumbent upon the university to develop student leaders with desirable characteristics. This leads to my own experience (the author of this book) with student leadership development.

When I was given responsibility for students and transformation in 1998 as a deputy vice chancellor of the former University of Natal (now the University of KwaZulu-Natal) I found out that when a new SRC was elected, an orientation workshop was held for the members in which they were informed about student governance. I changed that to a leadership and governance course for the student leaders. This entailed bringing together student leaders from the then four campuses of the university: Howard College in Durban (then the headquarters of the university), Pietermaritzburg Campus, in Pietermaritzburg, the Medical School in Durban and Edgewood College for teachers in Pinetown. (The Westville Campus was still an independent university for Indian people – the former University of Durban Westville). First, the students enjoyed coming together and learning about student leadership and governance. Second, the relationship between the student leaders and the deputy vice chancellor, and consequently between student leaders and the university executive team, became less formal. The students could relate to the deputy vice chancellor as someone they could talk to informally and even enjoy light drinks with, not as someone sitting in a high office in the main administration block. That kind of relationship enhances opportunities for solving student problems without the students resorting to protests and violence.

The idea in a student leadership development course is not only to develop the leadership potential and skills of these future leaders but also to help them see they are part of the university, not customers. In order for students to see themselves as part of the university, they need to be involved in the life and activities of the university, not only in student politics. They need to be involved in faculty and departmental boards, getting to know about debates that relate to the development of programmes. They need to be actively involved in the university's community services and in university committees such as Senate and Council. They need to develop a deeper sense of responsibility for student activities and for the needs of the various categories of students, including female students and those with disabilities. In the student leadership development course, student leaders need to have time to reflect on, and to debate and discuss, relevant issues and topics. In this regard a student leadership development programme could be a two- to three-day programme covering the following topics:

1. Leadership, management and student governance
2. Personal Leadership Development, with a focus on:
   - Finding your mission and developing a personal mission statement
   - Team leadership
   - Self-awareness and leadership qualities
3. The mission, vision and structure of the university
4. The role of students in the structures of the university, for example, departmental and faculty boards, Senate and Council
5. Student leadership representation in matters to do with teaching and learning
6. Financial management with special reference to SRC finances and the finances of clubs and societies
7. The role of student leaders in the areas of health facilities for students; transport; sports; the interests and challenges of differently abled students (i.e. students with disability); female students; student counselling; and accommodation issues and off-campus students
8. Relationships with academics, the executive and workers
9. Testimonials on such topics as 'The Great Leader I Know' and 'The Leader I Would Like to Be'

Programmes for educational leaders

In this part of the chapter we refer to kinds of training programmes that may be available for certain categories of university personnel and other educational leaders. There is no intention to propose an actual course as such but to show an indication of the principles involved and some of the key elements that such a programme might contain. We make a distinction between degree/diploma programmes and short courses.

A master's or diploma in Educational Leadership

For a master's or diploma in Educational Leadership, this book could work as the compulsory text or one of two key texts complimented by some modules in Education as indicated below. A book that could serve as a supplementary text in addition to *Learning to Lead for Transformation* is Bush et al. (2019) *Principles of Educational Leadership and Management* (Sage). The purpose of the supplementary book would be to add to and enrich the Leadership and Educational Leadership components that are covered in this book. Two other books could be added as recommended resource books with specific chapters being recommended for students to read. These are: Paulo Freire, *Pedagogy of the Oppressed* (Penguin); and P. Hallinger (2003), *Reshaping the Landscape of School Leadership: A Global Perspective* (Mahidol University, Thailand; online: Swets & Zeitlinger, Lisse, Netherlands). The main text, that is, this book, presents enough material for a complete course complemented by some modules as shown below and in Chapter 15. A consideration in an MA or postgraduate diploma programme in Educational Leadership is to have two streams of students:

Stream A: School Leadership
Stream B: Higher Education Leadership

To the content of the prescribed texts identified above could be added modules on the following topics:

Stream A:
- Educational Philosophy and Psychology
- Managing Diversity in Schools
- Technology and Instruction
- Financial Management

Stream B:
- University Education in Selected Countries, for example, the UK, America, China
- Colonialism and Education, with Special Reference to University Education
- Online Teaching and Learning
- Financial Management

Short courses for on-the-job training

Here we present courses for on-the-job training. The courses proposed here may be taken over a period of five days (where funds and time allow, these courses could be run over a period of two weeks, but five days should suffice taking into account budgetary and time considerations). Many university leadership courses focus on the senior management, with emphasis on vice chancellors and deans. The approach taken here is based on 'the family concept'. In a nuclear family there are three essential figures: father, mother and child or children. My late wife and I used to use the concept of the 'three-legged pot'. With reference to a school this referred to teachers, students and parents. If any of these 'legs' is missing, the pot cannot stand. The same is true of a family – it is a three-legged pot. If any of the 'legs' is missing, the family ceases to be a family. A husband and wife together constitute a couple, not a family as such. If either the father or mother is missing, and you have children and one of the parents, what you have is a single-parent phenomenon, not a complete family. Very often such a scenario is the result of a broken family and a broken marriage with its usual problems. What we are getting to here is that it is well and good to have leadership courses for the executive management and senior academics – it is better for a university to have this arrangement than not to have leadership training at all. But ideally an institutional leadership course should include all three categories of personnel: the executive management and administrators, the academics led by the deans and the student leadership component, with a special student leadership course being run for student leaders as shown above.

Before presenting the types of courses or programmes that deal with all categories of the university family, it is appropriate to point out the following: First, the evidence from the literature (e.g. Greicar 2009; Seale 2015) is that on-the-job training is one of the most effective ways of preparation for deans. It should also be very effective for vice chancellors and other senior management staff. Second, it is important for vice chancellors and other executives to have the opportunity for interaction with people who hold equivalent positions. Such interaction is enriching in that the individuals learn much from the process of exchanging ideas and experiences with others. Third, there is no reason why a vice chancellor should not register for a specialist degree in Educational Leadership, such as the one referred to above. Now that online teaching and learning, as well as internationalization, have become part and parcel of professional training and development, a vice chancellor intent on improving herself/himself could organize their learning programme in a manner that does not unduly interfere with daily duties. Fourth and finally, it is important for each university to have a leadership development strategy for various categories of personnel from the vice chancellor to student leaders. Part of the discourse today is about leading the university in the context of complexity. For those in responsible positions at the various levels of university leadership to cope with the challenges presented by the context of complexity, they need to be involved in lifelong learning.

Two types of programmes that offer lifelong learning opportunities for various categories of university leaders are presented here: The first is a national or regional programme in terms of which different universities come together for leadership development. A team of specialists in leadership would need to be engaged to run the course which could take about five days to complete. The second is an Institutional Transformation Course for a single university aimed at facilitating the transformation process of the university in line with the philosophy advocated in this book. The former programme is referred to as a Type A course and the latter Type B.

Type A: A national or regional programme

Different universities have come together for the training of the following groups:

1. Vice chancellors, members of the executive management and senior administrators
2. Deans and heads of department
3. Student leaders

The training team would organize the course in such a way that all the groups come together at the start of the programme where the overall agenda, the topics to be covered and the principles to be followed would be explained by the facilitators before the participants split into their different categories as outlined above with each group focussing on content that is most relevant for its work. For example, deans and academics could focus a lot on teaching and learning, indigenous knowledge systems, research and innovation, the use of technology and the challenges of internationalization in the context of globalization. The vice chancellors and executive management could focus on leadership, governance and management; internationalization, globalization and the colonial legacy; the interaction between the meso and macro levels in university leadership; and the social and learning problems of students. Students could work on issues of particular interest to students such as learning problems of students, including the challenges of online teaching and learning; the quality of degrees and employability of graduates; arrangements for attachment of students to industry; the funding of students; issues to do with accommodation, student social life and financial support for the SRCs and the students' unions; comparability of degrees and student international exchange; and so on. Registrars and senior administrators could deal with such issues as efficiency in the administration, registration and examination of students; issues of corruption in student administration; the use of technology in the management of the university; professionalism and ethical conduct in all the operations of the university; and so on.

It would be good to set up commissions to deal with the various issues, which commissions would report at plenary sessions the day before the programmes ends so that the recommendations of the commissions are debated in the plenary sessions by all groups. Key issues would be identified which would be summarized and adopted on the last day as recommendations to the universities of the country or region. During the course of the week vice chancellors would have the opportunity to exchange notes with fellow vice chancellors. Similarly deans would meet with fellow deans, registrars with fellow registrars and so on.

Type B: The institutional transformation programme

This is a five- to six-day programme for a single institution run by a team of at least three facilitators, each of whom would be attached to one of the following: the executive and administration, the academic staff and students. The university team would be organized along the following lines:

1. The management subdivided into (i) the vice chancellor and executive and (ii) the registrar and administration staff
2. Faculty deans and chairpersons or heads of department
3. The president and members of the student representative council and chairpersons of clubs and societies

Post-Covid-19, parts of the programme could be presented online while the rest is conducted face to face. There would be at least three common sessions when all the three groups come together. The common sessions could be arranged as follows:

1. The Opening Session during which the vice chancellor presents a compelling vision like the African storyteller as explained in Chapter 10, making sure she articulately develops a new consciousness in the people; creating awareness of the present undesirable state of affairs and painting a realistic desirable future which the participants see themselves creating and making real; and setting SMART goals.
2. A Mid-Week Session during which each of the three groups presents progress made so far, challenges met and plans for the next stage of the process. In this session each group would open itself to interrogation by and advice from the other groups. There could also be a subsession in which the vice chancellor practices the Mutapa-Moshoeshoe leadership style. As a Mutapa, there would be questions for her to answer from both students and staff, some of which may not be directly related to the transformational programme. As a Moshoeshoe, she would have her executive members and the registrar to help her answer the questions and solve the problems presented to her by the students and staff.
3. A Third Session before the Closing Session: During this session the final reports from the various groups would be presented, interrogated and revised as necessary. These would be compiled into the final programme report that would in turn be interrogated and adopted by the whole assembly before departure.

'All work and no play makes Jack a dull boy.' The Institutional Transformation Week should not only be about work. The participants should have time for relaxation with various activities such as music and dance and cultural displays. People should be free, particularly in the evenings, for showing their talents and skills and sharing jokes. The participants should work hard but also enjoy their time at the Institutional Transformation Programme venue.

Ideally, the following week the vice chancellor would hold a *General Pitso* to which everyone is invited for the academic leader, assisted by representatives of the academic staff, executive, administration staff and student leaders, to present the outcome of the Transformation Programme before the report is submitted to Senate and Council. Those who did not attend the transformation programme should be free to ask questions and to make more suggestions for the way forward. The idea is to develop a common understanding of the mission, vision and goals of the institution.

Some months after the Institutional Transformation Week, and after the resolutions have been presented to Senate and Council, an Innovation, Research and Leadership Week could be held to which members of the public are invited. It would be something of an Open Day lasting over several days during which scholarship, leadership and innovation are displayed faculty by faculty and in terms of groups such as the Student Representative Council and others. The displays could include:

- The results of scientific research and innovation
- The incorporation of indigenous knowledge systems into curricula
- Demonstration of the incorporation of positive foreign cultures into curricula and leadership practices
- The results of overall curriculum reform by faculties
- Examples of university/industry collaboration
- Examples of internationalization, demonstrating fruitful collaboration with overseas institutions
- Displays of involvement with community organizations, including traditional and women's organizations

The Institutional Transformation Week and other activities would be guided by the following principles (for African institutions) and by equivalent principles and practices (for institutions on other continents):

- The development of interactive collaborative leadership practices as reflected in the traditional African discussion groups such as *Umhlangano*, *Khotla*, *Legotla* or *Dare*.
- The spirit of a public *Pitso* where the people are free to express their responsible views and to advise the leader without fear of retribution.

- The spirit of *Utu/Ubuntu* in terms of which the leader knows that without the people there is no leader, and the individual knows that she/he becomes a full human being in relation to other beings and must therefore respect others.
- The principle of interdependence that is an important part of the philosophy of *Ubuntu* in terms of which the king or leader realizes that he/she depends on the people just as much the people depend on him/her and consequently the leader must consult and listen to the people or their representatives.
- The Japanese concept of respect which led Toyota to develop the philosophy of 'We make people while we make cars. It's our people who make cars, not machines' (Anderson 2020: 68).
- The Japanese principle that John Adair (2003: 211–12) learnt from Kunosuke Matsushita that manpower, technology, funding, plant and equipment are important, but it is even more important 'that the chief executive should set up sound company goals and ideas and make sure that all the employees are thoroughly acquainted and in agreement with them', leading Adair to comment, 'The key to the Japanese success was "management by collective wisdom."'

In the next chapter, the closing chapter of the book, we examine ideas, information and principles that complement the proposals made in this chapter.

15

A new globalization and a new epistemology

Repositioning leadership and educational leadership in the twenty-first century

The book presents an approach to educational leadership which foregrounds African traditional values and practices, combined with Western approaches, and brings in Japanese concepts and practices to bear. The disciplines of leadership and education are brought together to create an enriched concept of educational leadership. The position taken here is: First, leadership is one of the most important issues of our time: Nations rise and fall on account of leadership. Organizations rise and fall on account of leadership. Institutions blossom or deteriorate depending on the leadership capacity of those who head them. The population of a nation can either prosper or suffer on account of leadership. In view of this one author (Sanders 1999: 10) has commented: 'Each generation has to meet and resolve its own leadership problems and today we are facing an acute crisis in leadership in many spheres.' Another (van Maurik 2001: 1) has said of leadership, 'The fact remains that as a concept it is vital, and the quality of its use or misuse arguably makes it *the most important issue in the world today*' (this writer's italics). With reference to today's advances in technology, the late Nobel Prize laureate Wangari Maathai (2009: 155) has said, 'The point is to recognize that, just as one develops new technologies and expands the potential for breakthroughs in computer science and engineering through technical colleges, so advances in leadership and the application of values must receive similar impetus.'

While I, as author of this book, would agree with John van Maurik that leadership is the most important *issue* in the world today, I would argue that education is one of the most important, if not *the most important, processes* of human development. The kind of education we go through defines our conception of the world and the role we play in that world. The education of humans starts with parents who teach us to talk, to walk, to eat what is good for our health and to understand society. As we grow into young girls and boys, and women and men, the kind of formal education we receive moulds us into the kind of people and professionals we become and the way we view the world and play our leadership roles in it. Paulo Freire talks about the narrative character of the education system: Two plus two equals four. Four times four is sixteen. We memorize facts that are deposited into our heads by the teacher. This kind of education is what he calls 'banking education' as we saw in Chapter 1. This kind of education is not liberating. Similarly, those Whites who lived under the apartheid system of South Africa were taught to believe they were superior beings to Blacks, and they believed they were. Those Africans who, like this writer, received a Western education came to believe the Western concept of leadership was the only form of leadership there was in the world. We did not even realize that, based as it was on the philosophies of certain leaders such as Machiavelli, it did not encompass everything Westerners had inherited. Similarly, we came to believe the Western epistemology was the only valid approach to knowledge. That which was not written in books was not knowledge, and that which came from oral traditions was not knowledge, history or literature.

This book has attempted to show there is much that can be learned about leadership from traditional African culture and practice with a specific example of how *Utu/Ubuntu* was practised in two kingdoms: the Mutapa Empire of Zimbabwe and the Kingdom of Lesotho under the founder, King Moshoeshoe I. Wangari Maathai (2009: 154) has challenged Africans to collectively understand that the current situation where corruption, incompetence and oppression are rife was not always the case, arguing that Africans should understand that 'the majority of their forebears were honest, fair and just and that their societies were functional and people's basic needs were met – and challenge themselves to emulate some of these values'. The book presents the two kingdoms as examples of what Maathai refers to. She goes on to connect the rampant corruption and the degradation of the environment in Africa with the loss of cultural traditions (ibid.: 167). She is also careful to point out that the intersection of the loss of culture with the degradation of the environment and political corruption is not only an African problem: 'People all over the world, rich and poor, are short-sightedly stripping the Earth of her bounty in favor of acquiring wealth today, at the expense of the survival of future generations, whether theirs or other peoples' (ibid.: 167). In educating African leaders about what Black people were able to do in the past, educational leaders should also interrogate Sheikh Anta Diop's argument (1974: xiv) that: 'Ancient Egypt was a Negro civilization. The history of Black Africa will remain suspended in air and cannot be written correctly until African historians dare to connect it with the history of Egypt.' That argument further supports the point made by citing the two kingdoms, that Africa has had capable leaders in the past. There is no reason to think that Africans are genetically incapable of running successful nations. What is needed is a new orientation resulting from an appropriate education system.

What the foregoing paragraphs are suggesting is that the world is at a particular point in its development where both leadership and education as separate disciplines and practices have an important role to play in shaping the future of both the South and the North. After the Second World War there were signs of optimism on separate fronts. With leaders like Winston Churchill of the UK and Harry Truman of America followed by the likes of J. F. Kennedy, the West was optimistic about a better future with capitalism as the model of economic development. On the other hand, the communist/socialist world led by the Soviet Union had its own vision of where the world was going. In the South, the people of the colonies were waking up to the dream of self-rule and independence. The Cold War was a threat but the two sides involved in that threat, the capitalist West and the communist bloc, were each optimistic about a future grounded on its own ideology.

Today, memories of the Cold War have been revived by the Russian invasion of Ukraine. Importantly, there is the phenomenon of globalization dominated by the capitalist West and China with its form of what might be called capitalistic socialism playing a major role. In the globalized world forces such as technology, trade and market forces are at the centre of the stage, with issues of what makes humans human not being a major concern. Terrorism is a major threat to world peace. The optimism of former colonies, especially in Africa, has given way to a new understanding: Independence did not necessarily mean freedom for the people. The majority of Africans in sub-Saharan Africa are poorer than ever. There is now a realization that 'blackness is not all' – the fact that you have a government led by Africans does not necessarily mean you are better off than you were under colonialism. It was indeed necessary to fight for freedom, but in many of the countries the people expected much more than what has turned out to be the fruit of their labour. In Europe and other Western nations there is a new form of nationalism which might threaten the unity of existing nations such as the UK and might give rise to a new form of racism against immigrants. At the same time, there is now a fear of the death of what Europe symbolized for centuries and centuries as evidenced by the publication of Douglas Murray's book, *The Strange Death of Europe: Immigration, Identity, Islam* (Murray 2017). In Africa and other colonies there is a glimmer of hope in the stories of Rwanda and Indonesia. The former, a country torn and devastated by genocide unthinkable in the modern world, is becoming a model of development for other African countries, while Indonesia is a model of development by world standards. Another country to reckon with in Africa is South Africa with democratic practices and an economy that are more advanced than the majority of African countries.

All this has a story to tell: There is now a great need in the world: good and effective leaders; a sound education system for the world; and truly educated and wise educational leaders who can develop a sound education system that can produce leaders of tomorrow who will help save the world. This is a time for educators to realize that depending on the direction given by politicians is not enough. It is time for educators to stop and reflect on where the world is going and where the world should be going. It is time for educators, and in particular educational leaders, to reflect on what role education should play in redirecting the course of history. It is time for educators to be true to their profession of educating society and developing leaders. To be able to do that, educational leaders should, among other things, engage in *hansei* – the discipline of self-awareness. In the next section we discuss some of the issues educational leaders should reflect upon, beginning with African academics.

The challenge to educational leaders – some things to understand

The challenge to African academics and educational leaders

Many African politicians continue to blame all the woes of the African people on colonialism without admitting that much as colonialism is to blame, they are part of the problem: It is dishonest to continue to blame on colonialism such ills as corruption, the lack of freedom in independent countries and the lack of development. Intellectuals too may continue to blame all the ills of the African people on colonialism. Fortunately some are beginning to admit that we, the educated Africans, are part of the problem. And why are we part of the problem? First, because of the Western education we received, we do not know enough about traditional African culture, African values and African history. Second, because of the education we received, based on Western epistemology, we tend to think the only approach to knowledge is the Western approach. Third, when we wake up to the fact that there is something of value in traditional African culture, history and practices, we sometimes react emotionally to the two cultures: glorifying the African past without identifying that which is bad in that culture; and denigrating everything Western, failing to distinguish between the good and the bad, and thereby throwing the baby out with the bathwater. I have listened to a video in which Jordan Peterson was saying something to the effect that the purpose of memory is to extract lessons out of the past to structure the future. The idea, therefore, is not to import wholesale everything from the past but to 'extract' lessons from the past.

Way back in the 1980s, Fay Chung and the author of this book (Chung & Ngara 1985: 71–81) wrote about the positive and negative aspects of the culture of pre-capitalist societies, pointing out, among other things, that 'chief among the negative elements of such cultures are superstition, an irrational world view and blind obedience to authorities'. One of the negative aspects we pointed out (ibid.: 78) is that many businessmen and some farmers in Zimbabwe were believed to have killed their own children or relatives in order to get *muti* (medicine) which would enable their businesses to flourish and compete favourably with other people's businesses. We pointed out the belief was quite common in many countries including Eswatini (Swaziland) where ritual murder was quite widely spread. The point of citing these examples is to emphasize the need to weed out that which is bad in traditional culture so as to purify the cultural traditions of the elders so that they can positively and adequately serve the needs of a modern society.

What, then, should African educational leaders do? In a recent paper (Ngara 2021), I argued that as a first stage, those who want to Africanize the African university should start by understanding the following concepts, among others: imperialism, colonialism, neo-colonialism, decoloniality and nationalistic populism. To these I shall add 'coloniality', which is briefly discussed in that paper and is referred to in Chapter 1 of this book, and what I have called 'colonizerlity', because its meaning is not included in the existing terminology. I comment briefly on each of these:

1. *Imperialism*: This is the enrichment of one country at the expense of another, often through military conquest and the establishment of an oppressive occupying force. A classical example of this is Rome in Judea, Galilee and Samaria (or Palestine).
2. *Colonization/Colonialism*: A form of imperialism through which the imperial power not only occupies the country militarily but also establishes a full-scale government and sends out settlers to live in the conquered territories and to rule the conquered people on its behalf. In this regard Britain, France, Germany, Portugal and Belgium were among the colonial powers in Africa. Now through colonization the culture, values and traditions of the indigenous people are undermined with the colonized people assimilating the culture and values of their conquerors. The education system becomes the major instrument in this process. Referring to colonial education, Julius Nyerere (1968: 47) commented, 'It emphasized and encouraged the individualistic instincts of mankind, instead of his co-operative instincts. It led to the possession of individual material wealth being the major criterion of social merit and worth.' One can see how colonial education undermined and had the effect of subverting the traditional values of *Utu/Ubuntu*. As Nyerere went on to explain (ibid.), 'Colonial education in this country was therefore not transmitting the values and knowledge of Tanzanian society from one generation to the next; it was a deliberate attempt to change those values and to replace traditional knowledge by the knowledge from a different society.'

3. *Coloniality*: This is the effect of colonialism on the colonized people which is explained in very brief terms here. Scholars (e.g. Seroto 2018) identify three dimensions of coloniality: coloniality of power, coloniality of knowledge and coloniality of being. The coloniality of power is difficult to define simply but has to do with the global-political power structure of the modern world which, among other characteristics, is Euro-American-centric, capitalist, patriarchal and racially hierarchized. The coloniality of knowledge has to do with the impact of colonization on how the different areas of knowledge and knowledge production are dominated by the West, resulting in an epistemology that defines knowledge only in relation to modern Western knowledge systems and conceptions of reality, and consequently sidelining other types of knowledge, such as indigenous knowledge systems. The coloniality of being is the understanding that 'colonial relations of power did not only leave indelible marks in the areas of authority, sexuality, knowledge and the economy, but also on the general understanding of being' (Seroto 2018: 5). In other words, the colonized see who they are through colonial lenses. It is perhaps pertinent to point out that debates on these issues are not only carried out in Africa but in South America as well.

4. *Colonizerlity*: This denotes the mind, psychology and attitude of the colonizer in relation to the colonized. The colonizer has a predetermined attitude about the humanness, culture and mental capabilities of the colonized people which tends to express itself in the form of racialism. In its raw nature, at the colonizer's first encounter with the colonized, colonizerlity sees a being that is not fully human, whose culture is inferior if not savage, who is not as fully mentally developed as the people of his/her own race. The concept of colonizerlity is fully expressed in Joseph Conrad's novel, *The Heart of Darkness*. In the novel Marlow, Conrad's spokesperson, states that the conquest of the earth means 'taking it away from those who have a different complexion'. Having 'different complexions and flattened nose' meant that Europeans had the right to exploit the land for ivory and other treasures and take it away from them.

5. *Neo-colonialism*: Because of pressure for freedom by the colonized people, the European colonial powers divested themselves of direct political control of the colonies, but wealth from these colonies continued to flow to the metropolitan powers through multinational corporations (also known as transnational corporations) such as Anglo-American, Lonrho and Lever Brothers. Kwame Nkrumah (1965: ix) defined neo-colonialism as follows: 'The essence of neo-colonialism is that the State which is subject to it is, in theory, independent and has all the outward trappings of international sovereignty. In reality its economic system and thus its political policy, is directed from outside.' The sad thing is it would appear that many of the leaders of independent Africa

continue to exploit the citizens of their countries for their own benefit, doing so in alliance with the forces of neo-colonialism.
6. *Decoloniality*: This is a term that refers to the process of undoing colonialism, neo-colonialism, coloniality, imperialism and underdevelopment.
7. *Nationalistic populism*: This is the overvaluing of 'the golden past' and turning a blind eye to the negative aspects of traditional culture. Also included in this concept is the refusal to accept that there are positive elements in colonial cultures, values and traditions.

As part of the process of grappling with decoloniality and creating an education system that both liberates the African and facilitates development on the continent, African academics and academics from former colonies elsewhere need to understand these concepts. I once quoted Frantz Fanon presenting Africans with a challenge in these words (Ngara 2013: 166): 'Each generation must, out of relative obscurity, discover its mission, fulfil it, or betray it.' Many African thinkers would agree that the purpose of liberation struggles in some countries that had to fight for independence and freedom has been betrayed by political leaders who have failed to fulfil the aspirations of the people. In the last two decades or so, there has been much talk about the African Renaissance. The African Renaissance cannot take place without Africa rediscovering itself and using the past to develop a noble purpose for the future.

African intellectuals will also have betrayed their mission if they do not turn the African university into an institution that moulds leaders who can change the fortunes of the African continent for the better. The developing leaders of today, many of whom have gone through a university education, must be imbued with the hope of a future where freedom, true independence and development are possible and palpable. The university is a very conservative institution, but it can learn from other conservative organizations. As a follower of Jesus I am ashamed at what the Christian Church has done to itself and to the peoples of the world. As mentioned earlier, the church was one of the weapons used by colonizers to denigrate African cultural traditions. It is such a shame, for example, that the Bible was used to justify the ideology of apartheid which was anchored on racism and the idea of the Africans as an inferior race to Whites. The Christian Church worldwide is a very conservative institution and still has much to do to reflect what its founder wanted to see in his followers; but I have been impressed by some of the transformations that have taken place in some countries in line with African culture and tradition.

The Catholic Church, for instance, is a very conservative organization that in the early twentieth century would have been appropriately described as a dinosaur, but the changes that have been made in the liturgy, and especially in music, in countries such as Zimbabwe, are quite admirable. In this regard, Wangari Maathai (2009: 178–9) reports that one of the Popes, Pope John Paul II, on his visit to Kenya in 1995, apologized for the sins committed by Christian missionaries against African culture. He urged religious leaders to recognize that culture is dynamic and incorporates elements from other cultures but that it is Africans themselves who should decide what they want to take from other cultures. Maathai goes on to report, 'Others cannot do this for Africans, the pope emphasized, without perpetuating the culture of patronizing the African people.' If the church can adopt this attitude and effect such changes, why cannot the university do the same? Needless to say, African universities are expected to do more: As centres of research and innovation, they are expected to be places where, in part, the wisdom of humanity, not only of the West, is researched, preserved and applied, working on projects that foster the development of communities and nations. In Africa where there is dire need for development, one of the preoccupations of the university should be to research on development models of more successful nations, both Western and non-Western.

With reference to nationalistic populism, the peoples of Africa and other formerly colonized nations can learn lessons from some other non-Western peoples and cultures. For example, the Japanese were conquered in the Second World War, but they did not for that reason cut themselves off completely from Western ways. I learned that their motto was 'imitate and overtake'. In 1988 as visiting professor at Duke University in North Carolina, I had the opportunity to casually examine foreign products on the American market. I was amazed to see how that market was flooded with Japanese cars. When my late wife and I went on a tour of Chinese institutions in 1987, we were struck by how some of the best hotels we were accommodated in were said to have been built by Chinese people in the diaspora (mostly based in America and other Western countries) who were investing in their own country. These examples show there is nothing wrong in being both patriotic and accepting and incorporating that which is good and valuable from other peoples and cultures.

Some challenges to all educational leaders – Westerners and the rest

Western educational leaders should have an understanding of what their counterparts in the former colonies are grappling with. If Western educators want to play a role in creating a better world, they should have some understanding of what educators in the developing world have to deal with. In this regard, discussing the concepts defined above such as colonialism, coloniality, decoloniality and so on will lead them to a better understanding of what Europe has done to former colonies, leading to a more objective view of why Africa is where it is now. The building of a more balanced and better world will in part depend on cooperation between the North and the South, and the quality of that cooperation in part depends on mutual understanding between educators in the North and the South. This leads us to some of the universal problems of the modern world.

The world is riddled with unethical practices and the drive for individual success at the expense of what Mike Bottery (Bush et al. 2019: 48) calls 'elements of care, cooperation, public good and equality'. Bottery here is inadvertently referring to the values that the philosophy of *Utu/Ubuntu* promotes – the idea of the individual seeing herself/himself as part of the many, the community; the individual seeing self-fulfilment in the context of community fulfilment. As it turns out, this is also in line with traditional Japanese thinking: through respect for others and teamwork you maximize individual and team performance.

The question is what role has education played in the undesirable practices referred to in the immediately preceding paragraph? Bottery (ibid.) presents two scenarios: one based on a neo-Darwinism form of market competition between potential winners and losers (the survival of the fittest) in terms of which educational leadership, management, curricula and teaching are imbued with the same perspective; and one in which competition is only one element 'in a more complex multi-hued educational endeavour, where elements of care, cooperation, public good, and equality have large roles to play'. The latter is clearly in line with the philosophy of *Ubuntu* about which Archbishop Desmond Tutu (2011: 22) says: 'This concept speaks of how people are more important than things, than profits, than material possessions. It speaks about the intrinsic worth of persons as not dependent on extraneous things such as status, race, creed, gender, or achievement.' This reminds one of Mwalimu Julius Nyerere (1968: 47) saying colonial education emphasized and encouraged the individualistic instincts of mankind, instead of his cooperative instincts, as was quoted in a previous paragraph. The question is: If Western education did this to African learners, would it not have done the same (or even worse) to Western learners?

Wangari Maathai noticed a connection between loss of culture and loss of care for the environment and between loss of culture and corruption. There is so much talk about the environment today. By not caring for the environment as we seek to maximize profit through machines that pollute that environment, we forget to care for future generations. Those who will be impacted by the polluted environment will not only be Africans and other peoples of the developing South but the whole world, the developed North included. The lesson for both the South and the North is: Culture and the environment are important for human survival. A people without a culture will be lost when what matters are competition and personal wealth acquired through technology, trade and market forces. By rediscovering their cultures, the people of the South will rediscover their humanity. By learning about traditional African culture and other cultures of the South, the people of the North may also begin to think about the value of their own cultural traditions that have been forgotten for thousands of years. Is there something, for example, that the English, the Scots and the Irish people can learn from the culture of the Anglo-Saxons and the Anglo-Celtic people? The counterargument may be it is too far back to go. To this, Sir Winston Churchill might respond: 'The farther back you can look, the farther forward you are likely to see.' Another of Churchill's quotes that is relevant to this discussion is this: 'If we open a quarrel between the past and the present we shall find that we have lost the future' (see BBC America Editors, 9 April 2015). The veracity of this statement finds support in Maathai who sees a connection between loss of culture on the one hand and corruption and lack of care for the environment on the other.

In Chapter 13 we discussed some of the problems of globalization – how our values and mindsets are determined for us by forces such as news agents, the internet, the race to maximize profit and so on. These are what have been called 'macro issues' which this writer prefers to call 'supra-macro issues' as they are beyond ordinary national governments. In 1987 the World Commission on Environment and Development (WCED) published a report entitled *Our common future*, also called *The Bruntland Report* after its chairwoman, Gro Harlem Bruntland. The report called for a strategy that united development and the environment, defining sustainable development as follows: 'Sustainable development is development that meets the needs of the present without compromising the ability of future generations to meet their own needs.' Mike Bottery (Bush et al. 2019: 45) points to the fact that the Bruntland Report is asking both humanity and educational leaders to look to 'a road requiring the adoption of global, inter-species visions, because increasingly, the things that will most affect us … are precisely these macro-issues, the ones that can have huge effects upon us without our necessarily realising their causes'. These things, which Bottery correctly says our students need to understand, are likely to negatively impact future generations. Bottery lists the following among the changes that are taking place: temperature rises, climate control, energy challenges, species decline and so on. These arguments are in line with the importance of putting humanity at the centre of what we do. The philosophy of *Ubuntu* can be extended to mean that if the people of today forget about what makes humans human by destroying all that makes human life possible in our 'common home', the quality of life for future generations will be severely negatively affected. If I am because you, the community, are, future generations will be because we, the present generation, are. If we destroy the humanity of humans today, we will have destroyed the humanity of future generations, and God knows what kind of future that will be!

As educational leaders we promote sustainable development through the education process, and if, as posited above, education is *the most important process* or *one of the most important processes* of human development, then we must pay attention not only to the Gruntland Report but also to the Sustainable Development Goal 4 of the United Nations (SDG 4) which states, 'Ensure inclusive and equitable quality education and promote lifelong learning opportunities for all.' SDG 4 is divided into seven targets. Of special reference to our argument in this chapter is Target 4.7: 'By 2030 ensure that all learners acquire the knowledge and skills needed to promote sustainable development, including, among others, through education for sustainable development and sustainable lifestyles, human rights, gender equality, promotion of a culture of peace and non-violence, global citizenship and appreciation of cultural diversity and of culture's contribution to sustainable development.'

Target 4.7 resonates with the *Utu/Ubuntu* philosophy and with the Japanese principle of *Respect* in that it focuses on human principles – human rights, gender equality, peace and non-violence, appreciation of cultural diversity – and goes on to recognize the contribution of culture to sustainable development. This target or indicator challenges educators to see the extent to which these values are mainstreamed in curricula, with learners being led to reflect on their own cultures and perspectives and on those of groups different from theirs. The indicator facilitates the development of the practice of recognizing the perspectives of others, leading to an understanding of the importance of the principle of peaceful coexistence between different ethnic, racial and religious groups. This leads us back to the argument about the need for the people of the North to familiarize themselves with some of the issues the people of the South have to grapple with – issues such as colonialism, neo-colonialism, coloniality and decoloniality and so on. It is necessary for Europeans and Americans to understand that without the African continent, they would not have a large measure of the resources that make life more comfortable for them and their children. If educated Africans are what they are partly as a result of the education they or their parents received from European missionaries, Europeans enjoy the kind of life they enjoy today partly as a result of the raw materials that come from the African continent. Consequently, in terms of the *Ubuntu* philosophy, Europe is because Africa is.

The question that arises is: Whereto for educational leaders now – both in the North and the South? Both in Europe and Africa? Is it enough to learn leadership lessons from Africa and Japan? We attempt to address this important question in the next two sections. But first, is there a European model to learn from?

A European model of good leadership

If the transformation of the education systems is going to bear fruit, education must aim at reorientating society, not educators only. The education systems of both the North and the South should aim at not only changing the attitudes and practices of educational leaders but should also be designed to produce good, effective, democratic and ethical leaders in government and business. For educators to be able to develop such a system, they need to have models of governments that satisfy the citizens of the countries concerned. It is not enough for African educational leaders to design a system that is aligned to the values and traditions of Africa, if practices such as corruption, oppression and election rigging are going to continue unabated. The citizens of Africa will continue to migrate to countries where they can enjoy relative freedom of expression and a decent income with which to maintain their families. There are a few African countries, such as South Africa, where such opportunities are relatively available. For the bulk of Africans, the destinations tend to be Western countries – ironically. Ironically also, it is also in the West where we can find examples of countries that can satisfy their own citizens to such an extent they would rather not go anywhere else. The examples this author has come across are the Nordic or Scandinavian countries – Denmark, Finland, Sweden, Norway as well as Iceland and the Faroe Islands. These are very cold countries, and taxation levels are said to be extremely high, but their citizens are considered to be the happiest in the world. Why is that?

Every year, a group of happiness experts from around the world rank 156 countries and publish their report in the *World Happiness Report (WHR)*. Scandinavian countries tend to consistently come top where the United States is said to typically land around eighteenth or nineteenth. So it is not necessarily the size and success of the economy that decides how satisfied the citizens are by their government. Readers are referred to the following articles that can be found on the internet:

1. 'Why Finland and Denmark are the happiest countries in the world' (cnbc.com/2020/01/09/)
2. "'The Nordic Exceptionalism: What Explains Why the Nordic Countries Are Constantly among the Happiest in the World' (Martela et al., WHR, 20 March 2020)

In the former article, Jeff Sachs, co-creator of the WHR, among other things, highlights what he calls 'balance' as a key factor in the happiness of the citizens of these countries. The countries prioritize a good balance of life, which is the 'formula for happiness'. Consequently, 'we find happiness in our own pursuits' and this includes professional work and 'passions'. He also highlights freedom as a value that matters and determines someone's well-being. Among other things freedom means the freedom to shape your life the way you want without being trapped by such things as debt and poverty.

The authors of the second report are more detailed and scholarly in their explanation. They start by quoting what they say Thomas Jefferson said in 1809: 'The care of human life and happiness and not their destruction is the first and only legitimate object of good government.' Here was a leader who understood leadership the *Utu/Ubuntu* way: *Morena ke morena ka batho* 'A king is a king on account of the people'. The leader owes his/her position to the people and so should see the good life and happiness of the people as his/her first and only duty. The authors list the following with detailed researched explanations. Here we can only make very brief explanations:

1. *Welfare state generosity*: Satisfaction with public common goods such as healthcare, education and public transport. People are happy where there is easy access to such benefits and where labour is regulated to avoid labour exploitation.
2. *Institutional quality*: The authors explain that the Nordic countries occupy top positions alongside such countries as New Zealand and Switzerland in respect of this indicator. Government quality is divided into two dimensions: democratic quality and delivery quality. Democratic quality refers to people's *access* to power, for example, ability to participate in selecting the government, freedom of expression and political stability. Delivery quality, which is even more important, is about the *exercise* of power, and this includes the rule of law, control of corruption, regulatory quality and government effectiveness. From our examples of traditional African leaders we can, for example, consider how the Mutapa would spend the whole day solving people's problems while others were resting and how the people had so much confidence in the protection of the emperor that they would build houses without doors.
3. *Income equality*: This indicator is not clear in terms of comparative studies with other countries, but the authors point out that low levels of inequality *might be* important for the happiness of Nordic citizens – although the same direct effect is not visible in many other countries.
4. *Freedom to make life choices*: The extent to which a country is able to provide individuals with a sense of freedom and autonomy plays a significant role in the happiness of citizens. The authors explain that autonomy and freedom combined with relatively high material prosperity, a well-functioning democracy and liberal values play a significant role in the happiness of Nordic citizens.
5. *Trust in people and social cohesion*: Three countries – Denmark, Finland and Sweden – occupy top three positions in their index of social cohesion, making trust and social cohesion an additional explanation for the happiness of Nordic citizens.

This is a model that is very useful for those who hold government positions in particular and those preparing to hold government positions. It is a model which developing countries would do well to try and emulate. In a training programme there would have to be a lot more detail for the trainees. However, the information provided here gives an indication that vices such as corruption, oppression and inefficiency and a whole lot of others can be avoided, and that a government can effectively rule in the interests of the people and in line with the principles of *Utu/Ubuntu*.

What are the implications of the issues raised in the chapter for leadership development?

A diversified epistemology

The book has presented some approaches to leadership development that can be used to develop leaders of tomorrow in the face of the present globalized world and the incompetence and oppressive practices of many leaders in many African countries and other countries of the South. As Sir Winston Churchill has explained, 'The first duty of the university is to teach wisdom, not a trade; character, not technicalities. We want a lot of engineers in the modern world, but we do not want a world of engineers' (BBC America Editors 2015.). In view of what the book presents it might be imperative to adopt an approach to educational leadership development that takes the best from different cultures, with special reference to the following:

- The *Utu/Ubuntu* approach which is akin to servant leadership as defined and developed by Robert Greenleaf but with a deeper philosophical basis that determines why the leader should serve as something of a servant of the people
- The Japanese approach as explained and demonstrated by Isao Yoshino in Katie Anderson's book (2020)
- A combination of servant leadership as developed by Robert Greenleaf (1977) and the government practices of the Nordic countries

In view of the above, a leadership development programme which facilitates the moulding of a future generation of leaders who recognize the imperatives of globalization but are at the same time conscious of the need to develop an ethical people-centred approach to leadership could, in brief, be structured along the following lines:

1. *A Study of the Utu/Ubuntu philosophy* with a focus on:
    i. Humanness; the relationship between the individual and the community; the values of *Ubuntu*; the relationship between the king/chief and the people; traditional interactive leadership practices
    ii. Examples of leaders (such as the Mutapas and Moshoshoe I) who put that philosophy into practice
    iii. How the philosophy can be applied today in domains such as politics, business and education (both in schools and higher education, and in respect of learning and teaching as well as in governance, leadership and management)

2. *The Japanese or Chinese approach*
   i. For the Japanese the focus could be on such principles and practices as the fabric concept (the warp and weft threads); *hansei* (self-reflection); respect for people (with the key elements of respect and teamwork); collective wisdom, going to gemba; fall down seven times, get up eight; and so on
   ii. The Toyota Way, including the Foundational Leadership Lessons (Anderson 2020: 73–131)
3. *Western people-centred approaches*

   i. Servant leadership as developed by Robert Greenleaf
   ii. The Nordic example of how governments can rule in the interest of the people

Such a programme can be presented against the background of the following:

1. Understanding education and leadership
2. The leadership of domination
3. Personal leadership development.

A course of this kind can be part of a degree or diploma programme as explained in Chapter 14 or as a stand-alone short course. Such a programme presents an epistemology that is not based solely on Western ideas but on an approach that recognizes the diversity of human knowledge and understanding of leadership. Furthermore, the approach facilitates the internationalization of higher education. In terms of this it would be enriching for students to have a European university, an African university and a Japanese university jointly running the kind of programme proposed here – and this could be done online. The approach recommended to the British Council by the University of Cambridge Institute of Sustainable Leadership seems to be generally in support of what is proposed here. The Institute (CISL 2017) presented to the British Council a proposal with nine (9) recommendations. One of these (Recommendation 8) states:

> A hybrid model of leadership development is likely to add most value – focusing on knowledge, values, and skills – although there may need to be some adaptations as some nations are further than others along the prescriptive-interactive-experiential learning spectrum.

Conclusion: Hearing the voices of wisdom

There is a need for change in the world – both in the South and the North. As stated earlier, the disciplines of leadership and education have a key role to play in the task of redirecting the world. We might think, what is it that educationists can do? The politically powerful have the means and the power, and the world will continue to move in the direction in which they want it to move. Against this spirit of pessimism, we might do well to listen to the collective wisdom of some of the greatest people of our time. Their collective voice and advice can be heard in the following statements:

> *Statement one*: 'The world is a dangerous place to live, not because of the people who are evil, but because of the people who won't do anything about it' (eminent twentieth-century physicist Albert Einstein 1879–1955).
>
> *Statement two*: 'The single most important thing I can do is to help in any way I can to prepare the next generation of leadership to take up the baton and to take their own crack at changing the world' (first African American US president, Barack Obama, born 1961).
>
> *Statement three*: 'Education is the most powerful weapon which you can use to change the world' (Nelson Rolihlahla Mandela, arguably one of the greatest people to have ever lived, 1918–2013).

Together these great people are inviting educational leaders to take responsibility for redirecting the world and to use education to develop leaders who care enough for humanity to change the world. Obama also said, 'Change will not come if we wait for some other person or some other time', adding, 'We are the change that we seek'. Let us use the power of a sound education system to mould the leaders who will change the world.

Appendix

Reflection exercises for students and interested practitioners

These exercises are meant to help the user of this book to see whether he/she has grasped some of the key points raised in the various chapters and sections of the book. Some are ideally done in groups with participants sharing ideas. Individual readers can also do some of the exercises as individuals. Tutors can use the exercises as assignments for students, while a few of the exercises can be worked on in the form of debates.

Chapter 1: Education for development and leadership

1. (a) Using the contents of this chapter as your yardstick, assess the education system you have gone through and explain the extent to which the system reflected or did not reflect the following approaches to learning:
    (i) The reproductive approach
    (ii) The constructive approach
    (iii) The technical interest

    (b) What can be done to ensure the system is more reflective of:
    (i) The emancipatory interest
    (ii) Problem posing education
    (iii) The dialectical and developmental concept of education?

2. Using the guidelines to African institutions of higher education proposed in this chapter, do a critical analysis of an undergraduate or postgraduate programme you know and suggest improvements that could be made to it so that it reflects the characteristics of:
   (a) A truly Africa-centred consciousness programme (if the institution that offers the programme is in sub-Saharan Africa), or
   (b) A programme that truly reflects the ideals of your own country and people (if your country is not in sub-Saharan Africa).

Chapter 2: What is leadership?

1. Read the questions asked by Mr Mafa and Ms Temba in this chapter and do the following exercise: Add what you consider to be typically management questions to Mr Mafa's list and what you consider to be typically leadership questions to Ms Temba's list. Explain why you think each set of questions you have provided can be appropriately referred to as 'management questions' and 'leadership questions', respectively.
2. Reflect on the organization you work for (or make up one you think is an ideal organization), and write a report (five hundred to seven hundred words) on the interaction of *leadership*, *management* and *administration* in the organization. Think of any *governance* issues that may need attention and comment on them. Conclude your report with recommendations you may wish to make for the improvement of the organization/institution.

Chapter 3: General and educational theories of leadership

1. Write notes on what you consider to be the usefulness or otherwise of theory to leadership practice, with special reference to educational leadership.
2. Discuss how transformational leadership and distributed leadership can be applied to a school or a higher education institution.

Chapter 4: Educating people for domination

1. Discuss the following topic with fellow students or colleagues:

'The Leadership of Domination in Schools and other Institutions of Education in our Country'

What are your findings as a group? Are there any improvements you would like to see made in the system?

2. Consider the following scenarios:
   (a) You are a female officer. There are opportunities for promotion and you believe you deserve a promotion. You submit an application. The CEO then approaches you suggesting the promotion is yours on condition you spend a night with him in a hotel. What would be your reaction?
   (b) You have just been appointed the CEO of a state-owned enterprise (SOE). Soon after you have taken up the post, the permanent secretary (or director general) of the ministry (or government department) to which you report tells you that the salaries of your staff are too high compared to those of ministry officials, and the ministry was just waiting for you to come so that you can help to adjust the salaries downwards without negotiating with the staff. You are between the rock and the hard place. The permanent secretary has the power to protect you against your staff, but the staff look up to you for protection against what they see as an injustice. What would you do?

Chapter 5: The *Ubuntu* approach to relationships and leadership

In this exercise, learners and practitioners from any part of the world can substitute the Mutapas of Zimbabwe and Moshoeshoe I of Lesotho with traditional leaders from their part of the world.

1. Extrapolating from some of the practices of the leaders of the two kingdoms studied in this chapter, how can today's educational leaders use the *Ubuntu* philosophy (or the traditional philosophy of your people) to enhance their leadership practices?
2. Carry out a debate on the following topics:
   Team A: 'There is much that the leaders of our time can learn from the leadership practices of traditional leaders such as the Mutapas of Zimbabwe and King Moshoeshoe I of Lesotho.'
   Team B: 'There is not much that the leaders of today can learn from traditional leaders of any culture. Such leadership practices are too outmoded to be applicable to the twenty-first century.'

Chapter 6: Educating people to serve: Servant leadership

1. *Personal reflection*
   Reflect on your own leadership style and say which of the following modes of leadership most accurately reflect your own natural inclinations to date:
   - Democratic leadership
   - Autocratic leadership
   - The leadership of domination
   - Servant leadership

2. For your own education, write notes on at least two of the following topics:
   (a) Servant Leadership as exemplified by the Nyerere and Leo stories narrated in this chapter.
   (b) A comparison of *either* Servant Leadership and the Leadership of Domination *or* between Servant Leadership and *Ubuntu*-Based Leadership.
   (c) Robert Greenleaf's contribution to our understanding of leadership.
   (d) How the education system can be used to facilitate the development of servant leaders.

Chapter 7: Discovering one's purpose in life

1. Reflect on the following topic and write notes or a short essay on it: 'What I Consider to be My Purpose in Life'.
2. Do some research on personal mission statements and compose your own mission statement in a short paragraph.

Chapter 8: Personal mastery, self-awareness and leadership qualities and habits

1. There is a competition that is intended to encourage developing leaders to think seriously about the kind of leaders they would like to be. The participants are

expected to examine their current reality in relation to what each of them sees as the ideal leader he/she would like to be; they are expected to demonstrate their capacity for self-awareness and to show the steps they will take to become the ideal leader of their imagination. You have qualified to participate in the competition. Write your essay doing your best to ensure it is a winning essay.

2. Consider the following: Your goal is to become a college or school principal, a successful entrepreneur, or a master farmer. You know there are a number of things you must do before you achieve your goal, and there are also other things you desire to do in life. Among these are the following:
   (a) Getting married
   (b) Training to be a principal, entrepreneur or master farmer
   (c) Travelling the world
   (d) Purchasing business premises
   (e) Recruiting and training people to assist you in your desired career
   (f) Getting employed to live a fairly comfortable life
   (g) Training to be a soccer coach as a hobby
   (h) Applying for a loan to set up the business

Which of the above would you decide to attend to and in what order? Depending on which career you have chosen, would you decide to abandon or ignore any of the above? Explain your response.

Chapter 9: Educational leadership and the development of intelligences

1. On a five-point scale where
   i. stands for *Weak to Very Weak*
   ii. stands for *Average*
   iii. stands for *Above Average*
   iv. stands for *Very Good*
   v. stands for *Excellent*

   (a) Objectively assess your own level of development in each of the four intelligences we have dealt with in this chapter by giving each intelligence the appropriate rating.
   (b) Explain what you are going to do to improve your intelligence where your level of development is below 4.

2. Try to recall occasions when you have not performed well in emotional intelligence (EI). What is it that caused you not to do well in EI on each

occasion? How would you behave if you were to find yourself in a similar situation in future?

Chapter 10: Vision and organizational leadership

Practical Organizational Exercise 1

You have been appointed to lead an organization. It may be doing reasonably well; it may be a dysfunctional organization. Think of a real organization, institution or company in your area of expertise. The institution/company is comprised of three to five units/divisions or departments. Give it a name. Do the equivalent of a preliminary investigation that will enable you to assess the level of performance of the organization, and write notes on what you find out. Develop a compelling vision for it.

Chapter 11: Strategy as the road map to the desired state

Practical Organizational Exercise 2

Go back to the organization for which you created a vision in Practical Organizational Exercise 1 (Chapter 10). Guided by the vision, develop a simple strategic plan for the organization. The plan should include the following:

1. Evidence of a SWOT analysis – which takes into account the two types of questions asked in this chapter.
2. Set three to five SMART goals for the organization.
3. The goals should be divided into short-term, medium-term and long-term milestones.

Chapter 12: Execution as the key to the actual destination

Practical Organizational Exercise 3

Go back to the organization you conceptualized in Practical Organisational Exercise 1 and Practical Organisational Exercise 2, and do the following:

1. Briefly discuss the corporate culture of the organization, and explain what you are going to do to reshape it so that the people in it develop a strong culture of execution. Pay attention to both the hardware and software of the organization's culture.
2. Develop a simple operational plan (for one year) making sure that the operational plan is based on the strategic plan you developed in Practical Organizational Exercise 2.
3. Briefly refer to some of the leader's strategic operational behaviours you will rely on to get things done.

Chapter 13: Issues and principles of educational leadership

1. Carry out a debate based on the arguments of two teams as explained below:
   Team A: Globalization as it presently operates means that the future of the human race is going to be based on essentially one culture: A culture dominated by (i) Western ideas and languages, (ii) technology and (iii) market forces. On the contrary, it is necessary that the diversity of world cultures be reflected in what is taught in schools, colleges and higher education institutions.
   Team B: For mutual understanding between the nations, it is essential that there be one universal culture in terms of which there are four major components of human culture: (i) Western culture, (ii) technology, (iii) market forces and (4) the English language. An ideal education for the future should be based on these four elements.

2. As an aspiring university leader or a group of aspiring university leaders studying together or attending a meeting of university leaders together, consider the following issues, write some notes on at least two of them and share your ideas:
   (a) The complexity of the modern university – taking into account the issues discussed in this chapter and any other issues you consider important and relevant to the topic.
   (b) You are the vice chancellor of a university. You want to give a public speech on the interaction of the following levels in a modern higher education institution: the micro, meso, macro and supra-macro levels. Write your speech.
   (c) Discuss what you consider to be the ideal interplay of the following in a modern university: academic freedom and autonomy, the role of quality assurance agencies and institutional entrepreneurship.

Chapter 14: Leadership development at meso level

Answer one of the following questions:

1. Carry out a research project on training programmes for *one* of the leadership levels listed below, concluding your report with a comment on the lessons you have learnt from the exercise. Avoid a simple repetition of the information given in this chapter:
   (a) University vice chancellors
   (b) Academic deans and chairpersons or heads of academic departments
   (c) Student leaders

2. Discuss what you consider to be the relative importance of each of the following to an academic dean or chairperson/head of department:
   (a) Interpersonal relationships and communication skills
   (b) Leadership and innovation
   (c) Professional development of staff
   (d) Understanding of the quality of content and technical design of programmes
   (e) Sensitivity to issues of institutional diversity and student needs

3. To what extent should the following issues feature in the vision of the vice chancellor or academic dean?
   (a) The context of the university with special reference to cultural traditions, indigenous knowledge systems and the development needs of the nation
   (b) The role of technology in education
   (c) The impact of globalization on education

Chapter 15: A new globalization and a new epistemology

Imagine that you are the deputy minister of higher education and training in your country. Your minister and government have charged you with the responsibility of proposing the outlines of a leadership development programme for future leaders in your country with the assistance of a team of academic leaders and some captains of industry. You are expected to pay special attention to the subject matter of Chapter 15 of this book. Suggest some of the ideas you would put to your team for discussion.

References

Part I: Understanding education and leadership

Adair, J. (2003). *Effective Strategic Leadership*. London: Pan Books.
Adair, J. (2018). *Lessons in Leadership*. London: Bloomsbury Business.
Anderson, K. (2020). *Learning to Lead, Leading to Learn: Lessons from Toyota Leader ISAO YOSHINO on a Lifetime of Continuous Learning*. California: Integrand Press.
Bass, B. M. (1990). *Bass and Stogdill's Handbook of Leadership: Theory, Research and Management Applications*, 3rd edn. New York: Free Press.
Behr, A. L. (1980). *Teaching and Learning at University*. Durban: Butterworths.
Bergstrom, A. (2002). 'An Interview with Dr Bernard M. Bass', Kravis Leadership Institute, *Leadership Review*, Winter 2003.
Bush, T., Bell, L. & Middlewood, D. (eds) (2019). *Principles of Educational Leadership and Management*. Los Angeles, CA: Sage.
Caspersz, D., & Olaru, D. (2014). 'Developing "Emancipatory Interest": Learning to Create Social Change', *Higher Education Research and Development*, 33(2), 226–41.
Courtney, S. J., Gunter, H. M., Niesche, R. & Trujillo, T. (2021). *Understanding Educational Leadership: Critical Perspectives and Approaches*. London: Bloomsbury.
Covey, S. R. (1992). *The 7 Habits of Highly Effective People*. London: Simon & Schuster.
Eskelin, N. (2001). *Leading with Love*. Grand Rapids, MI: Revell.
Fayol, H. (1930). *Industrial and General Administration*. London: Sir Pitman & Sons.
Freire, P. (1972). *Pedagogy of the Oppressed*. Harmondsworth: Penguin Books.
Gardner, H. (1995). *Leading Minds: An Anatomy of Leadership*. New York: Basic Books.
Gill, R., Levine N. & Pitt, D. C. (1998). 'Leadership and Organizations for the New Millennium'. *Journal of Leadership Studies*, 5(4), 46–59.
Grundy, S. (1987). *Curriculum: Product or Praxis*. London: Falmer Press (reprinted 1989).
Hagemann, B., Vetter, S. & Maketa, J. (2017). *Leading with Vision: The Leader's Blueprint for Creating a Compelling Vision and Engaging the Workforce*. Boston, MA: Nicholas Brealey.
Hallinger, P. (ed.) (2003). *Reshaping the Landscape of School Leadership Development: A Global Perspective*. Bangkok: Mahidol University. Online: Lisse: Swets & Zeitlinger.
Harris, A. (2004). 'Distributed Leadership in Schools: Leading or Misleading?' *Educational Management, Administration and Leadership*, 32(1), 11–24.

Hatchuel, A., & Segrestin, B. (2018). 'A Century Old and Still Visionary: Fayol's Innovative Theory of Management'. https://doi.org/10.1111/emre.12292.

Hersey, P., & Blanchard, K. (1977). *Management of Organizational Behavior: Utilizing Human Resources*. Englewood Cliffs, NJ: Prentice Hall.

King Jr., Martin Luther (1963). 'Martin Luther King's I Have a Dream Speech', 28 August 1963, https://www.npr.org >i-have-a-dream-speech-in-its-entirety. Accessed 1 February 2022.

Lead and Inspire School of Leadership (2010). *Introduction to the Phenomenon of Leadership*, Lead and Inspire Teaching Materials Series. Pretoria: Unpublished.

Lowney, C. (2003). *Heroic Leadership: Best Practice from a 450-Year-Old Company That Changed the World*. Chicago: Loyola Press.

Maxwell, J. C. (2007). *The 21 Irrefutable Laws of Leadership*. Nashville, TN: Thomas Nelson.

Melick, R. R., & Melick, S. (2010). *Teaching That Transforms*. Nashville, TN: B&H Publishing Group.

Ngara, E. (1995). *The African University and Its Mission: Strategies for Improving the Delivery of Higher Education Institutions*. Roma: Institute of Southern African Studies (National University of Lesotho).

Ngara, E. (2013). 'Transformational Leadership and Traditional African Leadership Practice: A Study of Two Kingdoms'. Paper read in Victoria Falls at a conference organized by the National University of Science and Technology.

Ngara, E. (2021). 'Reflections on the Further transformation of UNISA: Focus on Governance, Leadership and Response to National Policy'. Paper read as part of a series of University of South Africa presentations.

Ngulube, P. (ed.) (2017). *Handbook of Research on Theoretical Perspectives on Indigenous Knowledge Systems in Developing Countries*. Hershey, PA: IGI Global.

Nkomo, M. (ed.) (1990). *Pedagogy of Domination: Toward a Democratic Education in South Africa*. Trenton, NJ: Africa World Press, Inc.

Onana, C. A., Oyewole, O. B., Teferra, D., Beneitone, P., Gonzalez, J., & Wagenaar, R. (eds) (2014). *Tuning and Harmonization of Higher Education: The African Experience* (Tuning Africa Project). Bilbao: University of Deusto.

Rawat, S. (2016). 'Top 4 Theories of Leadership'. Business Management Ideas, https://www.coursehero.com >file>Leadership-Theories. Accessed 2 February 2022.

Sanders, J. O. (1999). *Dynamic Spiritual Leadership*. Grand Rapids, MI: Discovery House.

Seroto, J. (2018). 'Dynamics of Decoloniality in South Africa: A Critique of the History of Swiss Mission Education for Indigenous People'. UNISA: *Studia Historiae Ecclesiasticae*, 44(3), 1–14.

Tomlinson, H. (2004). *Educational Leadership: Personal Growth for Personal Development*. Thousand Oaks, CA: Sage.

van Maurik, J. (2001). *Writers on Leadership*. London: Penguin Books.

Wren, D. A. (2003). 'The Influence of Henry Fayol on Management Theory and Education in North America', Researchgate.net/

publication/250300021_The_Influence_of_Henri_Fayol_on_Management_Theory_and_Education_in_North_America. Accessed April 2021.

Part II: Approaches to leadership

Boehme, R. (1989). *Leadership for the 21st Century*. Seattle, WA: Frontline Communications.
Boon, M. (2007). *The African Way: The Power of Interactive Leadership*. Cape Town: Zebra Press.
Greenleaf, R. (1977). *Servant Leadership: A Journey into the Nature of Legitimate Power & Greatness*. New York: Paulist Press.
Holy Bible. New International Version (NIV) (1973). Grand Rapids, MI: Zondervan.
Kalungu-Banda, M. (2006). *Leading Like Madiba: Leadership Lessons from Nelson Mandela*. Cape Town: DoubleStorey.
Khoza, Reuel, J. (2005). *Let Africa Lead: African Transformational Leadership for 21st Century Business*. Johannesburg: Vezubuntu.
Lead and Inspire School of Leadership (2010). *Approaches to Leadership*, Lead and Inspire Teaching Materials Series. Pretoria: Unpublished.
Maxwell, John C. (2017). *The Power of Your Leadership: Making a Difference with Others*. New York: Center Street.
Mbigi, L. (2005). *The Spirit of African Leadership*. Johannesburg: Knowres.
Mudenge, S. I. G. (1988). *A Political History of Munhumutapa, c.1400–1902*. Harare: Zimbabwe Publishing House.
New World Encyclopaedia (2012). 'Mutapa Empire', 6 July 2012, https://www.newworldencyclopedia.org/entry/Mutapa_Empire.
Ngara, E. (2012) 'Traditional African Leadership and Accountability: A Study of Three Kingdoms'. Unpublished paper read at a conference organized by the Thabo Mbeki Leadership Institute, Pretoria.
Ngara, E. (2013). 'Transformational Leadership and Traditional African Leadership Practice: A Study of Two Kingdoms'. Paper read in Victoria Falls at a Conference on Transformational Leadership, organized by the National University of Science Technology, Bulawayo.
Ngara, R. (2017). 'Multiple Voices, Multiple Paths: Towards Dialogue between Western and Indigenous Knowledge Systems', in Ngulube, P. (ed.), *Handbook of Research on Theoretical Perspectives on Indigenous Knowledge Systems in Developing Countries*. Hershey, PA: IGI Global.
Oral history of the Basotho, especially as narrated by Bernice Teboho Ngara (Nee Motanyane).
Sansom, B. (1974). 'Traditional Rulers and Their Realms', in Hammond-Tooke, W. D. (ed.), *The Bantu Speaking People of Southern Africa*. London: Routledge & Kegan Paul.

Skinner, Q. (1981). *Machiavelli: A Very Short Introduction*. Oxford: Oxford University Press.
Stengel, R. (2010). *Mandela's Way: Lessons for an Uncertain Age*. New York: Crown Archetype.
Therborn, G. (1980). *The Ideology of Power and the Power of Ideology*. London: Verso.
Tutu, D. M. (2011). *God Is Not a Christian: Speaking Truth in Times of Crisis*. London: Rider.
UK Essays (2021). 'Description of Moshoeshoe's Leadership Style'. *UK Essays*, 3 August 2021.
van Maurik, J. (2001). *Writers on Leadership*. Harmondsworth: Penguin Books.
Wikipedia (2012). 'Moshoeshoe I', 10 July 2012, http://en.wikipedia.org/wiki/Moshoeshoe I.

Part III: Education for personal development and leadership

Bush, T., Bell, L. & Middlewood, D. (eds) (2019). *Principles of Educational Leadership and Management*. Los Angeles, CA: Sage.
Colom, R., Kamara, S., Jung, R. E. & Haier, R. J. (2010). 'Human Intelligence and Brain Networks'. *Dialogues in Clinical Neuroscience*, 12(4), 489–501. doi:10.31887/DCNS 2010.12.4/ridom(?).
Covey, S. R. (1989). *The 7 Habits of Highly Effective People*. London: Simon & Schuster.
Covey, S. R. (2004). *The 8th Habit: From Effectiveness to Greatness*. London: Simon & Schuster.
Cox, L. (2017). 'How to Develop Stephen Covey's 4 Intelligences', https:www.linkedin.com >pulse>how-develop-stephen-coveys-4-intelligences-layton-cox/.
De Mello, A. (1992). *Awareness*. New York: Image, Doubleday.
Denisova-Schmidt, E. (ed.) (2020). *Corruption in Higher Education: Global Challenges and Responses*. Leiden: Brill Sense.
Downey, L. A., Papageorgiou, V. & Stough, C. (2006). 'Examining the Relationship between Leadership, Emotional Intelligence and Intuition in Senior Female Managers'. *Leadership & Organization Development Journal*, 27(4), 250–64.
Frankl, Viktor E. (1985). *Man's Search for Meaning*. New York: Pocket Books.
Garcia, J. (2012). 'The Four Intelligences of a Leader'. *Leadership Advance Online – Issue XXII*, Regent University, ISSN: 2012 School of Global Leadership & Entrepreneurship.
Goleman, D., Boyatzis, R. E. & McKee, A. (2013). *Primal Leadership: Unleashing the Power of Emotional Intelligence*. Boston, MA: Harvard Business Press.
Herrnstein, R. J., & Murray, C. (1994). *The Bell Curve: Intelligence and Class Structure in American Life*. New York: Free Press.
Lohman, D. F. (Winter 1989). 'Human Intelligence: An Introduction to Advances in Theory and Research'. *Review of Educational Research*, 59(4), 333–73.

Mathew, M., & Gupta, K. S. (April–June 2015). 'Transformational Leadership: Emotional Intelligence'. *SCMS Journal of Indian Management, Kochi*, 12(2), 75–89.

Mundakel, T. T. (1998). *Blessed Mother Teresa: Her Journey to Your Heart*. London: Simon & Schuster.

Senge, Peter M. (1990). *The Fifth Discipline: The Art and Practice of the Learning Organization*. New York: Currency Doubleday.

Sinek, S. (2009). *Start with Why*. London: Portfolio Penguin.

https://www.andyandrews.com/personal-mission-statement/; https://fastcompany.com/3026791/personal-mission-statements-of-5-famous-ceos-and-you-sho uld-write-one-too.

Sternberg, R. J. (2005). 'A Model of Educational Leadership: Wisdom, Intelligence and Creativity Synthesized'. *International Journal of Leadership in Education*, 8(4), 347–64.

Warren, R. (2002). *The Purpose Driven Life: What on Earth Am I Here For?* Grand Rapids, MI: Zondervan.

Part IV: Education for transformational organizational leadership

Adair, J. (2003). *Effective Strategic Leadership*. London: Pan Books.

Andrews, K. R. (1971) *The Concept of Corporate Strategy*. New York: Dow Jones-Irwin.

Bossidy, L., & Charan, R. (2011). *Execution: The Discipline of Getting Things Done*. London: Random House Business Books.

Gardner, H. (1995). *Leading Minds: An Anatomy of Leadership*. New York: Basic Books.

Hagemann, B., Maketa, J., & Vetter, S. (2017). *Leading with Vision: The Leader's Blueprint for Creating a Compelling Vision and Engaging the Workforce*. Boston, MA: Nicholas Brealey.

Senge, Peter M. (1990). *The Fifth Discipline: The Art and Practice of the Learning Organization*. New York: Currency Doubleday.

Sharma, R. (2010). *The Leader Who Had No Title*. London: Simon & Schuster.

Part V: Beyond the organizational context of educational leadership

Ajayi, J. F. Ade, Goma, L. K. H., Johnson, A. G., & Association of African Universities (1996). *The African Experience with Higher Education*. Accra: Association of African Universities; London: James Currey; Athens: Ohio University Press.

BBC America Editors (2015). '50 Sir Winston Churchill Quotes to Live By', 9 April 2015.

Boeren, E. (2019). 'Understanding Sustainable Development Goal (SDG) 4 on "Quality Education" from Micro, Meso and Macro Perspectives'. *International Review of Education* 65, 277–94.

Boeren, E., Nicaise, I., & Baert, H. (2016). 'Comprehensive Lifelong Learning Participation Model'. https://www.researchgate.net/figure/Comprehensive-Lifelong-Learning-Participation-Model-Boeren-et-al_fig4_305115262.

Bottery, M. (2019). 'An Ethics of Educational Leadership for Turbulent and Complex Times', in Bush, T., Bell, L. & Middlewood, D. (eds), *Principles of Educational Leadership and Management*. Los Angeles, CA: Sage.

Chung, F., & Ngara, E. (1985). *Socialism, Education and Development: A Challenge to Zimbabwe*. Harare: Zimbabwe Publishing House.

CISL (2017). *Global Definitions of Leadership and Theories of Leadership Development: Literature Review*. Cambridge: University of Cambridge Institute of Sustainable Leadership.

Council on Higher Education (CHE) (2013). *The Higher Education Qualifications Sub-Framework*. Pretoria: CHE.

Council on Higher Education (CHE) (2016). *South African Higher Education Reviewed: Two Decades of Democracy*. Pretoria: CHE.

Diop, C. A. (1974). *The African Origin of Civilization: Myth or Reality*. Westport, CT: Lawrence Hill.

Greicar, M. (2009). *The Professional Preparation of Academic Deans*. Doctor of Education Degree (EdD). Bowling Green State University.

Heck, R. H., Johnsrud, L. K., & Rosser, V. J. (2000). 'Administrative Effectiveness in Higher Education: Improving Assessment Procedures'. *Research in Higher Education*, 41, 663–84.

Maathai, W. (2009). *The Challenge for Africa: A New Vision*. London: William Heinemann.

Martela, F., Greve, B., Rothstein, B., & Saari, J. (2020). 'The Nordic Exceptionalism: What Explains Why the Nordic Countries Are Constantly among the Happiest in the World'. *World Happiness Report*, 128–46. https://worldhappiness.report/ed/2020/the-nordic-exceptionalism-what-explains-why-the-nordic-countries-are-constantly-among-the-happiest-in-the-world/.

Murray, D. (2017). *The Strange Death of Europe: Immigration, Identity, Islam*. London: Bloomsbury.

Ngara, E. (1995). *The African University and Its Mission*. Roma: Institute of Southern African Studies (National University of Lesotho).

Ngara E. (2013). 'Leadership, the Oldest Practice and Youngest Discipline: Clearing the Path to the African Renaissance', in Kondlo, K. (ed.), *Perspectives on Thought Leadership for Africa's Renewal*. Pretoria: Africa Institute of South Africa.

Ngara, E. (2021). 'Reflections on the Further Transformation of UNISA: Focus on Governance, Leadership and Response to National Policy'. Paper read at the Reclaiming Africa's Intellectual Capital Seminar Series on 'Decolonial Thinking in Governance, Leadership and Management in Higher Education', UNISA, 14 April 2021.

Ngara, E., & the SADC HAQAA Group (2017). "Draft SADC Guidelines for Credit Accumulation and Transfer: Prepared for the HAQAA Initiative". The paper was developed in the framework of the Harmonisation, Accreditation and Quality Assurance Initiative (HAQAA 1) funded by the European Union, in partnership with the African Union, between 2015 and 2018. It was part of the work conducted for a continental African training course on a Common Language for Quality Assurance in Africa, which HAQAA 1 executed. The opinions expressed reflect those of the author and not those of the African Union or European Union Commissions.

Ngara, R. (2017). 'Multiple Voices, Multiple Paths: Towards Dialogue between Western and Indigenous Knowledge Systems", in Ngulube, P. (ed.), *Handbook of Research on Theoretical Perspectives on Indigenous Knowledge Systems in Developing Countries.* Hershey, PA: IGI Global.

Ngulube, P. (2017). *Handbook of Research on Theoretical Perspectives on Indigenous Knowledge Systems in Developing Countries.* Hershey, PA: IGI Global.

Nkrumah, K. (1965). *Neo-Colonialism: The Last Stage of Imperialism.* New York: International.

Nyerere, J. K. (1968). *UJAMAA: Essays on Socialism.* London: Oxford University Press.

Odora Hoppers, C., & Richards, H. (2011). *Rethinking Thinking: Modernity's 'Other' and the Transformation of the University.* Pretoria: University of South Africa (UNISA).

Odora Hoppers, C. A., Oyewole, O. B., Teferra, D., Beneitone, P., & Wagenaar, R. (eds) (2002). *Indigenous Knowledge and the Integration of Knowledge Systems: Towards a Philosophy of Articulation.* Claremont: New Africa Education (NAE).

Onana, C. A., Oyewole, O. B., Teferra, D., Beneitone, P., & Wagenaar, R. (eds) (2014). *Tuning and Harmonisation of Higher Education: The African Experience* (Tuning Africa Project). Bilbao: University of Deusto.

Pop, A. (2016). 'What You Need to Know about Academic Credit Systems in the U.S', https://www.distancelearningportal.com/articles/1110/what-you-need-to-know-about-academic-credit-systems-in-the us.html. Accessed 10 January 2022.

Seale, O. J. J. (2015). *Building Leadership and Management Capacity for Deans in South African Higher Education.* PhD Thesis. Johannesburg: University of the Witwatersrand.

Seroto, J. (2018). 'Dynamics of Decoloniality in South Africa: A Critique of the History of Swiss Mission Education for Indigenous People'. UNISA: *Studia Historiae Ecclesiasticae*, 44(3), 1–4.

The Africa-EU Partnership (2021). 'HAQAA Ambassadors Network Virtual Event', January 2021.

Tuck, R. (2007). *An Introduction to National Qualifications Frameworks: Conceptual and Practical Uses for Policy Makers.* Geneva: Skills and Employability Department, International Labour Organisation (ILO).

Tutu, D. M. (2011). *God Is Not a Christian: Speaking truth in times of crisis*. London: Rider.
UNESCO (2014). 'Addis Convention on Higher Education'. https://en.unesco.org/news/unesco-addis-convention-higher-education-enter-force.
University of Cambridge Institute of Sustainable Leadership (CISL) (2017). *Global Definitions of Leadership and Theories of Leadership Development*. Cambridge: University of Cambridge.
van Maurik, J. (2001). *Writers on Leadership*. London: Penguin Books.
Yesufu, T. M. (ed.). (1973). *Creating the African University: Emergi Issues of the 1970s*. Ibadan: Oxford University Press.

Index

academic freedom and autonomy 156
Adair, John 1, 39–40, 107, 131–3, 185, 195
Addis Ababa Convention 157, 158
administration 28, 31–2
   in relation to leadership and management 28
African academics/African intellectuals
   the challenges to 200
African culture, values and history 200
African tradition(s) 62–3
Anderson, Katie 1, 2, 6, 18, 210
Andrews, Kenneth (Professor) 133
Arena 100–1
Association of African Universities 106, 156

Bantu 60
Basotho 66
Bass, Bernard 41
BBC America Editors 206, 210
Behr, Abraham Leslie 14, 18
being
   leadership as a discipline that entails being, knowing, becoming and applying 5, 25
   See also coloniality of being
Bible, the 203
Blanchard, Kenneth 39, 45
blended education 169
Blind spot 100–1
Boehme, Ron 51, 81, 121
Boer Republic, the
Boeren, Ellen 154
Boon, Mike 1, 6, 62, 67
Bossidy, Larry and Charan, Ram 139, 140, 142–3, 186
Botho 60–2
   See also Ubuntu, Utu, Unhu etc
Bottery, Mike 1, 205, 206

Bruntland, Gro Harlem 206
   See also Bruntland Report, the 206
Burns, Jim 41
Bush, Tony 3, 44, 45, 105
Business Management Ideas 38

calling 89
Cambridge Institute of Sustainable Leadership (CISL) 211
Casalis, Eugene 67
Casperz, Donella 13
Catholic Church, the 203–4
Christian Church, the 203–4
Chung, Fay 200
Churchill, Sir Randolph 90
Churchill, Sir Winston 87, 90, 199, 206, 210
cognitive interests
   technical, practical and emancipatory 12, 20
   See also Habermas, Jurgen
collective decision making practice
   of King Moshoeshoe I 66–7
coloniality
   of being 202
   of knowledge 202
   of power 202
   See also colonizerlity & decoloniality
colonization/colonialism 201
colonizerlity 202
   See also coloniality
common factors affecting higher education institutions (HEIs) 163–70
competences 20
   of African graduates 20
   of university graduates 20
complexity
   of higher education 191
connectedness 42

Conrad, Joseph 202
context 3
   education and 2
   leadership and 2
continuous improvement 2
corporate governance 32–3
corpus of knowledge, the
   in connection with curriculum content 19
corruption
   in higher education 106–7
Council chairperson 33
Council on Higher Education (CHE) 45, 165
Covey, Stephen R. 1, 90, 98, 109–12, 115
Covid-19 165–6, 174–5
Cox, Layton 116
Credit Accumulation and Transfer System (CATS) 160–3
Credit hour approach, the 161
   See also Notional studies hours approach, the
culture
   African culture and tradition 203–4
   and the environment 22, 198, 205
   strategies for shaping organizational 142–4
curriculum 12
   culture context and the 22
   curriculum benchmarks 159
   curriculum content 18–22
   guiding principles for designing the 21–3
   and ways of knowing 12

Dambamupute, Chioko 63
Dare 71, 75
   See also Khotla, Pitso, Imbizo
dean/dean leadership
   desirable characteristics of 187
   qualities of a great 182
   seven dimensions of 181–2
decoloniality 21, 172, 203
   See also coloniality
deference 70, 74
De Mello, Anthony 99
Denisova-Schmidt, Elena 106
Descartes, Rene 60, 172

determinism
   three types of 110
developmental approach 7
dialectical and developmental concept of teaching and learning 16–18
dialectical relationship 11
dialogical relations 15
digitalization 166–70
Diop, Sheik Anta 198
discipline 97
   Personal mastery as a 97

education
   banking 14–15, 198
   problem-posing 14–15
   the purpose of 11–12
   Western 198
   See also Freire, Paulo
educational experience
   the how and the what of 19
educational leader(s) 12, 23, 105, 107, 153, 158–9, 199–200
   challenges to 200–7
   programmes for 189–95
educational leadership
   repositioning 197–20
educators 200
Einstein, Albert 2, 79, 212
employability
   of graduates 159–60
Enslin, Penny 13
epistemology 7, 21, 177, 197–211
   diversified 210–11
   Western 23
equivalences
   of credits/credit systems 163
European Higher Education Area, the 157
execution 137–47
   definition of 139, 140
   elements of 140
   seven essential behaviours of the leader 140
   VSE factor, the 139

fabric concept, the 2
Façade 100–1
Fanon, Frantz 203

Fayol, Henri 3, 30
    five functions of management, Fayol's 30
    fourteen management principles of 30
Fleming, Alexander 87, 88, 90–1
formation, in leadership development 5, 25
Frankl, Viktor, E. 89
Freire, Paulo 7, 14–15, 18, 23, 198
    See also banking education
    dialogical relations 15
    problem-posing education 15
fruits and roots, in leadership development 95–6
Fundamental Pedagogics 12, 15

gap, the gap nobody knows 139
Garcia, Joel 115
Gardner, Howard 1, 114, 117
generic competences 20
Gandhi, Mahatma 104, 143
globalization 164–5, 174–5
goals 127, 135–6
    setting 135–6
    SMART 135–6
God, belief in 89–90
    See also Superior Being
Going to Gemba 186
Goleman, Daniel 119
governance 28, 32–3
Greenleaf Center for Servant Leadership 79
    See also Servant Leadership Movement
Greenleaf, Robert 7, 72, 78–81
Greicar, Margo, B. 181

Habermas, Jurgen 7, 12, 15, 20, 23
    See also cognitive interests
Hagemann, Bonnie, Vetter, S., & Maketa, J. 108
Hallinger, Philip 2, 3, 31, 46
Hansei (hansei) 2, 99, 109, 185
HAQAA Initiative 157–8, 161
Heck, R. H., Johnsrud, L. K., & Rosser, V. J. 181–2, 187
Herrnstein, Richard, J. 114–15
Hersey, Paul 39, 45
Hesse, Herman 78

Higher education
    massification of 155
Hoppers, Catherine Odora 174, 175

imperialism 201
Imbizo 185
indigenous knowledge systems 2, 14, 21, 172
influence, ability to 104
Ingham, Harrington (& Luft, Joseph) 100
    See also Johari Window
intelligence
    definition of 114
    Gardner's nine 114
    human intelligence 114
    multiple intelligences 114–15
    the four: mental, physical, emotional & spiritual 115
interactive collaborative leadership 71, 75
interdependence principle of *Ubuntu* 61, 63
internationalization of higher education 76, 166–7, 173–4
Internet Encyclopedia of Philosophy 55
isithunzi 70, 107
    See also *sereti* and *chiremera*
Iviwe
    and leadership without position 26

Japanese approach, the 2, 210–11
Jefferson, Thomas 208
Jesus Christ
    and teaching on leadership 104
Johari Window 100–2

Keating, Charles 39
Khotla 71, 75
    See also *Dare, Imbizo, Pitso*
Khoza, Reuel 1
King Committee on Corporate Governance 33
    See also corporate governance
knowledge
    and competences (KCs) 159
    the corpus of (in relation to curriculum content) 19

leader/leaders 28–9, 34, 61, 75
    (See also under educational leaders)

born or made? 27
functions of the, (John Adair) 132–3
instructional 4
leader-first 79–80
leader's strategic operational behaviours, the 140–44
servant 77–84
servant-first 79–80
university 151–6, 179–89
leadership (*approaches to*)
of domination 6, 51–8
servant 6, 51
traditional African 5, 6
Ubuntu-based 5
See also transformational, responsible, shared, stewardship view of, and so on.
leadership (*styles*)
autocratic 38
collegial 44
contingent 38–9, 45
democratic 38
distributed 44–5
inspirational 73
laissez-faire 38
managerial/managerialism 45–6, 165
shared 44–5
See also Blanchard, Kenneth, and Hersey, Paul
See also transformational leadership
leadership (*general*)
and administration 28–32, 34
African leadership traditions 6
as a discipline 4–5
and governance 32–3
instructional 46
and management 27–32
and position 26
as a practice 5, 25
qualities and habits 103–12
repositioning 197–200
school leadership development 31
traditional African approaches to 5–6
transformational 41–4
what leadership is 4, 23, 25
with lower case l 5, 25
with upper case L 5, 25
See also under educational leadership, personal leadership development etc
leading and presiding over (an organization) 140
learning
constructive 14
reproductive 14
Leo 78
Lewin, Kurt 38, 41
Lowney, Chris 99, 109
Luft, Joseph (& Harrington, Ingham) 100
Luther King, Jr, Martin 98, 103–4

Maathai, Wangari 62, 197, 198, 203–4, 205, 206
Machiavelli, Niccolo 55, 198
macro/meso/micro 153–5
See also supra-macro 4, 153
Madiba 74, 104
See also under Mandela, Nelson
malimo (can also be spelt *madimo)* 59, 66
Mandela, Nelson 60, 74, 75, 104, 107, 212
See also Madiba
Martela, Frank 208
matona 59, 66
Maxwell, John 1, 26, 107, 108, 121
Mbigi, Lovemore 1, 6
McGregor, Douglas 56–7
Melick, Rick & Shera 3
Mfecane 66
Middlewood, David 105, 106
milestone 136
minimum body of knowledge (MBK) 159
See also curriculum benchmarks
mission 89, 127
one's 99, 100, 121
See also purpose, why, personal mission statement
mission and vision 106, 107
missionaries
Moshoeshoe and Protestant and Catholic 67–8
mobility
of staff and students 157

module
   in a programme and qualification 158–9
Mohamedbhai, Goolam 106–7, 173, 174
Mohammed, Prophet 104
Moshoeshoe I, King 45, 59, 65–8, 70, 71, 72, 75–6, 103, 172, 198
   and collective decision-making 66–7
   and consultation 66
   and peace 67–8
   and shared and democratic leadership 71
Mudenge, S. I. G. 63, 64, 65
Murray, Douglas 199
Mutapa Empire, the 62–5, 176
Mutapa/Mutapas, the
   and the affairs of the people 64
   and the economy 63–4, 70
   and foreign powers 65, 71–2
   and peace 70
   and provincial leaders 63, 71
   and reciprocity relationships 74
   and service of the people 72–3

nationalistic populism 203, 204
neo-colonialism 72, 202
   See also colonialism, coloniality, decoloniality
New World Encyclopedia, the 62, 63, 64, 176
Ngara, Bernice Teboho 4, 26
   See also Acknowledgements and Dedication
Ngara, Emmanuel 7, 16–17, 36, 62, 155, 161, 200, 201, 203
Ngara, Rutendo 2, 59
Nkomo, Mokubung 19
Nkrumah, Kwame 202
Nordic countries (or Scandinavia) 208–9, 210
North, the
   See the North and the South 23, 204, 205, 211
Notional study hours approach, the 161–3
   See also Credit Accumulation and Transfer System (CATS); credit hour approach, the
Nyerere, Julius 6, 74, 78, 185, 201, 205

Obama, Barack 104, 212
Onana, C. A., Oyewole, O. B., Teferra, D., Beneitone, P., Gonzalez, J., & Wagenaar, R. 20
operational plan, the 145–7
   characteristics of 145
   definition of 145
   example of 145–7
organizational/corporate culture 142–3
   the hardware and software of 142–3
   strategies for shaping 142
   ways of reshaping 143

Pan African Quality Assurance and Accreditation Framework (PAQAF) 157
people process, the 143–4
personal development and leadership 84, 91–3
Personal Mastery 95, 108–9, 112
   characteristics of people with high levels of 98
   and competence 97
   and creative tension 98
   and current reality 98
   principles of 97–8
personal mission statement 91–3
   See also mission, personal mission
PEST (Political, Economic, Social and Technological factors) 133
Pitso 71, 75, 194
   See also *Dare, Imbizo, Khotla*
politics, the, of knowledge generation 21
Portugal 65, 72
principal 3, 31, 32–3
   See also school head, school leadership development
professionalism 105–6
programmes for educational leaders 189–95
   and the family concept
   masters or diploma programmes 190
   for a qualification 158–9
   short courses for-on-the job training 190
   texts for short courses 190
   and the three-legged pot model 191
   two types of programmes 191–5
purpose 88, 99, 100, 121

quadrants
   of the Johari Window 100
   qualification 158–9
quality/qualities
   leadership
Quality Assurance 155–63
   definition of 156–7
   as an industry 156–8

Rakotswane and the cannibals 66
Rawat, Surbhi 38
reciprocity relationships between the ruler and the ruled 73, 74
representation
   obedience based on a sense of 72
Research and innovation 174–5, 184
Richards, Howard 174, 175
roots and fruits (in leadership) 95–6

Sachs, Jeff 208
SADC in relation to Credit Accumulation and Transfer System (CATS) 161, 163
Sanders, John Oswald 197
Scandinavian countries
   See under Nordic countries
school head 31
   See also principal
school leadership development 3
Seale, Oliver 181
self-awareness 95, 98–102, 109, 112
   definition of 98–9
   as *hansei* 99
   as part of knowing yourself 100–1, 102
   principles of 99
   as self-reflection 99
   and the Johari Window 100–2
Senge, Peter 144, 197
sereti 107, 120
   See also *chiremera, isithunzi*
Seroto, Johannes 21
servant-first-leader 72, 79–80
servant leader, the
   characteristics of 81–3
   and community
servant leadership 77–84
   definition of 80
   and democracy
   and faith 80
   and Jesus 80
   and service of people
   and *Ubuntu*-based leadership 83–4
   the test of 80
Servant Leadership Movement, the 79
Sesotho/Sotho 51, 60, 107
Shona 51, 60, 107
Sinek, Simon 127
Skinner, Quentin 55
Socrates
   and self-reflection 99
SOEs (State Owned Enterprises) 156
Solomon, King 64
STEM (Science, Technology, Engineering & Mathematics) 156
Sternberg, Robert 114, 115
stewardship view (of leadership), the 82
storytelling 6
strategic
   leader 131–2
   plan 133–4
   thinking 132
strategy 131–6
   etymology of 131
student leader(s) 188–9
   developing the ideal 188
   programmes for 188–9
student leadership development course 188
   topics for 189
Superior Being 121
   See also God, Creator
Swahili 51
SWOT analysis 133

Tanzania 60, 77, 78
teaching and learning 14–16
   dialectical and developmental concept of 16
technology, trade and market forces 199, 205
   See also globalization
Teresa, Mother, Blessed, Saint 104
Thaba Bosiu 65, 66
The Prince, by Machiavelli 55, 56

Theories of leadership
  educational theories of 43–7
  general (six) theories of 35–43
Theory, the
  Behavioural 37–8
  Contingency (Situational) 38
  Functional 39–40
  Great Man 37, 132
  Qualities or Trait 37
  Transformational 40, 43, 44
  Theory X 56–7
  Theory Y 56–7
Therborn, Goran 70, 72
Toyota
  Foundational Leadership Principles of 185–6, 211
Tuning Africa Project and Competences 160
  See also Tuning Project
Tuning in Exercise, the 7, 8, 25, 35, 51–3, 77, 87, 113, 126, 151, 179–80, 186
Tuning Project, the 160
Tutu, Desmond 60, 61

Ubuntu 1, 2, 17, 18, 20, 36, 43, 57–62, 69, 75, 78, 106, 172–3 195, 198, 201, 205, 207, 208, 209, 210
  See also *Botho, Unhu, Utu*
Ubuntu philosophy (*See under Ubuntu*)
United Nations Sustainable Development Goal 4 154, 176, 206
University World News, the 106, 173, 174
Unknown Area (of the Johari Window) 100–1

van Maurik, John 1, 56, 197
vice-chancellor, the 179, 181, 182–6
  desirable characteristics of a 183–6
  as a Mutapa, Moshoeshoe, Yoshino 184–6

training programmes for vice-chancellors
vision 30, 125–30
  creating, the 129
  communicating the 129–30
  definition of a 127
  developing a compelling 128
  examples of visions 128
  and organizational leadership 127–30
  preliminary analysis of 128–9
  publicizing and marketing the 130
  testing the 129
  vision, purpose and communication 103
VSE factor 139
vocation 89–90

Warren, Rick 89
ways of knowing 6, 12, 118
  See also curriculum, epistemology
Western tradition 35, 36
  See also globalization and Westernization
Western education 62, 156
Western epistemology 198
Western people-centred approaches 7, 207–9
Western scholars/thinkers 2, 60
Why, the, of one's life 88, 127
  See also mission, purpose
WICS (wisdom, intelligence and creativity synthesized) 115

Xhosa (language) 51, 60

Yesufu, T. M. (Yesufu, Tijani M.) 156
Yoshino, Isao 1, 2, 18, 210

Zulu 51, 60, 107